The Politics of Postmodernity

In his famous study *Modernity and the Holocaust* Zygmunt Bauman contrasted the hopes and expectations of the modernising world of the nineteenth century with the real outcomes of the twentieth century, where the very conditions of modernity have led to the mass destruction of humanity and of early hopes for the betterment of humankind. In *The Politics of Postmodernity* a distinguished international team of contributors explores the possibilities left to once modernising societies, not only in terms of the worlds they have constructed but also in discerning the novel conditions which the closure of modernity entails. That closure, in part the completion of industrialisation and the social order that went with it, and in part the dislocation of the kinds of social knowledge used to understand it, has raised profound and disturbing questions about the character of this brave new world, this postmodern society, and the new ways in which its governance and the goal of the good society can be understood. These issues are the focus of *The Politics of Postmodernity*, which seeks to explore some of the current vicissitudes of modernity, especially in relation to the crises of the political and the political consequences of new technologies.

In keeping with the breadth of its subject the contributors to *The Politics of Postmodernity* are drawn from contrasting disciplinary backgrounds, including sociology, anthropology, philosophy, history and political theory, and the whole represents one of the most significant collaborative interventions yet in the most important intellectual debate of our times.

JAMES GOOD teaches social psychology at the University of Durham where he is also Director of the Centre for the History of the Human Sciences. He is co-editor (with Richard Roberts) of *The Recovery of Rhetoric*.

IRVING VELODY is Visiting Research Fellow in the Department of Sociology at the University of Bristol and in the Faculty of Economics and Social Science at the University of the West of England. He is co-editor of *Rewriting the History of Madness: Studies in Foucault's 'Histoire de la folie'* (with Arthur Still) and of *Politics and Modernity* (with Robin Williams).

The Politics of Postmodernity

Edited by

James Good

and

Irving Velody

CAMBRIDGE
UNIVERSITY PRESS

PUBLISHED BY THE PRESS SYNDICATE OF THE UNIVERSITY OF CAMBRIDGE
The Pitt Building, Trumpington Street, Cambridge CB2 1RP, United Kingdom

CAMBRIDGE UNIVERSITY PRESS
The Edinburgh Building, Cambridge CB2 2RU, United Kingdom
  http://www.cup.cam.ac.uk
40 West 20th Street, New York, NY 10011-4211, USA   http://www.cup.org
10 Stamford Road, Oakleigh, Melbourne 3166, Australia

First published 1998

Printed in the United Kingdom at the University Press, Cambridge

Typeset in Plantin 10/12pt [CE]

A catalogue record for this book is available from the British Library

Library of Congress Cataloguing in Publication data
The politics of postmodernity / edited by James Good and Irving Velody.
     p.   cm.
   Includes bibliographical references (p.   ).
   ISBN 0 521 46162 6 (hc). – ISBN 0 521 46727 6 (pbk.)
   1. Postmodernism – Political aspects.   I. Good, James, 1941–   .
II Velody, Irving.
JA71.P643   1998
303.4–dc21   97–42128 CIP

ISBN 0 521 46162 6 hardback
ISBN 0 521 46727 6 paperback

Contents

Acknowledgements

We wish to acknowledge the valuable help and support of our colleagues in the Centre for the History of the Human Sciences in Durham during the preparation of this volume.

We are grateful for the financial support of the General Lectures Committee of the University of Durham without which the 1991–2 public lecture series from which many of these chapters derive would not have taken place.

In Durham we are much indebted to the late Joan Trowbridge who not only word processed successive drafts of some of the chapters but was invaluable in liaising with contributors. The index was prepared in Bristol by Maggie Studholme. We are especially appreciative of the scholarly way in which she dealt with this task.

We are grateful to the following for their permission to republish some of the material in this collection: the editor of the *Irish Journal of Philosophy* for David Cooper's chapter; to Blackwell for Raymond Plant's chapter; and, for Quentin Skinner's chapter, to Cambridge University Press.

A special debt is owed to our editor at Cambridge University Press, Richard Fisher, for his patience and readiness to be helpful at all stages in the preparation of the manuscript.

Above all we express our warm thanks to Halina and Harriet for their love and support; and to Jane and Katharine for believing that these longstanding editorial duties could come to an end and for constant reminders which helped to ensure that they did.

James Good
Irving Velody

Notes on contributors

ZYGMUNT BAUMAN is Emeritus Professor at Leeds University. Amongst his many publications are *Modernity and the Holocaust* (1989) and *Postmodernity and its Discontents* (1996).

ROY BOYNE is Professor of Sociology at the University of Durham. His study *Foucault and Derrida: The Other Side of Reason* was published in 1990. He is currently completing a book entitled *Postmodern Subjectivity*.

DIANA COOLE is Senior Lecturer in Political Theory at Queen Mary and Westfield College, University of London. She is author of *Women in Political Theory* (1988, 1993) and has written extensively on feminism, postmodernism and postwar French thought. She is currently completing a book entitled *Politics and Negativity*.

DAVID E. COOPER is Professor of Philosophy at the University of Durham. He has held Visiting Professorships in the USA, Europe and South Africa. His most recent books are *World Philosophies: An Historical Introduction* and *Heidegger*. He is currently editing the series *Philosophy: The Classic Readings*.

JAMES GOOD teaches social psychology at the University of Durham where he is Director of the Centre for the History of the Human Sciences. He is co-editor with Richard Roberts of *The Recovery of Rhetoric* (1993). He is currently completing a book entitled *Disciplining Social Psychology: A Case Study of Boundary Relations in the Human Sciences*.

GEOFFREY HAWTHORN teaches politics and sociology at Cambridge University. Among his publications is *Plausible Worlds: Possibility and Understanding in History and the Social Sciences* (1991).

CAMILLA LUND received her PhD from Cambridge University in 1995. She held the Carlsberg Visiting Fellowship at Clare Hall, Cambridge and a Research Fellowship at the Nobel Institute in Norway. She presently works in Copenhagen for *Huset Mandag Morgen.*

HERMINIO MARTINS, Fellow of St Antony's College (Oxford), has published papers on Brazil and Portugal; he has also contributed studies on the sociology of scientific knowledge. Recently a collection of his theoretical essays was published in Portuguese under the title *Hegel, Texas e outros ensaios de teoria social.*

RAYMOND PLANT, Master of St Catherine's College (Oxford), has published extensively in the field of political philosophy, including *Modern Political Thought* (1991).

QUENTIN SKINNER has been Regius Professor of Modern History in the University of Cambridge since 1996. His most recent publication is *Reason and Rhetoric in the Philosophy of Hobbes.*

JUDITH SQUIRES lectures in political theory at Bristol University. She is editor of the journal *New Formations* and has edited various collections including *Principled Positions: Postmodernism and the Rediscovery of Value* and *Feminisms* (with Sandra Kemp). She is currently writing a book entitled *Gender in Political Theory* for Polity Press.

MARILYN STRATHERN, William Wye Professor of Social Anthropology (Cambridge University), has researched on Melanesian gender relations (*The Gender of the Gift,* 1972). Her work on British consumer society (*After Nature,* 1992) and new reproductive technologies (*Reproducing the Future,* 1992) has sharpened her interest in new property forms.

IRVING VELODY is visiting research fellow at the University of Bristol and also the University of the West of England. He is co-editor of the journal *History of the Human Sciences* and has edited with Arthur Still *Rewriting the History of Madness: Studies in Michel Foucault's 'Histoire de la folie'* (1992).

1 Introduction: postmodernity and the political

James Good and Irving Velody

Truth was their model as they strove to build
A world of lasting objects to believe in.

W. H. Auden, 'The History of Truth'

Every beginning
is only a sequel, after all,
and the book of events
is always open halfway through.   Wisława Szymborska, 'Love at First Sight'

This volume explores the political possibilities left to those once modernising societies, an exploration that is made not only in terms of the worlds these societies have constructed but also in revealing the novel conditions and possibilities which the closure of modernity entails. That closure, in part the completion of industrialisation and the social order that went with it, and in part the dislocation and decay of the kinds of knowledge used to understand it, has raised profound and disturbing questions about the character of this brave new world and the new ways in which its governance and the goal of the good society can be measured.[1] This crisis, often taken as the central feature of post-modernity, is discussed throughout this volume, which essentially presumes the death of the foundational approach to political analysis and offers a variety of new perspectives to look forward to the post-modern social world.

This collection takes up issues concerned with the debate on the foundations of political thought, with special reference to the work of Richard Rorty, Jean-François Lyotard, Charles Taylor and Alasdair MacIntyre.[2] Inevitably it bears on matters which have been tangential to modernist political themes: issues of gender, ethnicity and ecology, which have become increasingly central to the social organisation of political activities. We take this term broadly to include both the role of formal political institutions as well as the public actions of those wide-ranging collectivities, which have become part of the manifesta-tion of the crisis of the political. It seems that the break-up of nation-states, of those bourgeois securities exterior to juristic processes which themselves mirror the interiorisation of the conscience and the soul, has run parallel to the breakdown of epistemological and ontic securities.

Such matters have an external quality, which has opened up discussion in new directions. The mass murders in Europe (including the more recent events in the former Republic of Yugoslavia), the rise of fundamentalist religious movements, the conflicts over human rights and attempts to control immigration in the European Union, certainly all these have contributed to an unease about the apparatus of analysis of the political; but also of the social as well.[3] Thus, the crisis in the political is very much an aspect of crises of interpretation and representation in the social sciences. That is to say, the crisis in the political is but one dimension of a more general sense of disintegration in the human sciences.[4]

A central aspect of this disintegration is the intellectual fragmentation that is a consequence of modernist disciplinary specialisation. This has led not only to a revival of interest in inter- and cross-disciplinary work but also to a recognition of the importance of 'boundary work' in the production of knowledge.[5] Writing about the problems facing archaeology as a discipline Michael Rowlands comments: 'Yet the dilemma of disciplinary confusion is a more widespread phenomenon. Everywhere the foundations of expert knowledge are being undermined . . . '[6] This intellectual shipwreck has been named in many ways but the term of central interest here is 'postmodernism'.[7]

While there is no copyright in academic usage, for present purposes 'postmodernism' can be equated with at least three rather different usages: as referring to a characteristic of cultural forms, typically as expressed in Jencks' *What is Post-Modernism?*[8]; as a type of social structure and set of economic relations, as in Lash and Urry's *The End of Organized Capitalism*[9]; and finally as a summation of a long-term trend in the re-evaluation of the procedures and methods of the social and human sciences. Here we have in mind Lyotard's *The Postmodern Condition* as providing a concise expression of the matter through his formula: scepticism towards grand narratives.[10]

When Lyotard famously wrote of the abounding scepticism towards grand narratives, he was doing little more than summarising the intellectual work of a half-century of endeavour. Indeed this evocation, sometimes noted as postmodernism, is itself but the consequence of modernity's own processes. His summatory account reflects a multiplicity of sources, although comparatively few of them are found in sociology. Heidegger, Nietzsche, Ludwik Fleck, Wittgenstein, Derrida,

Hayden White, and perhaps Garfinkel in sociology, have all contributed to this movement.[11]

As far as the human sciences and their traditions are concerned then, the consequences of the postmodernist moment are to rule out of court a number of central assumptions and topoi of this domain: that the character and nature of rationality can be established by any clear-cut procedure or formula; that there can be decisive foundational supports for such conceptions; that actors' meanings and utterances can be accounted for by external causal processes; that there is available a clear-cut technical language to report the character of the social world in, separable from ordinary language activities. A number of further consequences flow from this position including a recognition that the search for interior structures whether in 'society' or in 'the mind' is the quest for a mirage and also the denial of the concept of progress in the domain of the social.[12]

In attempting to renew our understanding of the polity at the point of closure of the modern era, the single most used tactic (itself a development of Lyotard's formula) is that put forward by Rorty in 'Postmodern Bourgeois Liberalism', namely the development of an anti-foundationalist stance towards both political and social theory.[13] That this has not gone unnoticed by John Rawls, that most representative figure of a Kantian and grounded approach to political theory, can be clearly seen in his recent statements, especially in *Political Liberalism*.[14] For Rorty this position has led to a project couched in terms of dialogue and exchange, but his view seems to take little account of what has, until quite recently at least, been known as the material world. Not all commentary, however, has remained satisfied by such a quiescent voice: in this volume Raymond Plant sketches out more clearly the character of a 'political theory without foundations'.[15]

But dispensing with foundations also leads to the loss of other procedures and 'data'. The hope that (for example) objective measurements of stratification or crime could resolve issues relating to poverty or deviant behaviour has proved as nugatory as the basis of measurement and conceptual equipment on which they depend. In particular, while it may be feasible to retain terms like class and justice, legitimacy and ideology, it may no longer make sense to retain the scaffolding that kept these terms together.

It is the value of historical research in the realm of ideas that such modernist programmes can be exhumed, dissected and precisely examined, and that they can be shown to be closely linked with more overt processes currently under way in our societies. If postmodernism is an attitude or a perspective encompassing past achievements in their failure and collapse, what then are the intellectual possibilities that can be opened up from this viewpoint? For the history of our past, collapsed and compressed in the traditional interrogations of the human sciences, can no longer make sense of what can be said of the future. Yet it is not that these stories are without meaning. Rather it is the task of our generation to give some coherence and direction to the kind of world the year 2000 will bring, the kind of world the makers of this book and its readers will have helped to create.

In the remainder of this introduction we note some dilemmas of the postmodern, which revolve around themes of identity, utopia and legitimation, as well as the kinds of crises facing the political. We consider too the consequences for a realm of politics bounded by novel technologies and further discuss the prospects for political theory in the context of a new vision of historical process.

Dilemmas of the postmodern

In the previous section of this introduction we alluded to the dilemma of an increasing tension between the global and the local, between globalisation and the burgeoning proliferation and resurgence of national identities. In a sense this is a manifestation of a modernist universalism/particularism dualism. Yet this resurgence of ethnic, religious and national identity raises fundamental issues for the human sciences, issues which they remain poorly equipped to tackle, trapped as they are within a broader set of crippling dualisms or binary oppositions, often tied to particular disciplinary formations.[16]

At the heart of such matters lie notions of identity and belonging, ostensibly key terms in psychology and social psychology. Yet despite the pioneering work of William Sumner on ethnocentrism and William James on the self at the beginning of the century, psychology with its individualised mental representational model of the mind has been tardy in developing an adequate grasp of the social or collective sources of identity. Nowadays, thanks to the efforts of Henri Tajfel and a generation of his social psychological colleagues, a more adequate conceptualisation of the links between the personal and collective dimensions of identity is available. It is clear that one's sense of identity, of who one is, is powerfully bound up with salient group memberships. Moreover there is a strong tendency to promote the well-being of one's own group and its members at the expense of out-group members.[17] Yet even in this literature a residual essentialism is still discernible.[18]

With modernity, as Douglas Kellner has pointed out, 'identity becomes more mobile, fluid, multiple, self-reflexive, and subject to

change and innovation'. Nonetheless identities are relatively circumscribed, fixed and limited.[19] This lingering essentialism, however, has
sustained a further attack in the writings of Kenneth Gergen and John
Shotter who have developed a relational notion of identity in which
identity cannot be understood independently of the relationships in
which it is embedded.[20] Thus the postmodern self no longer possesses
the depth, substantiality and coherence of the modern self.[21] Yet we
agree with Kellner's conclusion that the features of postmodern identity
'could be read as an intensification of features already present in
modernity'.[22]

The kinds of selves offered up under the rubric of modernist social
science are beings with certain possibilities, but principally persons who
might be sent along a bifurcating path. One direction takes the self into
the clear and crystalline world of rationality and rational choosing –
occasionally among ends, but usually among means. The other path
offers the possibility of constant re-moulding and plasticity, leading to
the socially produced self. In different ways both selves are available for
the grand encounter with political and social utopias.

While More's *Utopia* as a golden fiction has no location, in a brilliant
reversal of fortunes, Engels' *Socialism: Utopian and Scientific*[23] discovers
a precise geography for this vision. For Engels, Utopianism is the work
of the pre-scientific, the pre-modern mind. Admirable as the Anabap-
tists, or the Diggers, were their writings were also but the theoretical
enunciations corresponding to the 'revolutionary uprisings of a class not
yet developed; in the sixteenth and seventeenth centuries, Utopian
pictures of ideal social conditions; in the eighteenth, actual communistic
theories . . .' and so on.

Engels' sensibility understood immediately that only adequate scientific analysis of the causal processes underlying the surface characteristics
of society could offer a solution to the problems of injustice and
inequality. And with varying emphases and stratagems this can be seen
as the main thrust of both social and political theorising in the modern
period. The dilemma, indeed the paradox, of this approach is that the
methodologies of social and political scientists can now be seen to be
effectively utopian in terms of their assumptions about these very underlying processes. It is no longer quite so clear that the Diggers were more
lacking in clear vision than the leaders of the Third Reich, or the
Revolution which took the Communist Party to power in Russia in 1917.

As Kolakowski puts it in his essay 'The Death of Utopia Reconsid-
ered', the notion can be widened so that it applies not only to global
visions of a saved society but also to epistemological utopias, the search
for a source of ultimate cognitive perfection.[24] Thus, that modernist

theories of the good society, or indeed of any society, import epistemological utopias into their account (frequently marrying them to substantive societal projects) is very much the point of commentators like Lyotard or, for that matter, MacIntyre. It is this move that brings out the impossibility of these undertakings or at least reduces their plausibility as convincing narratives.

These kinds of fundamental critical assessments of the working assumptions of modernism, however, as in the demolition of the mental machinery model of selves and their identities, have opened up rather than constrained the vision of thinkers in the political. Such visions may themselves be unrealisable but, insofar as they have disbanded the apparatus of modernist thinking, it is inadequate to characterise them as utopian.

In contrast, the collapse of grand narratives in the human sciences has coincided with the failure of those positivist projects, with their utopian concerns about value-neutral objectivity and epistemological grounding.[25] This has in turn brought about an intense preoccupation with issues of reflexivity, rhetoric and meaning-making practices.[26] Yet this recognition of the positioned and positioning character of human inquiry need not lead, as John Dewey and other pragmatist philosophers so clearly argued earlier this century, to the abandoning of the quest for secure knowledge. The recognition that there can be no cognitively privileged point of observation, no 'God's Eye-View' to use Hilary Putnam's term, opens the way for a more adequate grasp of the complex relationships between the knower and the objects of knowledge and the conditions of their production.[27] As Putnam puts it: 'the notion of *how things are* [Putnam's emphasis] makes no sense apart from the way in which we interact with such things'.[28]

Indeed the current 'resurgence of pragmatism' noted by Richard Bernstein and others has occurred not just in philosophical writing but in such diverse areas as aesthetics, history and philosophy of science, social theory, history and psychology.[29] It may also be seen as a timely response to the continuing domination of dualistic thinking in intellectual inquiry and the seemingly endless cycle of debates about realism and relativism, qualitative and quantitative methods, individualism and holism etc.[30]

Nor should a recognition of the positioned and positioning nature of human inquiry undermine attempts to foster the good society. Inevitably the loss of a sturdy epistemic anchor has had consequences in the moral and political spheres as well. Writers such as Susan Hekman in the moral domain, and Richard Rorty and Chantal Mouffe in the political, have begun the task of sketching non-foundational approaches which clearly show the influence of the pragmatists in these attempts to contemplate the possibility of what Joseph Margolis has called a 'life without principles'.[31] A renewed interest has also been fostered in pragmatist political ideas, especially those of John Dewey.[32] Pragmatist concerns about dualistic thinking have also been echoed recently by Nancy Fraser in her attempt to lay to rest 'false antitheses' in current debates about the politics of recognition and the politics of redistribution.[33]

Crises of the political

The claims of subordinated groups; beyond them, in particular, the claims of women; the claims of the rediscovered dangerous classes (of peoples holding bizarre views, clothed in outlandish dress, living in repugnant ways): such claims have not been stilled. Further, all these calls for recognition and identification appear as unexpected consequences, in terms of the civil and political programme, of the narratives of modernisation and the enlightenment vision of progress and equality.

For such collectivities have had scant recognition within the liberal democratic, and indeed socialist, traditions of the later nineteenth and twentieth centuries. Not only have the great exterior events confounded the hope of enfranchisement of the modern period. More even than the wars and genocide which the West has exacted from its own children, whole sectors of these societies have been quietly disposed of through a kind of indifference. It is these kinds of difficulties that have sustained the voice of Richard Rorty in taking a more committed version of postmodernist political expression, or given force to Raymond Plant's postmodernist brand of socialism as a possible reality. As Diana Coole points out: 'the Enlightenment discourses . . . spoke with a masculine voice . . . [A]ny theory which claimed mastery or truth necessarily did the same'(this volume).[34]

It is this sense of intellectual inadequacy which has determined the formulation of 'difference' as a key term in the work of Iris Young and Catherine MacKinnon among others.[35] The recognition of the worth of the person and the roots and conditions which may sustain and enhance it, have now become a central issue for the human sciences. Indeed the politics of recognition has been the focus of a great deal of sustained effort in recent debates about the relationships between multiculturalism, justice and the political institutions of liberal democracy – debates which are reflected in the chapters below.[36]

The rise of 'identity politics' has led not only to the assertion of a whole range of new voices in the public sphere, but also to new forms of political expression and participation. This change in what Nancy

Fraser has called the 'political imaginary' has resulted in the most salient social movements no longer being economically defined 'classes' struggling to defend their 'interests'.[37] Rather, a cultural politics focused on issues of gender, ethnicity, the environment etc. has been decoupled from social politics and there has been an eschewal of traditional (institutional) channels of political expression.[38] Group identity (rather than class interest) has become the chief medium of political mobilisation. In this 'postsocialist condition' as Fraser terms it, there has been a commensurate (and regrettable) privileging of recognition over redistribution.[39] Fraser is keen to see the development of a position which is adequate to both recognition and redistribution.

Fraser's work can be seen as reflecting the impact of some of Foucault's later work on political thought.[40] As Jon Simons has noted recently: 'Foucault's political thought is timely in ways which are not immediately obvious. The concern for "cultural" issues of identity politics and concern for the self, rather than allegedly "real" issues such as economics and social distribution should not be considered the luxury of the rich.'[41] Simons also notes that a position which is focused on group identity converges with concerns about ethnic inequalities and the feminisation of poverty.

New technologies, new politics?

While Max Weber in a telling phrase noted the collapse of the old gods, but simultaneously the emptiness of the newly erected idol of science, it is Walter Benjamin who displays the undermining power of technology at the most rarefied and ineffable of levels – in our cultural expressions. His essay 'The Work of Art in the Age of Mechanical Reproduction' does for cultural products what the new biotechnologies of reproduction both promise and threaten to undertake for the meaning of human relationships.[42] That science and technology could pose threats to human well-being became apparent from an unexpected direction in the Germany of the thirties and forties.

For Third Reich theorists science was of less account than technology; in a curious way they foreshadowed the late twentieth-century developments of consumer capitalism – an economy whose own driving force is linked neither to knowledge nor to culture, but only to devouring the products of the world. But other aspects of Third Reich technological *politik*, especially the racial purity projects, both positively through breeding scenarios and negatively through the chemical extirpation of unhealthy species, have resonances with current biotechnologies, as Marilyn Strathern reports elsewhere in this volume.

In rewriting the ideas of individual and person, the concomitant relations between those highly valued spheres of bourgeois political theory – the public and the private – now show other vulnerabilities, as can be so clearly seen in Strathern's discussion of reproductive technologies. In part these problems have been explored in the context of work on governmentality, a second strand of Foucault's political thought.[43] Such weaknesses had become apparent already in late modernity's mass-party phenomenon. Again, as has been observed by Benjamin, with the loss of the aura, fascism responds with the aesthetisation of violence and violence itself becomes an aspect of the sublime, Shoah revealing its horror as a spectacle paralleling the Nuremberg rallies and the Nazi torch-light parades.[44]

Yet everyday life proceeded in the Third Reich even as it did in Stalin's Russia. The questions that now face our society are more in the nature of a future so different that the radicality of change will make this usable notion of the everyday incredible, hard even to dream of. The cut-off between these spheres remains in spite of all the centralised forces marshalled against it. Yet in the contemporary scene the boundary, perhaps always exaggerated in its significance and exaggerated in its degree of impact, has begun to wither for other reasons, through processes which are linked to changes in the idea of a self, of identities and the kinds of goals that can serve and subserve human endeavour. As Hawthorn and Lund conclude, if 'modern liberal republics are not to be paralysingly overloaded . . . the line between the "public" and "private" does indeed have to be redrawn' (this volume).

Conclusion: facing the angel of history

A substantial section of this volume is devoted to discussing the history of the subject, and to surveying political theory. For the history of the disciplines is bound up with the more general readings of social processes as historical events and narratives. Just why history is so central to these endeavours is brought out in Roger Smith's *History of the Human Sciences*, where he concludes that the writing of history is inseparable from debates about the human sciences themselves.[45] And notably the writing of history itself has become central to the debate over postmodernity; for as Hans Kellner observes 'it was the early *historists* who were the postmoderns'.[46]

Herminio Martins points out in this volume that postmodernism is a notion that relates closely to *posthistoire*: the end of history – an end which is by turns beneficent and apocalyptic.[47] And postmodernism itself signals another end – or perhaps as Derrida has said more a closure than an end – that is the 'completion' of the modernist programme of explanation. That is some sense that we have reached an intellectual end in our attempts to offer explanations of social and political events in terms of rational, causal and law-like processes.

Currently, then, it is also understandable that a good deal of experimentation is on hand. From the use of Freudian insights through Foucauldian genealogical method to the application of social constructionism, a vast and confusing array of approaches have appeared on the horizon of the new millennium. Perhaps a novel kind of approach might be in view, which, in characteristically postmodernist terms, is paradoxically a much older procedure, a kind of philosophical anthropology. Certainly boundary-crossing projects like Charles Taylor's *Sources of the Self*, and Alasdair MacIntyre's *After Virtue* and its successors endeavour to bring together the social, moral and the political, while continuously aware of the limitations and absurdities of those attempts by the human sciences to mirror a late-nineteenth-century vision of the natural sciences and their developmental style.[48]

It is among the paradoxes of this condition (postmodernity) that it is yet possible, in a world of partiality and difference, to experience a claim to universality or a truth at least valid for the generality of human experience in our time. In writing that history we are compelled to rewrite the very direction of our intellectual past and what it can hold for us.[49] The significance of this historical rethinking and its links with the politics of postmodernity is epitomised in the work of Zygmunt Bauman.[50] As a twice-born exile he has been well placed both to experience and to analyse the meaning of exile and marginality in the politics of modernity, and the contradictions therein.[51] His views resonate with the critique of progress and history expressed by Benjamin. More specifically, and with great prescience, Benjamin writes: 'Social Democracy has inherited the old Protestant work ethic; it recognises only the progress in the mastery of nature, not the retrogression of society; it already displays the technocratic features later encountered in Fascism. It believes in the infinite perfectibility of mankind.' But for Benjamin the face of the angel of history is turned towards the past. And 'where we perceive a chain of events he sees one single catastrophe which piles wreckage upon wreckage'. While the debris before him grows, a storm is blowing from paradise which irresistibly propels the angel into the future. 'This storm is what we call progress.'[52] As Gillian Rose puts it, 'history is exilic not universalistic'.[53]

Much of the debate, both between modernist and postmodernist political theorists and within those collectivities themselves, has been over the residual possibilities of socialism and the feasibility of political visions for a future world. For Bauman such a vision remains open, but in a special way; for as he writes in his essay on Benjamin:

The strategy of Benjamin . . . is not a strategy of redemption. It is instead a strategy of keeping the ground ready for redemption, if the redemption comes . . . In a history without a telos or a pointer, without a deterministic chain pulled ahead and thus kept straight by its still invisible, yet fully defined end, without a pragmatically correct programme for what is to be done to assist that end in its effort – in such a history, every moment, every 'now' becomes pregnant with significance.[54]

NOTES

1 For some general discussions see Connolly (1988), Rengger (1995) and White (1991).
2 Especially Rorty (1989), Lyotard (1984), Taylor (1991a, 1991b) and MacIntyre (1981, 1988).
3 On the 'crisis of the representation of the social' see Moscovici (1990).
4 This sense of disintegration can be discerned in the humanities as well. In introducing a recent volume on hysteria, Roy Porter sees that one of the great gains of the last decade or two has been the breaking down of old disciplinary boundaries in the humanities. He notes that: 'Thanks to new approaches to texts stimulated by various forms of postmodernism, we can no longer regard poems and novels as disembodied . . . works of the spirit; we see them now as works that are subject to modes of production that have a challenging . . . physical life of their own' (Porter, 1997).
5 On interdisciplinarity see Klein (1990); on boundary work Gieryn (1983) and Fuller (1991); on some consequences for the organisation of the academy see Wallerstein (1996) and Readings (1995).
6 Rowlands (1994). See Sassower (1993) for an illuminating discussion of the politics of scientific expertise.
7 For two rather contrasted discussions see Wallerstein (1995) and Fuller (1993).
8 Jencks (1986).
9 Lash and Urry (1987).
10 Lyotard (1984).
11 For a recent history of postmodernism see Bertens (1995).
12 For some general discussions of social theory and postmodernism see Harvey (1989), Seidman and Wagner (1992), Smart (1993) and Tester (1993).
13 Rorty (1983).
14 Rawls (1993).
15 See also Plant (1992).
16 Such dualisms include those of body/mind, individual/social, subject/object, nature/culture, fact/value etc. At the beginning of the century the pragmatist philosophers, especially George Herbert Mead and John Dewey devoted much attention to the analysis of the consequences of such dualistic

thinking. For a recent discussion of the impact of such dualisms on the human sciences in general see Fay (1996).

17 See Tajfel (1981, 1982), Abrams and Hogg (1990) and Brown (1995).

18 But see Sampson (1993) for a relatively rare exception. Calhoun (1994a) provides a helpful discussion of recent debates about essentialism and constructionism in relation to identity issues. Michael (1996) draws on actor-network theory in his illuminating exploration of how 'the nonhuman' can play a part in the construction of identity.

19 Kellner (1992).

20 In Gergen (1991) and Shotter (1993). See R. Jenkins (1996) for a recent attempt to develop a more mutualist account of social identity that focuses on an 'internal-external dialectic of identification as the process whereby all identities – individual and collective – are constituted' (Jenkins, 1996, p. 20) and Somers (1994) for an approach which links narrative and identity in an instructive way.

21 Kellner (1992).

22 Kellner (1992), p. 174. For discussions of some general issues concerning postmodern identity see Lash and Friedman (1992) and Calhoun (1994b).

23 Engels (1978).

24 Kolakowski (1990).

25 For discussions of notions of objectivity and truth see Allen (1993), Harding (1992), Proctor (1991), and Longino (1990). On foundationalism and anti-foundationalism in relation to postmodernism see Crook (1991) and Rouse (1991a).

26 On reflexivity see Woolgar (1988) and Lynch (1995); on rhetoric see Billig (1996), Myerson (1994) and Roberts and Good (1993); on meaning-making see Bruner (1990) and Harré and Gillett (1994).

27 John Dewey's initial critique of the 'spectator theory of knowledge' is in his *The Quest for Certainty* (Dewey, 1930). His final attempt to develop a transactional approach to knowledge is the result of his long collaboration with Arthur Bentley (Dewey and Bentley, 1949). For a more recent approach which attempts a synthesis of pragmatism, Heideggerian philosophy and social studies of science see Rouse (1987, 1996). Rouse observes: 'There is no politically or epistemologically neutral standpoint for critical reflection . . . What remains to be achieved is to distinguish clearly and effectively the impossible and pernicious ideal of . . . neutrality, from what for the lack of a better word I would still call objectivity, an appropriate respect for the myriad ways in which the world transcends, remolds and resists our various interpretations' (Rouse, 1991b, p. 364).

28 Putnam (1995), p. 288.

29 Bernstein (1992). On pragmatist aesthetics see Shusterman (1992) and Benson (1993); on pragmatist approaches to the history and philosophy of science see Jardine (1986) and Ellis (1990). On pragmatist social theory see Joas (1993) and Shalin (1986); on psychology see Still and Good (1992).

30 See Margolis (1989), Bernstein (1991) and Fay (1996).

31 See Hekman (1995), Rorty (1989), Mouffe (1993, 1996) and Margolis (1996).

32 See Westbrook (1991) especially for his critical discussion of the relationship

between John Dewey's political ideas and those of Richard Rorty; and also Alan Ryan (1995) for his recent sympathetic and insightful account of Dewey's politics.

33 Fraser (1997).

34 See also her monograph *Women in Political Theory* (Coole, 1993).

35 For example in Young (1990) and MacKinnon (1991).

36 For example in Kymlicka (1995a 1995b), Taylor (1994), Nicholson and Seidman (1995) and Rajchman (1995).

37 Fraser (1997).

38 See Seidman (1994), Chapter 7, 'The new social movements and the making of new social knowledges', and Squires (this volume).

39 Fraser (1997).

40 Especially Foucault (1991). For some general discussions see Barry et al. (1996) and McNay (1994), Chapter 3, 'From discipline to government'.

41 Simons (1995) p. 123.

42 Benjamin (1968b).

43 For Andrew Barry, the study of governmentalities 'is the analysis of political reason itself, the mentalities of politics which have shaped our present'. This work 'lies somewhere between a history of political ideas and a sociology of the technologies of government' (Barry et al., 1996, p. 2). See further Burchell, Gordon and Miller (1991).

44 Benjamin (1968b).

45 Smith (1997).

46 Kellner (1995). Kellner's full expression is: 'to read the early historists . . . is to reverse the charges made against postmodernist students of historical discourse; far from being historicist in any classic sense, it was the early historists who were the postmoderns, as Jean-François Lyotard suggested when he noted that a postmodernism precedes every modernism.' (p. 15)

47 On the end of history thesis see Fukuyama (1992) and Niethammer (1992).

48 For example in Rorty (1989), Kolakowski (1990) and Blumenberg (1983). A central contribution to this task of reconstruction has been the work of feminist writers such as Sandra Harding (1991), Donna Haraway (1991) and Selya Benhabib (1992).

49 For some discussions of the impact of pragmatist, postmodern and feminist ideas on the writing of history see Joyce Appleby et al. (1994), Norman Bryson (1983), Michel Foucault (1972), Ian Hacking (1990), Keith Jenkins (1991, 1996), Ludy Jordanova (1989), Michael Krausz (1991), Joseph Margolis (1991), Joan Scott (1988) and Hayden White (1978).

50 For example in Bauman (1987, 1989, 1993a).

51 As a Pole exiled to Russia during the war; as a Jew exiled from Poland during the anti-Zionist campaign of the 1960s. Some of these exilic experiences are movingly brought out in Janina Bauman's (1988) autobiography: *A Dream of Belonging: My Years in Postwar Poland*.

52 The iconography of Benjamin's angel is derived from a painting by Paul Klee which he owned at one time; its title was the 'Angelus Novus'. Benjamin's comments and the reference to the painting can be found in his (1968a) 'Theses on the Philosophy of History'. For a detailed discussion of

this image see Gershom Scholem's incomparable essay 'Walter Benjamin and His Angel' (Scholem, 1988).
53 Rose (1993).
54 Bauman (1993b).

BIBLIOGRAPHY

Abrams, D. and Hogg, M. (1990) *Social Identity Theory: Constructive and Critical Advances*. Hemel Hempstead: Harvester Wheatsheaf.
Allen, B. (1993) *Truth in Philosophy*. Cambridge, MA: Harvard University Press.
Appleby, J., Hunt, L. and Jacob, M. (1994) *Telling the Truth about History*. New York: Norton.
Auden, W. H. (1966) *Collected Shorter Poems, 1927–1957*. London: Faber.
Barry, A., Osborne, T. and Rose, N. (eds.) (1996) *Foucault and the Political*. London: UCL Press.
Bauman, J. (1988) *A Dream of Belonging: My Years in Postwar Poland*. London: Virago.
Bauman, Z. (1987) *Legislators and Interpreters*. Cambridge: Polity Press.
  (1989) *Modernity and the Holocaust*. Cambridge: Polity Press.
  (1993a) *Postmodern Ethics*. Oxford: Blackwell.
  (1993b) 'Walter Benjamin, the Intellectual', *New Formations*, 20: 47–57.
Benhabib, S. (1992) *Situating the Self: Gender, Community and Postmodernism in Contemporary Ethics*. Cambridge: Polity Press.
Benjamin, W. (1968a) 'Theses on History', in *Illuminations*. London: Fontana.
  (1968b) 'The Work of Art in the Age of Mechanical Reproduction', in *Illuminations*. London: Fontana.
  (1992) *Illuminations*. London: Fontana.
Benson, C. (1993) *The Absorbed Self: Pragmatism, Psychology and Aesthetic Experience*. Hemel Hempstead: Harvester Wheatsheaf.
Bernstein, R. J. (1991) *The New Constellation: The Ethical-Political Horizons of Modernity/Postmodernity*. Cambridge: Polity Press.
  (1992) 'The Resurgence of Pragmatism', *Social Research*, 59: 813–40.
Bertens, H. (1995) *The Idea of the Postmodern: A History*. London: Routledge.
Billig, M. (1996) *Arguing and Thinking: A Rhetorical Approach to Social Psychology*. 2nd edn. Cambridge/Paris: Cambridge University Press/Editions de la Maison des Sciences de l'Homme.
Blumenberg, H. (1983) *The Legitimacy of the Modern Age*, trans. R. M. Wallace. Cambridge, MA: MIT Press.
Brown, R. J. (1995) *Prejudice: Its Social Psychology*. Oxford: Blackwell.
Bruner, J. (1990) *Acts of Meaning*. Cambridge, MA: Harvard University Press.
Bryson, N. (1983) *Vision and Painting*. Cambridge: Cambridge University Press.
Burchell, G., Gordon, C. and Miller, P. (eds.) (1991) *The Foucault Effect: Studies in Governmentality*. Hemel Hempstead: Harvester Wheatsheaf.
Calhoun, C. (1994a) 'Social Theory and the Politics of Identity', in C. Calhoun (ed.) *Social Theory and the Politics of Identity*. Oxford: Blackwell.
Calhoun, C. (ed.) (1994b) *Social Theory and the Politics of Identity*. Oxford: Blackwell.

Connolly, W. E. (1988) *Political Theory and Modernity*. Oxford: Blackwell.

Coole, D. (1993) *Women in Political Theory: From Ancient Misogyny to Contemporary Feminism*. 2nd edn. Hemel Hempstead: Harvester Wheatsheaf.

Crook, S. (1991) *Modernist Radicalism and its Aftermath: Foundationalism and Anti-foundationalism in Radical Social Theory*. London: Routledge.

Dewey, J. (1930) *The Quest for Certainty: A Study of the Relation of Knowledge and Action*. London: Allen & Unwin.

Dewey, J. and Bentley, A. (1949) *Knowing and the Known*. Boston: Beacon Press.

Ellis, B. (1990) *Truth and Objectivity*. Oxford: Blackwell.

Engels, F. (1978) *Socialism: Utopian and Scientific*. Moscow: Progress Publishers.

Fay, B. (1996) *Contemporary Philosophy of Social Science: A Multicultural Approach*. Oxford: Blackwell.

Foucault, M. (1972) *Histoire de la folie à l'âge classique*. Paris: Gallimard.

(1991) 'Governmentality', in G. Burchell, C. Gordon and P. Miller (eds.) *The Foucault Effect: Studies in Governmentality*. Hemel Hempstead: Harvester Wheatsheaf.

Fraser, Nancy (1997) *Justice Interruptus: Critical Reflections on the "Postsocialist" Condition*. New York: Routledge.

Fukuyama, F. (1992) *The End of History and the Last Man*. London: Penguin.

Fuller, S. (1991) 'Disciplinary Boundaries and the Rhetoric of the Social Sciences', *Poetics Today*, 12: 301–25.

(1993) *Philosophy, Rhetoric, and the End of Knowledge: The Coming of Science and Technology Studies*. Madison: University of Wisconsin Press.

Gergen, K. J. (1991) *The Saturated Self: Dilemmas of Identity in Contemporary Life*. New York: Basic Books.

Gieryn, T. (1983) 'Boundary Work and the Demarcation of Science from Non-science: Strains and Interests in the Professional Ideologies of Scientists', *American Sociological Review*, 48: 781–95.

Hacking, I. (1990) *The Taming of Chance*. Cambridge: Cambridge University Press.

Haraway, D. J. (1991) *Simians, Cyborgs, and Women: The Reinvention of Nature*. New York: Routledge.

Harding, S. (1991) *Whose Science? Whose Knowledge? Thinking from Women's Lives*. Milton Keynes, Bucks.: Open University Press.

(1992) 'After the Neutrality Ideal: Science, Politics, and "Strong Objectivity"', *Social Research*, 59: 567–87.

Harré, R. and Gillett, G. (1994) *The Discursive Mind*. London: Sage.

Harvey, D. (1989) *The Condition of Postmodernity: An Enquiry into the Origins of Cultural Change*. Oxford: Blackwell.

Hekman, S. J. (1995) *Moral Voices, Moral Selves: Carol Gilligan and Feminist Moral Theory*. Cambridge: Polity.

Jardine, N. (1986) *The Fortunes of Inquiry*. Oxford: Clarendon Press.

Jencks, C. (1986) *What is Post-Modernism?* London: Academy Editions.

Jenkins, K. (1991) *Re-thinking History*. London: Routledge.

(1996) *On 'What is History?': From Carr and Elton to Rorty and White*. London: Routledge.

Jenkins, R. (1996) *Social Identity*. London: Routledge.

Joas, H. (1993) *Pragmatism and Social Theory*. Chicago: University of Chicago Press.

Jordanova, L. (1989) *Sexual Visions*. Hemel Hempstead: Harvester Wheatsheaf.

Kellner, D. (1992) 'Popular Culture and the Construction of Postmodern Identities', in S. Lash and J. Friedman (eds.) *Modernity and Identity*. Oxford: Blackwell, 141–77.

Kellner, H. (1995) 'Introduction', in Frank Ankersmit and Hans Kellner (eds.) *A New Philosophy of History*. London: Reaktion Books, 15.

Klein, J. T. (1990) *Interdisciplinarity: History, Theory and Practice*. Detroit: Wayne State University Press.

Kolakowski, L. (1990) *Modernity on Endless Trial*. Chicago: University of Chicago Press.

Krausz, M. (1991) 'History and its Objects', *The Monist* 74: 217–29.

Kymlicka, W. (1995a) *The Rights of Minority Cultures*. Oxford: Oxford University Press.

(1995b) *Multicultural Citizenship: A Liberal Theory of Minority Rights*. Oxford: Clarendon Press.

Lash, S. and Friedman, J., (eds.) (1992) *Modernity and Identity*. Oxford: Blackwell.

Lash, S. and Urry, J. (1987) *The End of Organized Capitalism*. Cambridge: Polity Press.

Longino, H. E. (1990) *Science as Social Knowledge: Values and Objectivity in Scientific Inquiry*. Princeton, NJ: Princeton University Press.

Lynch, M. (1995) *Scientific Practice and Ordinary Action: Ethnomethodology and Social Studies of Science*. Cambridge: Cambridge University Press.

Lyotard, J.-F. (1984) *The Postmodern Condition: A Report on Knowledge*. Manchester: Manchester University Press.

MacIntyre, A. (1981) *After Virtue*. London: Duckworth.

(1988) *Whose Justice? Which Rationality?* London: Duckworth.

MacKinnon, C. (1991) *Towards a Feminist Theory of the State*. Cambridge, MA: Harvard University Press.

Margolis, J. (1989) 'Postscript on Modernism and Postmodernism, both', *Theory, Culture & Society*, 6: 5–30.

(1991) 'Prospects for a Theory of Radical History', *The Monist*, 74: 268–92.

(1996) *Life Without Principles: Reconciling Theory and Practice*. Oxford: Blackwell.

McNay, L. (1994) *Foucault: A Critical Introduction*. Cambridge: Polity.

Michael, M. (1996) *Constructing Identities: The Social, the Nonhuman and Change* London: Sage.

Moscovici, S. (1990) 'Questions for the Twenty-first Century', *Theory, Culture & Society*, 7: 1–19.

Mouffe, C. (1993) *The Return of the Political*. London: Verso.

Mouffe, C. (ed.) (1996) *Deconstruction and Pragmatism*. London: Routledge.

Myerson, G. (1994) *Rhetoric, Reason and Society: Rationality as Dialogue*. London: Sage.

Nicholson, L. and Seidman, S. (1995) *Social Postmodernism: Beyond Identity Politics*. New York: Cambridge University Press.

Niethammer, L. (1992) *Posthistoire: Has History Come to an End?* Trans. Patrick Camiller. London: Verso.

Plant, R. (1992) 'Political Theory Without Foundations', *History of the Human Sciences*, 5 (3): 137–44.

Porter, R. (1997) 'Foreword', in P. M. Logan, *Nerves and Narratives: A Cultural History of Hysteria in 19th-Century Prose*. Berkeley: University of California Press.

Proctor, R. N. (1991) *Value-Free Science: Purity and Power in Modern Knowledge*. Cambridge, MA: Harvard University Press.

Putnam, H. (1995) 'Comments and Replies', in P. Clark and B. Hale (eds.) *Reading Putnam*. Oxford: Blackwell.

Rajchman, J. (1995) *The Identity in Question*. New York: Routledge.

Rawls, J. (1993) *Political Liberalism*. New York: Columbia University Press.

Readings, B. (1995) 'Dwelling in the Ruins', *The Oxford Literary Review*, 17: 15–28.

Rengger, N. J. (1995) *Political Theory, Modernity and Postmodernity*. Oxford: Blackwell.

Roberts, R. H. and Good, J. M. M. (eds.) (1993) *The Recovery of Rhetoric: Persuasive Discourse and Disciplinarity in the Human Sciences*. Bristol: The Bristol Press.

Rorty, R. (1983) 'Postmodern Bourgeois Liberalism', *Journal of Philosophy*, 80 (10): 583–9.

(1989) *Contingency, Irony, and Solidarity*. Cambridge: Cambridge University Press.

Rose, G. (1993) 'Walter Benjamin – Out of the Sources of Modern Judaism', *New Formations*, 20: 59–81.

Rouse, J. (1987) *Knowledge and Power: Toward a Political Philosophy of Science*. Ithaca: Cornell University Press.

(1991a) 'Philosophy of Science and the Persistent Narratives of Modernity', *Studies in the History and Philosophy of Science*, 22: 141–62.

(1991b) 'Policing Knowledge: Disembodied Policy for Embodied Knowledge', *Inquiry*, 34: 353–64.

(1996) *Engaging Science. How to Understand its Practices Scientifically*. Ithaca: Cornell University Press.

Rowlands, M. (1994) 'The Politics of Identity in Archaeology', in G. C. Bond and A. Gilliam (eds.) *Social Construction of the Past: Representation and Power*. London: Routledge.

Ryan, A. (1995) *John Dewey and the High Tide of American Liberalism*. New York: Norton.

Sampson, E. E. (1993) 'Identity Politics: Challenges to Psychology's Understanding, *American Psychologist*, 48: 1219–30.

Sassower, R. (1993) *Knowledge without Expertise: On the Status of Scientists*. Albany, NY: State University of New York Press.

Scholem, G. (1988) 'Walter Benjamin and His Angel', in G. Smith (ed.) *On Walter Benjamin: Critical Essays and Recollections*. Cambridge, MA: MIT Press, 51–89.

Scott, J. W. (1988) *Gender and the Politics of History*. New York: Columbia University Press.

Seidman, S. (1994) *Contested Knowledge: Social Theory in the Postmodern Era.* Oxford: Blackwell.

Seidman, S. and Wagner, D. G. (1992) *Postmodernism and Social Theory: The Debate over General Theory.* Cambridge, MA: Blackwell.

Shalin, D. N. (1986) 'Pragmatism and Social Interactionism', *American Sociological Review,* 51: 9–29.

Shotter, J. (1993) *Cultural Politics of Everyday Life: Social Constructionism, Rhetoric and Knowing of the Third Kind.* Buckingham: Open University Press.

Shusterman, R. (1992) *Pragmatist Aesthetics: Living Beauty, Rethinking Art.* Oxford: Blackwell.

Simons, J. (1995) *Foucault and the Political.* London: Routledge.

Smart, B. (1993) *Postmodernity.* London: Routledge.

Smith, R. (1997) *The Fontana History of the Human Sciences.* London: Fontana.

Somers, M. R. (1994) 'The Narrative Constitution of Identity: A Relational and Network Approach', *Theory and Society,* 23: 605–49.

Still, A. W. and Good, J. M. M. (1992) 'Mutualism in the Human Sciences: Towards the Implementation of a Theory', *Journal for the Theory of Social Behaviour,* 22: 105–28.

Szymborska, W. (1996) *View with a Grain of Sand.* Trans. S. Barańczak and C. Cavanagh. London: Faber.

Tajfel, H. (1981) *Human Groups and Social Categories: Studies in Social Psychology.* Cambridge: Cambridge University Press.

(1982) *Social Identity and Intergroup Relations.* Cambridge/Paris: Cambridge University Press/ Maison des Sciences de l'Homme.

Taylor, C. (1991a) *Sources of the Self: The Making of the Modern Identity.* Cambridge: Cambridge University Press.

(1991b) 'Justice After Virtue', in J. Horton and S. Mendus (eds.) *After MacIntyre: Critical Perspectives on the Work of Alasdair MacIntyre.* Cambridge: Polity Press, 16–43.

(1994) *Multiculturalism: Examining the Politics of Recognition.* Ed. Amy Gutmann. Princeton, NJ: Princeton University Press.

Tester, K (1993) *The Life and Times of Post-Modernity.* London: Routledge.

Wallerstein, I. (1995) 'What are we Bounding, and Whom, When we Bound Research?', *Social Research,* 62: 839–56.

(1996) *Open the Social Sciences: Report of the Gulbenkian Commission into the Restructuring of the Social Sciences.* Stanford, CA: Stanford University Press.

Westbrook, R. B. (1991) *John Dewey and American Democracy.* Ithaca: Cornell University Press.

White, H. (1978) *Tropics of Discourse.* Baltimore: Johns Hopkins University Press.

White, S. K. (1991) *Political Theory and Postmodernism.* Cambridge: Cambridge University Press.

Woolgar, S. (1988) *Knowledge and Reflexivity: New Frontiers in the Sociology of Knowledge.* London: Sage.

Young, I. M. (1990) *Justice and the Politics of Difference.* New Jersey: Princeton University Press.

Part I

Modernity and its vicissitudes

Precisely why an age of anxiety has been created by the term 'post-modernity' and why in spite of vociferous opposition from quarters both Left and Right it has nevertheless made its presence increasingly felt can be seen in the chapters in this section.

Perhaps most prominent among those presenting critiques of modernity and its associated theoretical apparatus in the human sciences has been Zygmunt Bauman: in many ways a product of one of the strongest modernist visions, Marxism and the communist movement. Bauman as a member of an ethnic minority has been exceptionally well placed to both read and offer his own commentaries on this world.

Bauman's chapter explores aspects of the changing relationships between modernity and postmodernity. For Bauman, social modernity is about standards, hope and guilt; psychically, modernity is about identity, about the truth of being as not-yet-here. Both socially and psychically modernity is incurably self-critical: an endless exercise in self-cancelling and self-invalidating. Bauman develops his themes of parvenu and pariah by noting that in such a world all residents are nomads, but nomads who wander in order to settle. Wherever they come and dearly wish to stay, these nomads find themselves to be *parvenus*: someone already in but not quite of the place. Parvenus are people in frantic search for identities, chasing identities because from the start they had been denied definitions. For the parvenu the game is unwinnable, at least as long as it goes on being played by the set rules. Only the explosion of the myth of belonging can bring out the truth of the incompleteness of nomadic existence.

On the other hand, modernity, in proclaiming no order is untouchable, is the hope of the *pariah*. But the pariah can only stop being a pariah by becoming – struggling to become – a parvenu. What modernity sought to destroy – community, variety, contingency, ambivalence – is now rehabilitated. While this *may* be a postmodern age, in one sense modernity is very much with us. Hope, for Bauman, the hope of making things better than they are, is at least one surviving trait of modernity.

Yet he sees the postmodern accolade of difference as likely to embrace a conflictual ambivalence veering between the equally unpalatable and indefensible extremes of a 'wet liberalism' which meekly surrenders the right to compare and evaluate the others and a rampant tribalism which denies the others the right to compare and evaluate. What seems probable is that the parvenu route of escape from the pariah status will be closed.

Like Bauman, Geoffrey Hawthorn and Camilla Lund are concerned about institutional arrangements which in their modernist guise appear to be under extreme pressure, but here the focus is on the political constitutions and political identities which although the products of modernity, seem unable to cope with the changing states of affairs facing in particular the 'late-modern' democracies.

Their chapter elaborates the question of how, if at all, modern or postmodern conceptions of identity can be made more compatible with modern politics. They suggest that in republican political theory, classical and early modern, the individual's identity is that of the 'citizen', and he or she is a citizen of the 'community' of all citizens in the state. Whereas in radical democratic theory her identity is that of the 'individual' itself, and he or she exists in a 'civil society' that is distinct from the state. In the first of these two models, politics is that arena in which the citizens discuss their individual interests and those of the community and having done so, and having reflected on the discussion, come to an agreed conclusion. In the second, politics is simply where interests are represented and negotiated; there is no suggestion that politics itself will change them or the identities that embody them, and it would be unacceptable if it did.

In actually existing modern democracies, the idea of 'citizen' is abstract (and has been so since the French Revolution); for the purposes of political mobilisation and the competition for power, individuals are encouraged to see themselves as having individual interests (on the radical democratic model) which nevertheless can be subsumed in those of others, a class or confession or *ethnos*. Ironically, since it is so remote from existing democracies, it is only the picture of possible identities in republicanism that is consistent with present ('postmodern') conceptions: that is to say of identities as 'situational' – 'domestic' or private and 'political' or public – and in politics, as the subject for reflection, discussion and possible change. In radical democratic theory and the practice of modern democracies, by contrast, identities are fixed – politics is expected at best to 'respond' to them and the interests they embody – and the distinction between the private and the public is more difficult to draw.

Where Bauman, Hawthorn and Lund consider the problems of modernity at the institutional level, Quentin Skinner is concerned to take up analytical problems, and in particular one specific aspect of the modern self. Here Skinner examines Charles Taylor's approach to the 'who' in modernity. In parallel with some of Foucault's researches on identity, Skinner prises apart the buried banalities which haunt so many claimants to the role of the authentic self in the absence of the rational citizen.

His chapter concentrates on two connected features of Charles Taylor's argument in *Sources of the Self*. The first part of this investigation examines Taylor's list of the moral imperatives allegedly felt with particular force in the contemporary world and puts in question the extent to which the values listed by Taylor are genuinely shared. Further Skinner points to a range of criticisms put forward by conservatives, Marxists, feminists, and other opponents of liberalism, all of whose doubts Taylor appears to underestimate. Secondly, the chapter addresses Taylor's underlying claim that a religious dimension is indispensable if the highest human potentialities are to be realised; and concludes with a critique of his theistic arguments.

This section concludes with David Cooper's assessment of theoretical claims in the philosophical domain and particularly the collision between postmodernist stances and traditional modernist epistemic practices. Cooper's purpose is to diagnose the verdict of postmodernists like Lyotard, and of their 'heroes', like Heidegger, that philosophy, as traditionally pursued, is or should be dead. He sees this verdict as harsher than earlier 'death of philosophy' pronouncements. Cooper argues that Lyotard's well-known characterisation of postmodernism as 'incredulity towards metanarratives' does not bring out the radical character of his attitude to philosophy. Just how radical his position is can be seen in the dispute between Lyotard and Habermas over 'universal consensus' which shows that, for the former, no notion recognisably similar to that of truth is required to explain how scientific practice and linguistic communication are possible. The central critical question is whether the notion of truth or the 'truth-like' is presupposed by our intelligent activities. The postmodernist view that it is not is defended against some predictable objections (e.g. that the concept of progress in science requires such a notion).

Finally, Cooper attempts to relate this hostile attitude towards the traditional aims of philosophy to the wider culture of postmodernism. Following Jameson, he concludes that a characteristic of postmodernist views on art, literature, politics, etc. is a concentration on the surface of things, a rejection of 'depth'. This is also the outstanding characteristic of the postmodernist criticism of philosophy as a misguided search for the 'deep' foundations of our practices – a criticism strikingly similar to the later Wittgenstein and the later Heidegger.

2   Parvenu and pariah: heroes and victims of modernity

Zygmunt Bauman

Socially, modernity is about standards, hope and guilt. Standards – beckoning, alluring, or prodding; but always stretching, always a step or two ahead of the pursuers, always forging onward just a little bit quicker than their chasers. And always promising that the morrow will be better than the now. And always keeping the promise fresh and unsullied, since the morrow will forever be a day after. And always mixing the hope of reaching the promised land with the guilt of not walking fast enough. The guilt protects the hope from frustration; the hope sees to it that the guilt never dries up. 'L'homme est coupable' – observed Camus, that watchful correspondent from the land of modernity – 'mais il l'est de n'avoir su tirer de lui-même.'[1]

Psychically, modernity is about identity: about the truth of being as not-yet-here, as a task, a mission, a responsibility. Like the rest of standards, identity stays stubbornly ahead: one needs to run breathlessly to reach it. And so one runs, pulled by hope and pushed by guilt, though the running, however fast, feels eerily like crawling. Surging ahead towards enticing and yet unfulfilled identity looks uncannily like recoiling from the flawed, illegitimate reality of the present.

Both socially and psychically, modernity is incurably self-critical: an endless, and in the end prospectless, exercise in self-cancelling and self-invalidating. Truly modern is not the *readiness* to delay gratification, but the *impossibility* of being gratified. All achievement is but a pale copy of its paragon. Today is but an inchoate premonition of tomorrow; or, rather, its inferior, marred reflection. *What is* is cancelled in advance by *what is to come*. But it draws its significance and its meaning – its only meaning – from that cancellation.

Modernity is the impossibility of staying put. To be modern means to be on the move. One does not necessarily choose to be on the move – as one does not choose to be modern. One is set on the move by being cast in the world torn between the beauty of the vision and the ugliness of reality – a reality made ugly by the beauty of the vision. In such a world, all residents are nomads; but nomads who wander in order to settle.

Round the corner, there is, there should be, there must be, a hospitable land in which to settle; but behind every corner new corners appear, with new frustrations and new, yet undashed hopes.

The habitat of nomads is the desert – that place-no-place of which Edmond Jabès wrote that in it 'there are no avenues, no boulevards, no blind alleys and no streets. Only – here and there – fragmentary imprints of steps, quickly effaced and denied.'[2] Effacing yesterday's footprints is all there is to the chimeric homeliness of the overnight stay; it makes the arrival feel, comfortingly, like being at home – that is, until it also turns into an imprint to be denied and effaced. The sight of tents pitched yesterday on the site of the overnight stay is reassuring: it fences off a plot of the desert so that it may feel like an oasis and give a sense of purpose to yesterday's wanderings. These tents pitched yesterday, being but tents, also call, however, the bluff of self-congratulation. They prove, were proof needed, the self-deception of existence which wants to forget its nomadic past; it shows home to be but a point of arrival, and an arrival pregnant with new departure.

Wherever they come and dearly wish to stay, the nomads find themselves to be parvenus. Parvenu; *arriviste*; someone already *in*, but not quite *of* the place, an aspiring resident without a residence permit. Someone reminding the older tenants of the past which they want to forget and the future they would rather wish away; someone who makes the older tenants run for shelter in hastily erected permit-issuing offices. The parvenu is told to carry the 'just arrived' label so that all the others may trust their tents to be cut in rock. The parvenu's stay must be declared temporary, so that the stay of all the others may feel eternal.

The older tenants hate the parvenus for awaking the memories and the premonitions they struggle hard to put to sleep. But they can hardly do without parvenus, without some of them being branded parvenu, set apart, charged with carrying the bacillus of restlessness in their bodies; it is thanks to such branded ones, and them only, that the rest may think that the bad dreams and the morbid premonitions are other people's tales and do not quite apply to themselves. The parvenu needs a parvenu in order not to feel a parvenu. And so nomads fight other nomads for the right to issue residence permits to each other. It is the only way they can make their own residence feel secure. The only way in which they can fix time which refuses to stay still is to mark the space and protect the marks against being effaced or moved. At least, such is their desperate hope.

In Robert Musil's incisive description, 'The train of events is a train unrolling its rails ahead of itself. The river of time is a river sweeping its banks along with it.'[3] It was the modern 'melting of solids and profaning the sacreds' that brought about such trains and such rivers. Premodern trains ran predictably and boringly in circles, much like children's toy trains do. And premodern rivers stayed in their beds for a time long enough to feel immemorial. As Wylie Sypher observed, 'in any society where the class structure is so closed that everyone has their place and knows it – and keeps it', there is no place for a parvenu nor is there a purpose a parvenu could conceivably serve; 'but the nineteenth century produced a horde of parvenus'.[4] Not that inordinately many people began to challenge their class-bound or otherwise-bound definitions and refused to heed their place; but the contours of places had been themselves washed up – the river banks having been swept along with the rivers, and uncertainty called *the new*, or *the better*, or *progress*, having become the only official destination of trains. Places and their names were now to be *made* (and, inevitably, re-made), 'as one goes'. In Hannah Arendt's memorable phrase, *man's autonomy turned into the tyranny of possibilities*. The small print of the great modern Act of Emancipation carried an injunction against the restfulness of certainty.

Definitions are *born with*; identities are *made*. Definitions tell you who you are, identities allure you by what you are not yet but may yet become. Parvenus were people in frantic search of identities. They chased identities because, from the start, they *had been denied* definitions. It was only too easy to conclude that it was their restlessness that put paid to definitions, and charge them with the criminal act of breaking the border-signposts. Once hurled in the vast expanse of unlimited possibilities, the parvenus were an easy prey: there were no fortified places to hide, no trusty definitions to wear as an armour. And from all places still protected by old ramparts, and from all places that strove to build new ones, poisonous arrows were showered.

Early in his life, Goethe's Wilhelm Meister found out that only young aristocrats can count on being taken for *what they are*; all others would be appraised or condemned for *what they do*. Wilhelm Meister drew the only logical conclusion to be drawn: he joined the theatre. On the stage, he took on and took off *roles*. This is what he was doomed to do in life anyway, but at least on stage – and only on stage – everyone expected roles to be but roles and to be played, and dropped, and replaced by other roles. In life, he would be expected to do the opposite or at least to pretend that he was doing it: he would be expected to be *what he is*, though this is precisely what he was denied the right to.

Most parvenus cannot follow Meister's choice. *Life* is their stage, and in life, unlike in the theatre, skilful acting is called insincerity, not finesse; it is precisely to squeeze it out from the daily and the normal that acting as an honourable activity has been confined inside theatre walls. In life, roles must deny being roles and pretend to be identities, even if identities are not available in any other shape or form but that of roles. No one learns this truth better than the parvenus – living as they do under constant, relentless pressure: to quote Hannah Arendt 'to have to adapt their taste, their lives, their desires'; who are 'denied the right to be themselves in anything and in any moment'.[5]

Having learned the rules of the game does not mean being wiser, though. Even less does it mean being successful. There is little the parvenus can do to change their plight, however strongly they desire to do so. 'One cannot modify one's image: neither the thought, nor freedom, lie, nausea, or disgust can help one to get out of one's proper skin.'[6] And yet this is exactly what one is expected to do. The other-directed, other-monitored and other-evaluated parvenus are asked to prove the legality of their presence by being self-directed, self-monitored and self-evaluating, and *being seen* to be such. Wilhelm Meister has prudently *chosen* to be an actor: his modern successors are *forced* to be actors – and risk condemnation and ridicule once they consent to their fate. A vicious circle, if there ever was one. And, as if to rub salt into the wound, there is that deafening silence, the overpowering indifference, the baffling aloofness, the 'I wash my hands' gesture of the Pontius Pilates who sit in judgement. As Kafka wrote in *The Trial*, 'The court wants nothing from you. It receives you when you come and dismisses you when you go.'

The silence of the court makes the defendant his own judge: or, rather, it seems to be the case. With the prosecutor abstaining from censorious speeches and no judge to brief the jury, it is up to the defendants to prove their innocence. But innocence of what? Their guilt, after all, is nothing else but the very fact of having been charged, of standing in judgement. And this is one guilt they cannot deny, however smartly they argue their innocence, and however massive the evidence they gather to support the argument.

By the whim of French legislature, the blacks of Martinique and Guadeloupe have been appointed Frenchmen, unlike the blacks of Sénégal or Côte d'Ivoire or the Arabs of Morocco. Whatever is said or written about the rights of the Frenchmen extends to them; nothing remains to be proved and thus no court summons has been issued or need to be issued. Yet the absence of a court does not mean innocence: it only means that no final judgement will be ever passed and that innocence will be never certified. The silence of the Law means the endlessness of trial. The blacks of Martinique and Guadeloupe have to prove that their Frenchness requires no proof. Not unlike Weber's Calvinists, they must live a life of virtue (a virtue which, in their case, is called 'the Frenchness') without the trust that the virtue will be rewarded and despite the agonising suspicion that even if it were, they would not know it anyway. All around agree that they acquit themselves of the task admirably. They excel in schools. They are the most loyal and dedicated civil servants. Louder still than their co-citizens of a paler shade of skin they demand that the French borders be closed to those alien blacks of Chad or Cameroon 'who have no right to be here'. They even join Le Pen's National Front to promote the purification of La Patrie from the hordes of the parvenus bound to dilute the very Frenchhood they wish to embrace. By the most finical of fastidious of standards, the blacks of Martinique and Guadeloupe are exemplary Frenchmen. To most exemplary Frenchmen this is exactly what they are: black Martiniquans and Guadeloupians passing for exemplary Frenchmen. Well, it is precisely this earnest effort to be exemplary Frenchmen that makes them the blacks of Martinique or Guadeloupe. The more they do to turn into something else than they are, the more they are what they have been called not to be. Or have they indeed been called?

To the many versions of Abraham's answer to God's call, considered by Kierkegaard, Franz Kafka, the great spokesman for the parvenus of this world, added his own: another Abraham – 'who really does want to perform the sacrifice properly' . . . 'but who cannot believe that he has been chosen, the repulsive old man and his dirty son'. 'Although he was afraid of being laughed at, and even more afraid of joining in the laughter, his greatest fear was that, if he were laughed at, he would look even older and even more repulsive, and his son even dirtier An Abraham who comes uncalled!'

For the parvenus the game is unwinnable, at least as long as it goes on being played by the set rules. And the exit from the game means rebellion against the rules; indeed, a reversal of rules. Although, as Max Frisch put it, *always* and *for everybody* in our restless world of modernity 'identity means refusing to be what others want you to be', you are refused the right to refuse; you have no such right, not in *this* game, not as long as the umpires have their way. And so the frustrated dedication turns into mutiny. The myth of belonging is exploded, and the dazzling light of the explosion draws out of its exilic darkness the truth of the incompleteness, until-further-noticeness of the wanderer's existence. Being in the world the way one is (or imagines oneself to be, or wants to be) at home, could be accomplished solely in another world, a world one can reach only through the act of *redemption*.

For parvenus like Lukács and Benjamin, as Ferenc Feher observed, 'the natural way of belonging, the desire for which never left either one, was blocked . . . neither could become assimilated or a nationalist'. The desire of belonging could only point towards the future, beyond the suffocating crampedness of the here and now. There was no belonging in sight except on the other side of redemption. And redemption 'can either come in the form of the Last Judgment, where there is one single yardstick to measure with, and the Supreme Authority sitting in court; or in the form of a conciliatory act of redeeming all those who shared in the community of endless human suffering'.[7] One could struggle for a new certitude to put paid to the uncomfortable pretensions of the present one; seek the as-yet-undiscredited authority hoped to proclaim and enforce new canons and new norms. Or one could part ways with certitudes old, new, and above all those still to come – and follow Adorno's injunction that only experiments are legitimate when certitudes are no more. Both alternatives have been embraced and tried.

The parvenu Lukács spent his life searching for the authority bold and mighty enough to dismiss the judgements of today and proclaim its own judgement as if it were the Last – be it aesthetically perfect form or the distant alliance of proletarian sufferings with universal truth. In this he followed a long string of other parvenus, from Karl Marx – announcing the universality of belonging imminent once universal man is stripped of humiliating and degrading parochial liveries – through Karl Mannheim, struggling to reforge the homelessness of the itinerant sophist into the patent of judgement superior to all and any of the settled opinions – to Husserl, making the truth-bearing subjectivity transcendental, and thus entitled to brush off the admittedly false pretensions of this-worldly subjectivities.

Benjamin's world, on the other hand, was a series of historical moments pregnant with premonitions yet littered with the corpses of miscarried hopes; one moment, for that reason is not particularly different from another. The twin dangers against which the life-work of Benjamin militates, are, in Pierre V. Zima's words, 'la différence absolue et la disjonction idéologique (la *position* d'un des deux termes)' and 'le dépassement (hégélien, marxien) vers l'affirmation, vers la *position* d'un troisième terme sur un plan plus élevé.[8] Under Benjamin's pen, ambivalence turns into the crow's nest from which the archipelago of strangled chances can be sighted; instead of a malady to be cured, ambivalence is now the value to be cherished and protected. The angels – Benjamin noted in his *Agesilaus Santander* (the anagram, deciphered by Scholem as *Der Angelus Satanus*) – 'new ones each moment in countless hosts, are created so that, after they have sung their hymn before God, they cease to exist and pass away into nothingness'. And Adorno commented: Benjamin was one of the first to note that the 'individual who thinks becomes problematic to the core, yet without the existence of anything supra-individual in which the isolated subject could gain spiritual transcendence without being oppressed; it is this that he expressed in defining himself as one who left his class without, however, belonging to another'.[9] Well, like Lukacs, Benjamin was not alone on the road he had chosen. Simmel, with his uncanny flair for decomposing any, however mighty, a structure, into a bunch of human, all-too-human thoughts and emotions, was there first; and many would follow, to mention but Lévi-Strauss debunking progressive history with a pointer as one more tribal myth, Foucault with the discourses that themselves spawn all the limits which stand to confine and channel their formation, or Derrida with realities dissembled into the texts embracing each other in the never-ending quadrille of interpretations.

As in so many similar cases, the modern revolution ended in parricide – so poetically intuited by Freud in his desperate effort to penetrate the mystery of culture. The most brilliant and most faithful children of modernity could not express their filial loyalty otherwise than by becoming its gravediggers. The more they were dedicated to the construction of the artifice which modernity set about to erect, having first dethroned and legally incapacitated nature, the more they sapped the foundations of the edifice. Modernity, one may say, was from the start pregnant with its own postmodern *Aufhebung*. Her children were genetically determined to be her detractors, and – ultimately – her demolition squad. Those cast as parvenus, yet refused the comfort of arrival, were bound sooner or later to decry the safety of *any* safe havens; in the end they were bound to question the arrival itself as a plausible or desirable end of the travel.

Hence the astonishing case of a culture engrossed in a tooth-and-nail struggle with the social reality it was supposed, as all cultures should, to reflect and serve. In this disarticulation and the ensuing enmity between culture and reified existence modernity stands perhaps alone among all known societal arrangements. One can confidently define modernity as form of life marked by such disarticulation: as a social condition under which *culture cannot serve reality otherwise than through undermining it*.

But hence also the uniquely tragic – or is it schizophrenic? – character of modern culture, the culture that feels truly at home only in its homelessness. In that culture, desire is stained with fear, while horror bears attractions difficult to resist. That culture dreams of belonging yet fears locks and barred windows; it dreads the solitude called freedom yet still more than anything else resents oaths of loyalty. At whatever direction it turns, that culture – like the hungry rats of Miller and Dollard's maze – finds itself suspended at the point of ambivalence, where the lines of falling allurement and rising repulsion cross. Walter Benjamin reproached his friend in entrapment and adversary in the search for escape, Gershon Scholem: 'I almost believe that you desire this in-between state, yet you ought to welcome any means of ending it.' To which Scholem replied: 'You are endangered more by your drive for community . . . than by the horror of loneliness that speaks from so many of your writings.'[10]

In the Indian caste system, a pariah was a member of the lowest caste *or of no caste*. In an immovable, unquestionable, untouchable order of belonging, who could be more untouchable than those who did not belong anywhere? Modernity proclaimed no order untouchable, as all untouchable orders were to be replaced with a new, artificial order where roads are built that lead from the bottom to the top and so no one belongs anywhere for ever. Modernity was thus the hope of the pariah. But the pariah could stop being a pariah only by becoming – struggling to become – a parvenu. And the parvenu, having never washed out the stain of his origin, laboured under a constant threat of deportation back to the land he tried to escape: deportation in case he failed; deportation in case he succeeded too spectacularly for the comfort of those around. Not for a moment did the hero stop being a potential victim. Hero today, victim tomorrow, the dividing wall between the two conditions but paper-thin. Being on the move meant belonging nowhere. And belonging nowhere meant not to count on anybody's protection: indeed, the quintessence of the pariah existence was not to be able to count on protection. The quicker you run, the faster you stay put. The greater the frenzy with which you struggle to cut yourself off from the caste of the pariah, the more you expose yourself as the pariah of non-belonging.

It was the alluring image of a majestic artifice shimmering at the end of the tunnel that set the pariah on his journey and transformed him into the parvenu. It was the agony of the endless travel that dimmed the shine of the artifice and dented its attraction: looking back on the road travelled, the seekers of homes would dismiss their past hopes as a mirage – and they would call their new frustrated sobriety the end of utopia, the end of ideology, the end of modernity, the advent of the postmodern age.

Artificial homelands are hallucinations at best, vicious delusions at worst. No more revolutions to end all revolutions. No more stretching oneself towards the sweet future that turns bitter the moment it becomes the present. No more philosopher kings. No more salvation by society. No more dreams about identities that are not – dreams that spoil the enjoyment of the definitions that are. Travel has not brought redemption to the parvenu. Perhaps once there is nowhere to arrive, the sorry plight of the *arriviste* will be cancelled together with the travel?

With the setting of the universal sun, wrote the schoolboy Karl Marx, moths gather to the light of the domestic lamp. With the drying up of the high-tech artificial lake of universality, yesteryear's putrescent bogs of parochiality glisten invitingly as the natural havens for all who need to swim safely. No more salvation by society – but perhaps *community* will make the salvation unnecessary? 'We should not look for skyhooks, but only for toeholds' is how Richard Rorty sums up the mood of the bereaved, and proceeds to sing the praises of ethnocentrism and to advise us, rather than wasting our time in the vain search for objectivity and universal standpoints, to apply ourselves to the questions 'With what communities should you identify?' and 'What should I do with my aloneness?'.[11] While Isaiah Berlin tells his interviewers that there is nationalism which is rapacious, intolerant, cruel, and bad in many other ways, but that there is also nationalism which is warm, cosy, at peace with nature and itself and therefore also, hopefully, with its neighbours. 'Le doux nationalisme', as conscientious Frenchmen, baffled by the spectactular successes of Le Pen, and desperately trying to steal a march on the sinister adversary, call it. The tired wanderer sentenced to a life of a parvenu agony still wants to belong. But he gave up the hope that belonging can be attained through universality. He believes no more in long round about routes. He dreams now of shortcuts. Or, better still – of arriving without travelling; coming home without really ever moving out.

Whatever used to be a virtue, turned into vice. And the vices of yore have been (one hopes, not posthumously) rehabilitated. The verdict has been quashed, those who passed it condemned or dismissed as incompetent judges. What modernity set to destroy, has its day of sweet vengeance. Community, tradition, the joy of being *chez soi*, the love of one's own, the sticking to one's kind, the pride of being so stuck, the roots, the blood, the soil, the nationhood – they no more stand condemned; on the contrary, it is their critics and detractors, the prophets of universal humanity, who are now challenged to prove their case and of whom it is doubted whether they ever will.

Perhaps we live in a postmodern age, perhaps not. But we do live in the age of tribes and tribalism. It is tribalism that injects juice and vigour into the eulogy of community, the acclaim of belonging, the passionate search for tradition. In this sense at least, the long roundabout of modernity has brought us to where our ancestors once started. Or so it may seem.

The end of modernity? Not necessarily. In another respect, after all, modernity is very much with us. It is with us in the form of the most defining of its defining traits: that of hope, the hope of making things better than they are – since they are, thus far, not good enough. Vulgar preachers of unadorned tribalism and elegant philosophers of communally based forms of life alike teach us what they do in the name of changing things for the better. 'Whatever good the ideas of "objectivity"

and "transcendence" have done for our culture can be attained equally
well by the idea of community', says Rorty – and this is precisely what
makes that latter idea attractive for yesterday's seekers of the universal
roads to a world fit for human habitation. Rational designs of artificial
perfection, and the revolutions meant to imprint them on the shape of
the world, all failed abominably to deliver on their promise. Perhaps
communities, warm and hospitable, will deliver what they could not
deliver. We still want the work to be done: we just let drop the tools
which have been proved useless and reach for others which – who
knows? – may still do the job. One may say that we still agree that
marital happiness is a good thing; only we would no longer endorse
Tolstoy's opinion that all happy marriages are happy in the same way.

We know quite well why we dislike the tools which we have
abandoned. For two centuries or so people deserving or demanding to
be listened to with attention and respect told the story of a human
habitat which curiously coincided with that of the political state and the
realm of its legislative powers and ambitions. The human world was, in
Parsons' memorable rendering, the 'principally coordinated' space – the
realm upheld or about to be upheld by uniform principles maintained
by the joint efforts of the legislators and the armed or unarmed
executors of their will. It was such an artificial space that was represented as a habitat which 'fits naturally' human needs and – most
importantly – fits the need to gratify the needs. The 'principally
coordinated', possibly rationally designed and monitored, society was to
be that good society modernity set about constructing. Two centuries is
a long time – enough for all of us to learn what solitary great minds of
Jeremy Bentham's type intuited from the start: that rationally designed
'principal coordination' fits equally well a school and hospital as it fits a
prison and a workhouse; and to find out that such a universality of
application makes even the school and the hospital feel like a prison or a
workhouse. That period has shown as well that the wall separating the
'benign' brand of rational engineering from its malignant, genocidal
variety is so rickety, slippery and porous that – to paraphrase Bertrand
Russell – one does not know when one should start to cry . . .

As for the communities – those allegedly uncontrived, naturally
growing organisms, toeholds instead of skyhooks – we do not yet know
all those things we know only too well about the Grand Artifice
modernity promised to build. But we may guess. We know that the
modern zest for designed perfection condensed the otherwise diffuse
heterophobia and time and again channelled it, Stalin- or Hitler-style,
towards genocidal outlets. We may only surmise that the messy tribalism
suspicious of universal solutions would gravitate towards exilic, rather

than genocidal, outlets for heterophobia. Separation rather than sub-
jugation, confinement or annihilation. As Le Pen put it, 'I adore North
Africans. But their place is in the Maghreb.' We know as well that the
major conflict of the modern setting grew from the inherent ambivalence
of the assimilatory pressures, which prodded towards effacing the
differences in the name of a universal human pattern, while simultaneously recoiling before the success of the operation – but we may only
hypothesise that a similarly conflict-pregnant ambivalence will be disclosed in the postmodern accolade of difference, which veers between
the equally unpalatable and indefensible extremes of 'wet liberalism',
that meekly surrenders the right to compare and evaluate the others,
and rampant tribalism, denying the others the right to compare and
evaluate.

There is no certainty – not even a high probability – that in the
universe populated by communities no room will be left for the pariah.
What seems to be more plausible, however, is that the parvenu's route of
escape from the pariah status will be closed. Mixophilia may well be
replaced with mixophobia; tolerance of difference may well be wedded
to the flat refusal of solidarity; monologic discourse, rather than giving
way to a dialogic one, will split into a series of soliloquies, with the
speakers no more insisting on being heard, yet refusing to listen into the
bargain.

These are real prospects, real enough to give a pause to the joyful
chorus of sociologists welcoming the new soft world of communities.
Sociology has a long and distinguished record of sycophancy. Since its
birth, it established itself as the principal poet-laureate of the state-
centred and state-coordinated society, of the state bent on prohibiting
everything which has not been first made obligatory. With the state no
more interested in uniformity, losing interest in culture as a drilling
routine and gladly leaving the job of social integration to variety-loving
market forces, sociology is desperately seeking new courts where the
skills and experience of pensioned courtiers could be gainfully employed. For many, the endemically fissiparous mini-courts of imagined
communities, home ideologies and tribally invented traditions seem to
be just the thing they need. Once more, though in a strikingly different
way from before, one can flatter the practice with theoretical groundings
by drawing elegant diagrams of messy reality. Once more one can herald
a new ambivalence as a logical solution, and a definitive improvement
on the old one. Courtiers' habits die hard.

In the course of the long, tortuous and convoluted march of modernity we should have learned our lesson: that the human existential
predicament is ambivalent beyond cure, that good is always mixed with

evil, that the line between the benign and the poisonous dose of medicine for our imperfections is impossible to draw safely. We should have learned this lesson. But we hardly did. Having discredited the medicine, we forget about the ailment it was meant to cure. Once more we announce, jubilantly, the discovery of a wonder-drug for human ills – only this time it is the old malady which has been proclaimed to be the medicine. Once more we try, confidently, to prescribe the right dose of the cure. There is a good, enabling, progressive form of belonging – we are told – and this is called ethnicity, cultural tradition, nationalism. People are different, and let them stay so. Well, there is also an ugly posturing called heterophobia, or xenophobia or racism – a view and a practice of separating, banishing, exiling. But do the two have anything in common? Is not a small dose of the drug a foolproof antidote against its poisonous effects?

The orthodox consensus of sociology has been found guilty of aiding and abetting the all-too-often unwholesome practices of the nation-state. Some time will yet pass before the new 'communalistically orientated' sociology, now relishing its honeymoon period and blithely self-congratulating, stands charged of complicity in the unprepossessing effects of the present fashions in identity-building. This, presumably, will not happen (not by common agreement at any rate) before those fashions are found, as usual in retrospect, to be wrong choices and lost chances.

NOTES

1 Camus (1964), p. 111.
2 Jabès (1989), p. 34.
3 Musil (1965), p. 174.
4 Sypher (1960).
5 Arendt (1986), p. 247.
6 Arendt (1986), p. 31.
7 Heller and Feher (1991), p. 303.
8 Zima (1981), p. 137.
9 Adorno (1988), p. 14.
10 Scholem (1982), pp. 229, 234.
11 Rorty (1991), pp. 14, 13.

BIBLIOGRAPHY

Adorno, T. W. (1988) 'Introduction to Benjamin's *Schriften* (1955)', in G. Smith (ed.) *On Walter Benjamin: Critical Essays and Recollections.* Cambridge, MA: MIT Press.

Arendt, H. (1986) *Rahel Varnhagen: La vie d'une Juive allemande à l'époque du Romantisme*. Trans. Henri Plard. Paris: Tierce.

Camus, A. (1964) *Carnets, janvier 1942–mars 1951*. Paris: Gallimard.

Heller, A. and Feher, F. (1991) *The Grandeur and Twilight of Radical Universalism*. New Brunswick: Transaction Books.

Jabès, E. (1969) *Un Etranger avec, sous le bras, un livre du petit format*. Paris: Gallimard.

Musil, R. (1965) *The Man without Qualities*. Trans. by Eithne Wilkins and Ernst Kaiser. Vol. II. New York: Capricorn Books.

Rorty, R. (1991) *Objectivity, Relativity and Truth: Philosophical Papers*, Vol. I, Cambridge: Cambridge University Press.

Scholem, G. (1982) *Walter Benjamin: The Story of a Friendship*. New York: Faber & Faber.

Sypher, W. (1960) *Rococo to Cubism in Art and Literature*. New York: Vintage Books.

Zima, P. V. (1981) 'L'ambivalence dialectique: entre Benjamin et Bakhtine', *Revue d'Esthetique*, 1: 137.

3 Private and public in 'late-modern' democracy

Geoffrey Hawthorn and Camilla Lund

The achievement of modernity, social theory has suggested, is to erase particularity and create a universality: to create an identity, it might be called, which turns on no particular save that of the nation-state whose nationality, as its citizens, we share, and turns on no properties beyond those we are given by law. This is not to say that we are not individuated. The state requires us to be. But the individuation it demands says nothing about who we are as persons or in society. It serves merely to identify our public status as private citizens of the state. If we retain anything of a more particular kind that is also public, it is our position in the market.

Conceptions of modernity and their origins are innumerable. The social theories of modernity are in their direction, and often their direct inspiration, Kantian. They present the possibility of potentially autonomous agents exercising the distinctively human faculty of reason; being willed to be treated and to treat others as autonomous rational agents; and being able to realise this ambition under the rational law, a form of life in which they can live together without contradiction. For Hegel, this would be the universalising state; for Marx, universalising communism; for Durkheim, the conscience collective of moral individualism; for Max Weber (the least optimistic, it is true, of the Kantian social theorists, and the most uncertain), the recovery of individual conscience and a mutual trust in one nation; for Habermas, a society of individuals able in a finally unconstrained convergence on the truth to realise their capacity for *Mündigkeit*; for Fukuyama, a liberal democracy under capitalism in which men are at last able to achieve 'recognition' and meet their needs. The images, to be sure, are different. But the hope that informs them is the same. We will lose our particularity in order to arrive at a non-particular and universal harmony, and shall do so in real time. In this respect, even the more recent and purportedly more 'critical' theorists of modernity are not as critical as they claim.

Postmodernists (or as some like to think of themselves, theorists of 'late modernity') see that this is so. William Connolly puts it well.

Liberal 'individualists think that civil society is the road to world mastery, that freedom for the individual involves control over personal destiny, and control over personal destiny is perfected to the extent that the impersonal structure of civil society succeeds in subjecting nature to human purposes'; collectivists argue that 'freedom involves mastery over nature and insist that its highest locus of expression is the collectivity (a state, a people, a class) that establishes a plan to achieve it'; communitarians see 'more than indifference in nature' and discern a 'direction in the world to which the self and the community must . . . become attuned' (Connolly, 1991: 29). Whatever their differences, the political theorists of modernity assume that our task is to complete and perhaps perfect it. They do not see, the postmodernists claim, that modernity itself is a myth, and may always have been: that the line between the private and the public is artificial, perhaps even sinister, and that our task is not to refine a politics which turns on this distinction, but to challenge it.

Each side, modernist and postmodernist, is partly correct. This is the complication of 'late-modern' politics in the democracies. But to continue to think in terms of particulars and universals, freedom and constraint, individuals and collectivities, is to compound the confusion that the complication causes. Two rather different sets of distinctions are necessary to resolve it. The first, as we hinted at the start of this chapter, is that between the 'private' and the 'public'. This is a distinction in law, and as such, is the outcome of politics. The second is the distinction between the 'personal' and the 'social'. Just as politics is ultimately responsible for the first, so it is politics, the constructed *political* identities of a liberal state, that give us our more informal sense of the latter.

On the neo-Kantian view (including Rousseau's, which inspired Kant and connects directly to some of the later theorists of modernity), the personal, that which makes us the distinct individuals we are, was, or should be, of no moral consequence. It was, in Kant's word, 'phenomenal', the object of mere causality, the seat of the passions, of what the French used to call 'egoism'. In its consequences, it was non-moral and asocial and what the truly social society should transcend.

This is not to say that it was very problematic. Kantians have in this respect been at one with the utilitarians. They have differed only in their conviction that individual desires and interests are antithetical to the public good and cannot therefore be its foundation. They have also tended to assume, with the utilitarians, that individual desires and interests are of generalisable kinds. Both are extrinsic to the actual individuals who have them. Individuals, actual persons, are simply and quite contingently their site (Sen and Williams, 1982). The postmodernists converge on the same kind of thought. For the utilitarians, Derek Parfit has argued that the idea of a single, separable and continuing self is redundant. The deeply rooted idea of the 'person' continuing through time is a loose and dispensable proxy for what are contingent causal 'relations' between wholly distinct states: those of our (own) bundle of properties at some previous point in time, and those of others in the present (the second, Parfit claims (1983), often being the causally more important of the two). For postmodernists, the conclusion is similar. What we conventionally take to be distinguishable and continuing persons are constituted not by a causally distinguishable 'experience' but by cultural 'discourses'. For both, 'person' is a conceptual mistake, a superstition, an item in humanist nostalgia. There are no 'selves'.

None of these three views is satisfactory. The experiential argument, Bernard Williams argues, the argument at the heart of Parfit, confuses mere similarity and difference over time with our sense of ourselves as ourselves, the sense that each of us has and indeed has to have if we are to find the impulse actually to live our lives; the sense that what we each are and do is distinctively our own. Kantians, by contrast, and the postmodernists also (although Williams does not discuss them), simply remove from what we do everything that is ours.

Most people have many categorical desires, which do not depend on the assumption of the person's existence, since they serve to prevent that assumption's being questioned, or to answer the question if it is raised. Thus one's patterns of interests, desires and projects not only provide the reason for an interest in what happens within the horizon of one's future, but also constitute the conditions of there being such a future at all (Williams, 1981: 11).

This we accept, and call the 'Williams self'.

This self, however, is minimal and unadorned. It is inalienably particular, for each of us, just ours. But thus defined, it has no substance. To that, the experientialists and postmodernists do have something to say. Their pictures, however, are passive. Our identities are not just imposed upon us by experience or 'discourses'. We ourselves, with an initially unformed sense of what is distinctively ours, can and do make what we are. Unless we are very remarkable people, of course, we do not do so entirely by ourselves. (If we did, we would in Rorty's sense of the word be thought 'mad' (1990: 288).) We do so from the materials there are. Experience is certainly important. What it is to have a gender and to be of one age rather than another, to have an ethnos and a religious belief (or not), and how we react to each, are central. What it is to live, work and play, to suffer power or exercise it with the people we do, and to react, are equally important. 'Discourses' also have an effect. The ways in which we react to our experience are guided by the categories that already exist to frame it. These categories are intrinsically relational, ways of defining ourselves with others, or against them, and can in turn shape experience itself. What they actually are and where they come from will vary from place to place. And they are rarely singular or enduring. We make and re-make sets of identities and continually edit them. Nor are these identities usually consistent over time, or within themselves, often inconsistent with each other at any one point in time.

Such categories are our personal identity: an identity which may change, depending on where we are, what we are doing, and who we are doing it with, but an identity that is for each of us grounded in an unalterable and inalienable 'Williams self'. They also contribute to our social identity: that set of identities which are the identities they are because they are acknowledged by others, and acknowledged by others because they play a part in politics. The distinction between the two kinds of identity, therefore, is a distinction in practical rather than theoretical reason (Hawthorn, 1991). In liberal politics, personal identities are those which have been confined to the private sphere. Social identities, by contrast, are those which are agreed in the political sense to be public. There is no distinction of principle. Where there is a discernible difference and where, as noticeably now in 'late-modern' democracies, there is not, this is solely because of political practice.

Not every modern republic is liberal. And in those which are, the line between the public and the private, the line that defines how much of the personal is also to be social, is drawn in a different place. The Indian constitution of 1950, for example, contains a set of supplementary schedules requiring discrimination in employment and other matters in favour of certain defined tribes and castes. The Brazilian constitution of 1988 gives rights and privileges to defined occupations. But even in other kinds of regimes, such as those that are affected by the older republican notion of 'ancient liberty' (Constant, 1988; Pocock, 1975), regimes (as in Spanish America, where they are now most common (Morse, 1954) and elsewhere) that have included some socialisms, in regimes over much of sub-Saharan Africa, where the distinction between the public and the private has rarely had any force at all (Hawthorn, 1993), or in states formally guided by a theology, there remains a private realm beyond even the most comprehensive of laws and the most intrusive politics. Even if tacitly, and with reluctance, most societies that have been touched by modernity do at least formally acknowledge the difference.

The line between the public and the private nevertheless remains most marked, and is certainly most explicit, in what Marxists used disparagingly to refer to as 'bourgeois liberal republics' (Dunn, 1994): in those states in which economic life and politics are directed to the maximisation of personal interests under the rule of law, and in which the law distinguishes the realm of the 'right' (social and because legal, also public, owed to all and required of all) from a personal and private 'good'. In practice in these republics, of course, matters are always less clear. This is the effect of their democracy. Citizens express aspirations and interests in both the right and the good. To attract votes in elections, the competing parties appeal to both, and in so doing, seek to construct a distinctively political identity.

This is at once their achievement and their difficulty. If political representation were (as early Americans put it) to be 'actual', and even if the identities and interests to be represented were just of one kind, say exclusively those given by the division of labour, the task would be impossible: there would simply be too many to be coherently and effectively represented by a necessarily limited number of representatives. Political representation has therefore (as the Federalists, for other reasons, insisted) to be 'virtual'. Most electors will have to be represented by people from elsewhere in the division of labour. Indeed, all virtual representation can be seen as representation by an aristocracy, persons whom the electors believe, or are persuaded to believe, will act more effectively on their behalf than they could themselves (Manin, 1997). (Otherwise, as Manin says, the citizens would do better, as in some earlier democracies they did, to cast lots.) Now, all representation is virtual and exercised by political professionals who (as both early Americans and many since have feared) can be inclined to promote themselves and their own particular interests (Wood, 1992). The professionals have formed parties to seek votes and to do so have repeatedly tried to capture the electors' social identities and interests in a few general categories. In electoral politics in Europe in the later nineteenth and twentieth centuries, the most common of these, as we have said, has been that of 'class'.

In this respect, the politics of the modern bourgeois liberal republic, it would seem, has passed through three phrases. In the first, it was assumed that there would be a single undivided republican public. There would be just one political identity. In Britain, for example, Mill argued in the early 1860s, in contrast to central Europe, where 'Magyars, Slovacks, Croats, Serbs, Roumans . . . [and] Germans' were 'so mixed up as to be incapable of local separation', there was a common nationhood and a common opinion (1977: 549). There was also, he believed, an increasing equality of condition, and in contrast to China, a habit of obedience and resistance to tyranny. One merely required proportional representation to ensure a voice for minorities. Legislation would be proposed by a Crown Commission. There is no consideration in Mill's 'Considerations' of the complications of competing parties.

In the second phase, which runs from the later nineteenth century to the 1960s, such competition increased, and in one democracy after another, distinct and incipiently divisive social identities were made political or were actually invented for politics. This was clearest in countries like Britain, where the dividing line between the two main parties had been clear, and politicians could as a result be reasonably well assured that the voters' allegiances would not shift for so long as those voters remained where they were in the division of labour. It was apparent, however, in other liberal states. Despite the divisive consequences of proportional representation, Social Democrats in Denmark, Norway and Sweden, for example, were for forty years able to count on the support of a third or more of the electorate. And it was apparent also in its obverse, in the attempts in Italy, Germany, Brazil and Argentina overtly to deny that there should be such competition at all.

In the third phase of liberal democratic politics, which began to emerge in the 1970s, the competitive identities have themselves been dividing. This has been the result of a blurring between the public and the private. Issues of gender, ethnicity and religion (as well as those that go beyond the nation-state, like the arms race between other states and the prospect of environmental decay), issues that had hitherto not appeared in politics and in many cases deliberately kept out of them, began to be pressed. The proliferation of political identities has also been caused by dramatic changes in the labour market. Identities and allegiances that were once secure have been shaken by sectoral changes and a degree of individual mobility and, increasingly, by unemployment also. As a result, the encompassing identities of 'class' and the more directly party-political identities, 'Christian Democrat', 'Liberal', 'Social Democrat', 'Socialist', have been increasingly less able to capture all the different interests that citizens see that they might have in the state. Hence the fact already remarked on by some commentators in the 1980s: competing mass parties can no longer contain all the different interests there are, and 'social movements' are bound to proliferate (Maier, 1987; Pizzorno, 1987). Political identity has been changing dramatically. It has done so because what was once personal is now political and, through that, social also. One of the central premises of liberal politics is weakening.

As it does, it puts a strain on the structure. In claiming politically to represent, and in competing to capture power, parties in democracies face a double dilemma. They are caught between trying to represent particular interests and trying to represent the general, and between the demands of representation itself and those of power. One might indeed go so far as to say that as they become more successful, they also become less so. The more socially inclusive they are, the less can they represent any one social interest; the more particular they decide to be, the less they represent also; and the less they represent, the more uncertain will they be of victory at the next election (and should they win, of their authority to act). In competing for power, political parties always run the risk of subverting the general political identities on which they must trade to succeed. In competing for power now, in 'late-modern' democracies, that risk is clear.

The most obvious way in which to reduce it is for politicians to try to construct (or to reconstruct) what John Rawls (1993) calls an 'over-lapping consensus', shared principles of the scope and nature of public life. What competitive identities divide, this could unite. Morally and practically, however, as Rawls himself concedes, this is a delicate achievement, and difficult. It is not easy to see how the often incompatible interests and identities that are being brought to politics can be reconciled to the extent they would have to be and yet remain the interests and identities they are. The simpler solution, which is to insist that all the citizens have an overriding interest simply as the citizens of the state, an interest, as it has often been put, of a 'national' kind, can threaten competitive democracy itself. This has been most obvious outside the North, but was evident in France in the Fourth Republic and the early years of the Fifth, in Christian Democracy in Italy from 1948 until 1993, and in Conservatism in Britain between 1979 and 1990. Elsewhere, the divisiveness is most marked in countries like Denmark, Belgium and the Netherlands, in which election is by proportional representation and the barriers to entry are low. But it is evident also in those in which election is secured simply by being 'first past the post' and the voters have no incentive to support small parties. The only difference in the second case is that instead of a proliferation of political parties, there is (as in both the Conservative and Labour parties in Britain) a proliferation of factions within those that already exist. The outcome, however, is everywhere the same. This new politics contributes to the structural weakness of mass parties, the weakness exacerbates the tendency to fragmentation, discipline within the parties becomes more difficult, their organisation is called into question (Pane-bianco, 1988), and some even wonder about their future.

There are three reactions to these changes. The first, the postmodernists', is to applaud it. Liberation from the modern in the postmodern, they argue, consists in escaping from the confining categories of modernist theory and daily life. From Heidegger, French 'post-structuralisms', 'difference-feminism', and other theoretical and polemical sources, we are encouraged, as Reiner Schürmann puts it, to accept and enjoy 'the play of flux in practice, without stabilisation . . . an incessant fluctuation in institutions [as] an end in itself' (1987: 18). We are free at last to invent and re-invent ourselves and to make and break alliances as we wish. And if we are persuaded of the philosophical 'anti-foundationalism' that is now fashionable among postmoderns, we are free to do so without any longer having to worry about which identity and interest to 'privilege'. We can rely solely on our feelings of the moment, on what Rorty (1989) has called our contingent 'solidarities'. We do not have to produce any principled defence of what we are doing at all.

The second reaction to the destruction of our established political practices, that of the 'radical liberals', has been equally enthusiastic. The old mass parties, such liberals have argued, and the states they have constructed, are economically and politically insupportable. There is not the revenue to sustain the demands being made on them, and the escalation of these demands is now beyond political control. The line between the public and the private has to be reasserted and redrawn. The responsibility of the state should be only to set and to sustain the rule of law within which private interests can compete with each other outside politics. Citizens should abandon their collective identities and consider themselves solely as individual producers and consumers in a market. It is no business of politics to provide what people want. That is their own affair. And the radical liberals' argument has now spread: a host of formerly socialist or social democratic parties, Labour in Britain, Socialists in Spain, Social Democrats in Sweden, Congress in India, the PRI in Mexico, Communists in China, and many more, as well as many parties of a more conservative kind, have in the 1980s and 1990s more or less explicitly acknowledged it. Almost everywhere, the unprecedented faith of the first three decades after the Second World War in the scope and powers of the state, the province of 'the public', is being abandoned.

The manner of these first two reactions, and the arguments for each, are plainly different. 'One side', as Connolly describes it, 'seeks to open up discourses that are too closed and self righteous . . . the other to protect established truths it considers threatened' (1991: 60). Yet there is an affinity between the two. Both could without difficulty unite and fight under the slogan 'Return Politics to Society' and then (as Margaret Thatcher once famously said that she wanted to do) 'Abolish Society'. But the continuously reconstructed and deconstructed political identities that the postmodernists wish to see are not incompatible with the individual 'interests' that the radical liberals would like to leave to the play of an unconstrained market. The only difference is that in all but their most extreme libertarian mode, the radical liberals do have a coherent conception of the state, and the postmodernists do not.

The third reaction to the destruction of our established political practices is that it is regressive and perhaps even dangerous. It is regressive insofar as it means that what is necessary for all voices to be heard in the postmodern conversation is pre-empted. There will be no public action to create a greater equality of the conditions necessary for people to be able to speak and be heard and to be able to press the outcome when they are. The more reflective postmodernists are aware of this. Connolly, for instance, agrees that for the kind of political conversation he would like to see succeed, the highest income must not be more than five to six times as large as the lowest, and there must be 'general access to economic, educational, and cultural opportunities'. But he then goes on to insist that 'the state, as the legitimate centre of sovereignty, citizen loyalty, and political dissent, must give more ground to other models of political identification . . . If democracy is not to become a political ghetto confined to the territorial state, the contemporary globalisation of capital, labour, and contingency must be shadowed by a corollary globalisation of politics' (1991: 215). But until this happens, and even when it has, it is not clear how distributions of income are going to be narrowed and opportunities equalised. In wanting to 'roll the state back', the radical liberals and the postmodernists have, whether they like it or not, to accept the restriction of rights.

The destruction of our established practices might be dangerous, this third reaction adds, because it is unsustainable. Just as sufficient reason to police the world ended with the confrontation between the United States and the Soviet Union and, it is argued, allowed suppressed antagonisms to emerge in places they had previously controlled, so the recent retreat of states could allow discontents to emerge within their borders. Together with the erosion of the lines between the spheres of the public and the private (and between politics as the realm of the right and the good) this could allow those social identities and interests which in liberal societies have hitherto been suppressed, the identities and interests of race, place, religion, ethnicity, gender, sexual preference and the rest, to surface. Some might see the persistence of these, in Algeria, Egypt and Jordan, for instance, in Israel, in India and Sri Lanka, in the former Yugoslavia, and in Northern Ireland, as a last protest against modernity, the agonies of one or another doomed 'tradition'. But this is too simple. The identities are weapons, some old, others new, with which to fight for advantage. Political identities are coming out of the closet of the personal, fuelled by the frustrations of those who feel themselves to have been ignored (and the despair of those who are not even acknowledged), and in 'late-modern' democracies threatening to diminish or altogether to override the old liberal lines. And these new identities are not confined to the South and the former republics of the Soviet Union. They are evident in Europe also, not only in those central and south-eastern areas of the continent that Mill disparaged, and in the United States. The hope in that country (what, perhaps two generations ago, might with selective attention have seemed to some to be the central achievement) of a unifying identity is thought by liberals of an older generation to be in danger. 'Instead of a transformative nation with an identity of its own, America . . . is seen as a preservative for diverse alien identities . . . The multi-ethnic dogma abandons historic purposes, replacing assimilation by fragmentation, integration by separatism. It belittles *unum* and glorifies *pluribus*' (Schlesinger, 1992: 16–17).

In modern liberal republics, competing mass parties have been impelled to abstract and to confine once disparate and often inchoate identities and interests, and having done so, politically to fix them. The consequence of the competition between the parties, however, has been the reverse. It has stimulated more selves to aspire to rule in the regime of supposed self-rule than the established practices of liberal democracy can easily allow. Hence the apprehension. If these practices were to continue, it seems, these rules of rule would become unworkable. The genie is out of the bottle. To restrict the public, as the radical liberals want to do, and enlarge the private can now only incite what these liberals hope to suppress. What then of the reverse? Can this politics be saved by letting the public sphere extend? Are the postmodernists right after all?

This is in part an institutional matter. The conventional institutions, that is to say mixed electoral constituencies, a representative assembly of a manageable size, political parties that can (by themselves or in coalitions) form a government and separate state powers, are increasingly unable to cope with the range and variety of demands that are now made on them. If the increasing number of political identities and the increasing confusion and conflict to which they might give rise were to continue to be concentrated on the state itself, the overload would indeed be unavoidable. The radical liberals would be right. But they are not.

Some of the interests in modern politics are best pursued, if the means to do so exist, beyond the state altogether. In Western Europe, for example, the independence of the Court of Human Rights from any state government has given it the authority and the power to rule for claimants against such governments. If there were a properly representative government at the federal level (the kind of government that was both proposed and evaded in the Maastricht Treaty), there is a reason to think that in a nationally less controllable global economy, some of the economic and social policies that have hitherto been the responsibility of states should be transferred to it (Council of the European Communities, 1992; Allott, 1992). At the same time, however, many of the newly excited interests and their associated identities are of an altogether more local kind. In many European countries, this is acknowledged in the growth of regional parties. At present, however, many of these parties are either competing for power within the central state or threatening to secede from it. If the threats to secede were also promises to accede to a democratically authoritative federal authority, such a move might, in principle, make sense. But until such an authority exists, this possibility is idle. What is not, and would meet the need, are renewed institutions at the local level itself.

This is not a new thought. Those who have recently been pressing it, however, sometimes in the name of a new form of market socialism (Miller, 1989), sometimes as a wider kind of 'associational democracy' (Hirst, 1993), have done so on the old assumption that a local politics can assume the responsibilities of credit, investment and management for production. This is impractical. It is all but impossible to see how a control that now escapes even national governments could be recaptured and effectively devolved. In any event, this is not what the predominant interests in the new identities are. (It may have been a mistake of former socialists to have supposed that they ever were.) Insofar as they are interests of a more conventional kind, they are interests in different principles of distribution. As interests in investment, they are interests at most in a greater or more pointed investment in human capital. Everywhere, however, they are more than interests of a conventional kind. They indicate a wish also (as Fukuyama (1992) would say) for simple 'recognition', an interest of a kind which (as Fukuyama does not see) is increasingly less met in the generalised identities of mass party politics. Whatever purposes the old generalised identities may have served, at a time when, sociologically, they made more sense, they were never sensitive to variety. And it is the variety of voices that is now so salient. It is a variety of voices each of which wants publicly to be heard, but each of which is lost in a generalised 'public'. It is a variety of voices each of which is particular and can best be heard where it matters, 'socially' (as it would previously have been thought 'personally'), to those whose voice it is.

If modern liberal republics are not to be paralysingly overloaded or in desperation shrunk, the line between the 'public' and 'private' does indeed have to be redrawn. In this postmodernists and the radical liberals are correct. The postmodern mistake is to suppose that the solution lies in overcoming the distinction. The radical liberals' mistake, by contrast, is to think that for all the contents of political debate, and at all levels, the distinctions can be successfully redrawn in the same place. The tendencies of late-modern democracy and their implications are at once more complex and, as yet, more obscure.

BIBLIOGRAPHY

Allott, P. (1992) 'The European Community at the Pain Barrier: The Significance of the Maastricht Treaty'. Unpublished paper. Evidence Submitted to the House of Commons Foreign Affairs Committee (Cambridge).

Connolly, W. (1991) Identity\difference: Democratic Negotiations of a Political Paradox. Ithaca: Cornell University Press.

Constant, B. (1988) [1820] 'The Liberty of the Ancients Compared with That of the Moderns', in Benjamin Constant: Political Writings. Ed. and Trans. B. Fontana. Cambridge: Cambridge University Press, 309–28.

Council of the European Communities, Commission of the European Communities (1992) Treaty on European Union. Luxembourg: Office of Official Publications of the European Communities.

Dunn, J. (1994) 'The Identity of the Bourgeois Liberal Republic', in The Invention of the Modern Republic. Ed. B. Fontana. Cambridge: Cambridge University Press, 206–28.

Fukuyama. F. (1992) The End of History and the Last Man. London: Hamish Hamilton.

Hawthorn, G. (1991) Plausible Worlds: Possibility and Understanding in History and the Social Sciences. Cambridge: Cambridge University Press.

(1993) 'Sub-Saharan Africa', in Prospects for Democracy: North, South, East, West. Ed. D. Held. Cambridge: Polity Press, 330–3.

Hirst, P. (1993) 'Associational Democracy', in Prospects for Democracy: North, South, East, West. Ed. D. Held. Cambridge: Polity Press, 112–35.

Maier, C. S. (1987) 'Introduction', in Changing Boundaries of the Political: Essays on the Evolving Balance Between State and Society, Public and Private in Europe. Ed. C. S. Maier. Cambridge: Cambridge University Press, 1–24.

Manin, B. (1997) *The Principles of Representative Government*. Cambridge: Cambridge University Press.

Mill, J. S. (1977) [1861] 'Considerations on Representative Government', in *Essays on Politics and Society*. Ed. J. M. Robson. *Collected Works of John Stuart Mill*, Vol. XIX. Toronto: University of Toronto Press, 371–577.

Miller, D. (1989) *Market, State and Community: Theoretical Foundations of Market Socialism*. Oxford: Clarendon Press.

Morse, R. M. (1954) 'The Heritage of Latin America', in *The Founding of New Societies*. Ed. L. Hartz. New York: Harcourt Brace, 123–77.

Panebianco, A. (1988) *Political Parties: Organisation and Power*. Cambridge: Cambridge University Press.

Parfit, D. (1983) *Reasons and Persons*. Oxford: Clarendon Press.

Pizzorno, A. (1987) 'Politics Unbound', in *Changing Boundaries of the Political: Essays on the Evolving Balance Between State and Society, Public and Private in Europe*. Ed. C. S. Maier. Cambridge: Cambridge University Press, 27–62.

Pocock, J. G. A. (1975) *The Machiavellian Moment: Florentine Political Thought and the Atlantic Republican Tradition*. Princeton: Princeton University Press.

Rawls, J. (1993) *Political Liberalism*. New York: Columbia University Press.

Rorty, R. (1989) *Contingency, Irony and Solidarity*. Cambridge: Cambridge University Press.

(1990) 'The Priority of Democracy to Philosophy', in *Reading Rorty: Critical Responses to Philosophy and the Mirror of Nature (and Beyond)*. Ed. A. Malachowski. Oxford: Blackwell, 279–302.

Schlesinger Jr., A. S. (1992) *The Disuniting of America*. New York: Norton.

Schürmann, R. (1987) *Heidegger on Being and Acting: From Principles to Anarchy*. Trans. C.-M. Gros. Bloomington: Indiana University Press.

Sen, A. and Williams, B. (1982) 'Introduction', in *Utilitarianism and Beyond*. Ed. A. Sen and B. Williams. Cambridge: Cambridge University Press, 1–21.

Williams, B. (1981) *Moral Luck: Philosophical Papers, 1973–1980*. Cambridge: Cambridge University Press.

Wood, G. S. (1992) 'Democracy and the American Revolution', in *Democracy: The Unfinished Journey, 580 BC to AD 1993*. Ed. J. Dunn. Oxford: Oxford University Press, 91–105.

4   Modernity and disenchantment: some reflections on Charles Taylor's diagnosis

Quentin Skinner

The historian Alexander Kinglake wanted the following inscription to be placed on all churches: *Important if true*.[1] The same motto could equally well be inscribed on Charles Taylor's masterly book, *Sources of the Self* (1990), the work I shall treat as both my point of departure and my stalking horse in this effort to contribute to the reflections on postmodernity that go to make up this volume.[2] In part the appropriateness of beginning with Kinglake's remark is simply a tribute to the intellectual weight of Taylor's achievement. But in part it stems from the fact that the final message of Taylor's book, like that of the churches, is that our present secularised outlook may be inadequate to meet the moral challenges posed by modernity.[3] It is this aspect of Taylor's diagnosis of the ills attending our modern condition that I chiefly want to examine in what follows.

Taylor's wish to question and transcend our 'stripped-down secular outlook' appears in *Sources of the Self* in connection with his analysis of what he takes to be 'the moral imperatives which are felt with particular force in modern culture' (pp. 495, 520).[4] Although Taylor states and restates his list of these imperatives at a number of different points, he cannot I think be said to do so at any stage with complete consistency. Without being over-schematic, however, I think one can say that he distinguishes four main elements in our modern vision of 'strongly valued' goods (pp. 4, 14, 20, 42).

One characteristic component of modern moral consciousness is said to derive from the emphasis we place on the need to avoid suffering. Put positively, the value we are held to cherish is that of considering the welfare of others (pp. 12–14; cf. p. 394). But Taylor is even more concerned with a second aspect of our contemporary sensibility, our disposition to attach the highest moral importance to respecting other people's rights. We have come to think of everyone as possessing such rights, in consequence of which we have come to think of rights themselves as having a universal character. This prompts us to espouse a global ideal of justice, a value we define mainly in terms of the need to ensure that human rights are recognised (pp. 10–12; cf. p. 395). At the same time, we attach a no less exalted importance to our own right to follow whatever lines of individual self-development we may choose for ourselves, which in turn means that we place a correspondingly strong emphasis on the values of autonomy and integrity (p. 12; cf. p. 314).

Taylor goes on to claim that our anxiety to acknowledge the rights and equal moral worth of every individual expresses itself in our culture in a distinctive style. We have come to believe, in a manner Taylor regards as unique among the higher civilisations, that the obligations and commitments of 'ordinary life' embody moral and spiritual values worthy of our deepest respect (pp. 11–13; cf. pp. 211–12). Taylor has in mind (p. 211) the obligations of production ('the making of the things needed for life') and of reproduction (the life of 'marriage and the family'). For Taylor, as for Max Weber, this 'affirmation of everyday life' represents the distinctive as well as the most far-reaching legacy of Protestant spirituality. It was Puritanism that gave rise to an ethic of work and a 'companionate' view of marriage, thereby acting as the main progenitor of a bourgeois scale of values in which ordinary callings came to be seen as sanctified (pp. 224–6).

Taylor's fourth and fundamental claim is that all these commitments are underpinned by a general moral outlook definitive of modernity. We have come to believe that we ourselves are the sources and creators of the values by which we live. This vision of the modern world as disenchanted, lacking any sense of God as an immanent force or morality as objectively grounded, again appears to owe a considerable debt to Max Weber. Nevertheless, Taylor develops the argument very much in his own style, retracing the steps by which we have arrived at our present position in an ambitious historical survey extending from ancient Greece to the philosophy of the Enlightenment.[5]

Taylor begins with Plato, for whom there was a 'tight connection' between 'awareness of right order in our lives and of the order of the cosmos' (p. 125). Taylor's main concern is to contrast this position with that of Descartes, but he first notices that 'on the way from Plato to Descartes stands Augustine' (p. 127). Augustine still believed that our values must be founded on common standards lying outside ourselves, but also began to emphasise the more subjective notion of an inner guiding light (pp. 132–3). Descartes took a second giant step towards modern subjectivity when he insisted that the sources of knowledge as well as morality must be sought entirely within us (p. 143). Locke went on to argue that we have no access to any innate ideas about morality or truth, inferring that all our beliefs, as well as our very personalities, must therefore be constantly re-created by our own mental activity (pp. 164,

171). By the time we come to Rousseau, the process by which our moral values became disengaged from external standards is more or less complete. Although Rousseau may not have taken the final step, he made it easy to arrive at the conclusion that, as Taylor puts it, 'the inner voice of my true sentiments *define* what is the good' (p. 362).

It is crucial to Taylor's argument that these are the beliefs 'we' affirm. Sometimes, it is true, he recognises that they can hardly be treated as the values of every denizen of planet Earth. They are merely the conceptions of the self and the good 'which are at home in the modern West' (p. ix). But he nevertheless thinks that this 'new moral culture', which first arose in 'England, America and (for some facets) France' at the beginning of the nineteenth century, has been radiating 'outward and downward' to the rest of the world ever since (p. 305). Taylor is, in short, offering us a portrait of ourselves. So the first question to ask is whether the likeness is satisfactory.

It seems to me that Taylor offers a number of genuinely illuminating insights into the distinctiveness of our modern condition. He is surely right in the first place to stress the peculiarity as well as the centrality of the modern belief that individuals should be seen as bearers of rights which can in some sense be viewed as personal properties. Moral philosophers in ancient and Medieval Europe were greatly concerned with the question of distributive justice, and thus with the question of what is due to us as a matter of right. But they lacked a vocabulary to articulate the suggestion that what is due to us as a matter of right is something which can in turn be called our rights. It was only during the later middle ages that this conception of 'subjective' right began to enter European political discourse.[6] And it was only in the course of the seventeenth century that the concept began to acquire that moral hegemony which it has never subsequently lost.[7]

Taylor also seems to me deeply perceptive in his comments on the modern preoccupation with everyday life and work. The Graeco-Roman vision of the good life certainly allowed no space for the development of anything resembling an ethic of work. It was a vision too firmly wedded to the presumed connection between the progress of civilisation and the enjoyment of leisure. Nor is it easy to find in pre-modern Europe any strong precedents for our modern belief that the lives of ordinary folk may be deserving of just as much respect as those of great heroes. The moralists of antiquity and the Renaissance were too much concerned with ideals of honour and glory for such a perspective to be admissible. Nor was their outlook fundamentally altered when these values were transmuted under Christianity into an admiration for those individuals whose way of life appeared to promise them heavenly as opposed to worldly glory. The main effect of this change was simply to replace the worship of heroes with the worship of saints. As Taylor indicates, it was only after the Reformation that the duties of everyday life came to seem a major site of moral value and commitment.

It is difficult, however, to feel altogether satisfied with Taylor's sketch of 'our' predicament. Consider first his discussion of the value of autonomy, summarised in his declaration that 'everyone in our civilisation feels the force' of John Stuart Mill's demand that we should 'accord people the freedom to develop in their own way' (p. 12). I am far from confident that everyone in our civilisation has heard of John Stuart Mill. But even among those who have, is it really true that there is general agreement about the relationship between the idea of 'legitimate development' and 'such things as pornography' (p. 12)? According to Taylor, 'no one doubts' in the case of pornography that, if its prohibition endangers such development, we have a reason for relaxing social controls (p. 12). But this is exactly what a number of recent writers *do* doubt.[8] Instead of concentrating on traditional questions about the possible effects of pornography, these theorists have raised an interpretative question about its meaning or character. Rather than asking what it does, they have asked what it is. They have answered that one way to characterise pornography is to see in it an expression of violence and hatred towards women. It follows that those who claim a right to distribute such materials are claiming a right to propagate violence and hatred. But 'we' already regard such behaviour not as a right but as a criminal offence, at least where racial hatred is involved. Why not in the case of women as well?

Taylor unrepentantly responds that 'we generally consider it *a* reason for some measure that it facilitates people developing in their own way'.[9] But this fails to come to grips with the ferocity of recent attacks on what are perceived as liberal complacencies. What is being suggested is that, even if pornography could be shown to be absolutely vital to the self-development of those who propagate and consume it, we should still have no good reason for relaxing social controls. This is one of several points at which Taylor's account of what 'we' believe appears to underestimate the extent to which a liberal consensus has been swept aside by the continuing march of modernity.[10]

Consider similarly Taylor's emphasis on 'our' conviction that 'the full human life' must in part be 'defined in terms of labour and production, on one hand, and marriage and family life, on the other' (p. 213). Taylor's view of labour occasionally seems rather sentimental or at least unduly optimistic in tone. When he celebrates the value of work, he lays all his emphasis on the claim that, through acting as 'producers', we are able to gain the satisfaction of creating 'the things needed for life' (p. 211). But as recent exponents of Green politics have above all emphasised, the sad truth is that much of the labour undertaken in modern capitalist economies is not in this sense productive, while much of what is produced is not in the least needed for life. Again, Taylor appears to underestimate the extent to which 'we' have begun to reject traditional assumptions about production, and to complain at the same time that the worlds of daily labour and self-realisation scarcely intersect.

A further question raised by this aspect of Taylor's argument is how far it is really true that 'we' still think of marriage and family life as constitutive of our identities. Taylor's response has been to insist that it 'rather severely misidentifies' his position to suppose that this is what he believes.[11] But his disavowal seems hard to reconcile with the end of *Sources of the Self*, and especially with the powerful passage in the concluding chapter where he examines the narcissism of American 'self-help' manuals. He convincingly criticises the 'thinness of ties and shallowness' which this literature implicitly recommends us to cultivate (p. 508). But it is striking that he makes his point by arguing that, if we insist on 'the primacy of self-fulfilment', the 'solidarities' that will be forced into second place will include those 'of birth, of marriage, of the family' (p. 507).

I still find troubling the way in which this contrast is drawn. One reason why the issue seems worth pressing is that historians have recently done so much to uncover the paradoxical role played by the institutions of marriage and the family in the development of modern liberal societies. Although the ideology of liberalism has always proclaimed the values of freedom and equality, liberal societies have always been underpinned by a sexual contract in which these ideals have been systematically violated. As a number of feminist historians have recently argued, the result has been to inhibit women from attaining the liberal goals of self-realisation and moral self-development.[12] Again, Taylor appears to me to underestimate the extent to which 'we' have come to accept this indictment. The institutions he invokes to save us from meaninglessness are just those which, according to many of 'us', are most likely to betray our interests and threaten our liberties.

It is not my principal aim, however, to criticise Taylor's portrait of 'our' modern predicament, especially as I not only admire but feel influenced by many features of it. I am more interested in the argument he goes on to develop about the right attitude to adopt towards the values he singles out.

Taylor makes two contrasting points, the first of which is that we cannot fail to see the story he recounts as one of 'epistemic gain'

(p. 313). A declared foe of relativism, he goes so far as to insist that the proper view to take of our own moral evolution must be strongly affirmative. Despite the barbarism of the present century, we should recognise that we have built 'higher standards' into 'the moral culture of our civilisation' than ever before (p. 397). More than this, Taylor thinks that (to adopt the current jargon) we cannot but be 'moral realists' about our culture itself (pp. 6–8). Even though we can see that our picture of the good has been historically formed, we are bound to accept that our inherited values and way of life *are* good, and constitute 'something that we have to embrace' (p. 347).

But does a knowledge of history really have the effect of tying us to the present in this way? My own view is that exactly the opposite tends to happen. To see why this might be so, consider again Taylor's account of our modern disposition to attach a high degree of moral and even spiritual significance to the values of everyday life and work. Before these commitments could come to figure in our contemporary sense of selfhood, a strongly contrasting picture of spirituality had to be widely challenged, a picture according to which the life of full moral commitment involved the abandonment of precisely these everyday ties. A number of rival images of political life also had to be obliterated, particularly the Renaissance ideal of the citizen not as a bearer of rights but rather as someone engaged in government who acknowledges an overarching duty to contribute to the common good. We need to recognise, in short, that the march of modernity left a number of casualties lying on the roadside of history, including such previously prominent and respected figures as the Citizen and the Monk.

Let us now suppose that, in learning this much history, we also come to understand something of the causal processes by which our modern 'everyday' values triumphed over these earlier and incommensurable images of spiritual and political life. No historian denies that the ethic of family life and work must have answered to some authentic and important aspirations among the peoples of Western Europe in the sixteenth century. Had this not been so, it is hard to see how anything could ever have been achieved or legitimised in its name. At the same time, however, historians have been impressed by the number of powerful groups that had an interest in patronising and encouraging the growth of these values at the expense of older and more familiar conceptions of the moral life. It was obviously in the interests of aspiring absolutist rulers to insist that, as Hobbes put it in *De Cive*, a citizen's primary duties lie not in the public but entirely in the private and familial spheres.[13] The prize for winning this argument was to permit the concentration of more and more political power in fewer and fewer hands. It was even more obviously in the interests of the same ruling groups to promote the view that monastic spirituality embodied a misuse of human labour and wealth. The prize in this case was to make it seem godly and progressive (rather than impious and avaricious) to confiscate the vast estates the monasteries had acquired.

What are the implications of coming to understand that these were among the causal processes that enabled the figure of the dutiful Subject to replace the Citizen and the Monk? One implication, it seems to me, is that we become disturbingly aware of the sheer contingency of the process by which our values were formed. To this Taylor responds that he is 'not sure what is being claimed here'.[14] But the claim is not complicated: only three simple components are involved. The first is that a classical and Renaissance conception of active citizenship was largely superseded at a particular historical period by our modern view that citizens should be treated essentially as consumers of government. The second is that this change largely took place because a number of early-modern European states happened to evolve in the direction I have been indicating. The third is that this evolution was partly engineered by powerful ruling groups, and thus that things could conceivably have been otherwise. Taylor's response to this, if I understand him, is that my emphasis on causal factors overlooks the fact that certain ideas have an inherent force which helps explain why they supersede others.[15] To this I can only reply that the modern concept of the Subject does not appear to me to embody any greater moral force than the Renaissance concept of the Citizen. But even if it does, I doubt if this forms any part of the causal explanation of why the Renaissance ideal was successfully killed off.

I have also tried to gesture at a closely connected implication which follows from accepting the kind of historical explanation I have sketched. We are left confronting the possibility that our forebears may to some degree have been coerced or even hoodwinked into exchanging their traditional pictures of spirituality and citizenship for the very different ones they subsequently bequeathed to us. This is not of course to deny that the new values unrelentingly drilled into them by Protestant pastors and humanist pedagogues were indeed valuable. But so were the old values they were at the same time urged to forget. The point is rather that the world we have lost was one that our ancestors, left to themselves, might never have wished to forsake.

What hangs on my claim that these are among the implications to be drawn from the story of the Subject, the Citizen and the Monk? My suggestion is that, once we see this much, we can see that the victory of our inherited values brought losses and even deprivations in addition to the obvious gains. Taylor retorts that he has already taken sufficient account of this balance-sheet.[16] But it seems to me that what it *means* to take sufficient account of it is to recognise that we cannot hope to affirm our view of the good – the one that happened to emerge victorious – in anything like the unambiguous style that Taylor asks of us. One effect of learning more about the causal story is to loosen the hold of our inherited values upon our emotional allegiances. Haunted by a sense of lost possibilities, historians are almost inevitably Laodicean in their attachment to the values of the present time.

I turn to the other claim Taylor makes about our modern predicament. While we must embrace our present values, we must also recognise that they are in crucial ways inadequate. Taylor's sense of their inadequacy stems from his vision of modernity as the offspring at once of the Enlightenment and the Romantic movement. From the Enlightenment we have inherited an atomised conception of the individual self; from Romanticism we have derived a sense of the need to concentrate on our inner natures and explore their potentialities. The effect has been to bring to final fruition our deeply rooted tendency to look for our values entirely within ourselves. But this is not only selfish and self-absorbed, a cause of the erosion of traditional communal ties; it also has the consequence of cutting us off from wider sources of meaning and moral significance.[17]

According to Taylor, this outcome is untrue to some of the finest elements in our natures. We have a 'craving for being in contact with or being rightly placed in relation to the good' (p. 45). But as we 'struggle to hold on to a vision of the incomparably higher', we cannot hope to derive much comfort or inspiration from prevailing images of the self and the good (p. 24). The way we live now 'involves stifling the response in us to some of the deepest and most powerful spiritual aspirations that humans have conceived' (p. 520).

It is striking that, by contrast with so many sages who have recently bewailed our loss of spirituality, Taylor never suggests that the solution to our dilemma may lie in putting ourselves in contact with other cultures less contaminated by Western individualism and science. He looks for his solutions entirely within the resources of our own civilisation, describing his work as an attempt to 'retrieve' a number of neglected values and thereby 'bring the air back again into the half-collapsed lungs of the spirit' (p. 520).

I find many of Taylor's proposed remedies very congenial, although they strike me at the same time as a bit optimistic and perhaps unavoidably vague. One of his suggestions is that we may still be able to discover in the values of everyday life a haven in a heartless world.[18] A second is that we may be able to 'get outside' ourselves by enjoying the 'epiphanic' powers of art and literature. We can take advantage, that is, of the romantic and modernist insight that great works of art bring us 'into the presence of something which is otherwise inaccessible, and which is of the highest moral or spiritual significance' (p. 419). Finally, Taylor suggests that we may be able to satisfy our craving to make ourselves part of some larger design by devoting ourselves to a life of public and political activity.[19]

Even if all these hopes were to be realised, however, it remains Taylor's 'hunch' that none of this would be adequate to meet the full force of 'the modern moral challenge'.[20] We need to recognise that life is a quest, and that what we are in quest of, as part of 'our telos as human beings', is a scale of values that will 'command our awe', not merely our admiration or respect.[21] Put positively, Taylor's hunch is that 'the significance of human life' needs to be explained and vindicated in theistic terms, not in our present 'non-theistic, non-cosmic, purely immanent-human fashion' (p. 342). If we remain 'closed to any theistic perspective' we shall condemn ourselves to our present narrow subjectivism (p. 506). This is why 'the potential of a certain theistic perspective is incomparably greater' than any purely secularised vision of the moral life (p. 518). The fullest 'affirmation of humans' requires a belief in God.[22]

I confess to being disappointed by this *dénouement*, especially as Taylor presents it with so much rhetorical skill that he makes it appear as the climax and not just the conclusion of his book. My disappointment stems from the fact that, speaking once more as an historian, Taylor's argument strikes me as incomplete in two important respects. First of all, he makes it clear that the 'theistic perspective' he has in mind is specifically the Judaeo-Christian one, with 'its central promise of a divine affirmation of the human, more total than humans can ever attain unaided' (p. 521). As any historian can relate, however, the outcome of imposing this perspective on Western Europe over more than a millennium was at many stages catastrophic in human terms. The Medieval centuries were marked by frequent persecutions, while the attempt to challenge the powers of the Catholic Church in the sixteenth century gave rise to several generations of religious war. Given this background, the idea of recommending the re-adoption of the same theistic perspective is I think likely to strike anyone familiar with the historical record as a case of offering a cure for our ills potentially worse than the disease.

Taylor has of course thought of this objection, and freely recognises 'the appalling destruction wrought in history in the name of the faith' (p. 520). But he insists that it must be a cardinal mistake to believe 'that a good must be *invalid* if it leads to suffering or destruction' (p. 519).

The historical record of Christianity gives us no reason to doubt its value or applicability. But the fallacy in this line of reasoning is surely obvious. It is only true that we have no reason to fear the Christian faith if we can be confident that the horrors perpetrated in its name were unconnected with its character or aspirations as a creed. Once again, however, it is hard for an historian to offer such reassurances. The historical record makes it all too evident that Christianity has often proved an intolerant religion, and that some at least of the wars and persecutions with which it has been associated have partly followed from its character as a creed.

I turn finally to the other way in which Taylor's argument strikes me as incomplete. His intuition is that we need to believe in God if we are to appreciate the full significance of human life. But it is hard for an historian to avoid reflecting that one of the most important elements in the so-called Enlightenment project was to disabuse us of precisely that intuition. For Hume and his modern descendants there is no reason whatever to suppose that human life in its full significance cannot be appreciated in the absence of God. Not only have they argued that theism is a dangerously irrational creed; they have added that the death of God leaves us with an opportunity, perhaps even a duty, to affirm the value of our humanity more fully than ever before. Their arguments strike me as decisive, but that is not the point. The point is rather that, given the force of their claims, the task for contemporary theism must surely be to answer them. Theists need to convince us that, in spite of everything urged to the contrary for the past two centuries, the case for theism can still be rationally reaffirmed.

What, then, does Taylor take to be mistaken about the arguments underpinning modern unbelief? What reasons can he give us for sharing his doubts? Taylor has taken me to task, and quite rightly, for having merely asserted my own faith in the atheistic values bequeathed by the Enlightenment. But I remain disappointed that he for his part evidently feels it sufficient to present us with his alternative hunch, without making any attempt to show us that it amounts to more than whistling in the dark.

NOTES

1 The proposal is recorded in G. Madan, *Notebooks*, ed. J. A. Gere and J. Sparrow (Oxford: Oxford University Press, 1981), p. 11.
2 This chapter reprints, with only very minor changes, my contribution to the *festschrift* for Charles Taylor, *Philosophy in an Age of Pluralism: The Philosophy of Charles Taylor in Question*, ed. J. H. Tully (Cambridge: Cambridge University Press, 1994), pp. 37–48. That contribution in turn drew heavily

on an article I had earlier published about *Sources of the Self*. See Q. Skinner, 'Who Are "We"? Ambiguities of the Modern Self', *Inquiry*, 34 (1991): 133–53. For permission to make use of material from that earlier essay, both here and in my contribution to the *festschrift*, I owe many thanks to the editor of *Inquiry*. For helping me to recast and strengthen my original argument I am deeply grateful to Raymond Geuss and Jonathan Lear. I also owe a large debt to the audience at Durham University for the questions they raised after hearing me deliver the first draft of the present version as a lecture in the series on postmodernity out of which the present volume has grown.

3 This is the formula Taylor employs in his own contribution to the symposium on *Sources of the Self* published in *Inquiry* in June 1991. See C. Taylor, 'Comments and Replies', *Inquiry*, 34 (1991): 237–54, at p. 240.

4 Here and in all subsequent page references in the body of the text I am referring to Charles Taylor, *Sources of the Self: The Making of the Modern Identity* (Cambridge: Cambridge University Press, 1990).

5 This survey occupies most of Part II of Taylor's book. See *Sources of the Self*, pp. 109–207.

6 For contrasting suggestions about when exactly this came about, see M. Villey, 'La genèse du droit subjectif chez Guillaume d'Occam', *Archives de philosophie du droit*, 9 (1964): 97–127; A. S. McGrade, 'Ockham and the Birth of Individual Rights', in *Authority and Power*, ed. B. Tierney and P. Linehan (Cambridge: Cambridge University Press, 1980), pp. 149–65; B. Tierney, 'Villey, Ockham and the Origin of Individual Rights', in *The Weightier Matters of the Law*, ed. T. Witte and F. S. Alexander (Atlanta: Scholars Press, 1988), pp. 1–31; and B. Tierney, 'Origins of Natural Rights Language: Texts and Contexts, 1150–1250', *History of Political Thought*, 10 (1989): 615–46.

7 I have in mind here especially the centrality of the concept of natural rights, and the idea of liberty as a right, to be found in seventeenth-century contractarian thought. On these themes see J. Dunn, *The Political Thought of John Locke* (Cambridge: Cambridge University Press, 1969); R. Tuck, *Natural Rights Theories: Their Origin and Development* (Cambridge: Cambridge University Press, 1979); J. Tully, *A Discourse on Property: John Locke and his Adversaries* (Cambridge: Cambridge University Press, 1980); and Q. Skinner, 'Thomas Hobbes on the Proper Signification of Liberty', *Transactions of the Royal Historical Society*, 40 (1990): 121–51.

8 The claim has been advanced with the greatest vehemence by Andrea Dworkin. For a discussion see S. Mendus, 'Harm, Offence and Censorship', in *Aspects of Toleration*, ed. J. Horton and S. Mendus (London: Methuen, 1985), pp. 99–112. See also S. Kappeler, *The Pornography of Representation* (Cambridge: Polity Press, 1986).

9 Taylor, 'Comments and Replies', *Inquiry*, 34 (1991): 253.

10 For a fuller discussion of this point see S. R. L. Clark, 'Taylor's Waking Dream: No one's Reply', *Inquiry*, 34 (1991): 195–215, esp. at pp. 198–200 and 202.

11 Taylor, 'Comments and Replies, *Inquiry*, 34 (1991): 239.

12 For the best recent statement of the theoretical and historical case, see C. Pateman, *The Sexual Contract* (Cambridge: Polity Press, 1988).

13 Thomas Hobbes, *De Cive*, ed. H. Warrender (Oxford: Oxford University Press, 1983), esp. pp. 176–7. Hobbes' *De Cive* constitutes a crucial document in the legitimising of the change with which I am here concerned. Although his book is entitled *The Citizen*, part of his aim is to show citizens that they ought to think of themselves as subjects.

14 Taylor, 'Comments and Replies', *Inquiry*, 34 (1991): 240.

15 Ibid., 239–40.

16 Ibid., 240.

17 For the development of these claims see Taylor, *Sources of the Self*, pp. 37–40 and 495–521.

18 For the exploration of this theme see ibid., pp. 47–50, 292, 458.

19 See, for example, ibid., pp. 27–30.

20 Taylor, 'Comments and Replies', *Inquiry*, 34 (1991): 240.

21 For this theme see especially Taylor, *Sources of the Self*, pp. 17–20.

22 This is Taylor's own summary of the point he wishes to make about theism. See his 'Comments and Replies', *Inquiry*, 34 (1991): 240–1. As Taylor also notes in that passage, I placed an exaggerated emphasis on his claims in my original critique (cited in footnote 2, *supra*). I am glad of the chance to correct this misunderstanding and restate my own point.

5 Postmodernism and 'the end of philosophy'

David E. Cooper

Writing of such recent fashions as deconstruction and Foucauldian 'genealogy', Habermas concludes that 'the drapery of philosophical concepts' they display only 'serves as the cloak for a scantily concealed end of philosophy'.[1] In fact, several self-proclaimed postmodernists, like Lyotard and Rorty, as well as some of their heroes, like Heidegger, have been willing to lay it all bare and announce the end of philosophy.

My aim in this chapter is diagnosis. I want to understand the character of this verdict on philosophy, to locate it in relation to earlier obituaries, and to identify the exact issue on which assessment of the verdict must hang.

First, though, a disclaimer. Rorty now wishes he had not used 'postmodernist' in earlier essays, since he has 'given up on the attempt to find something in common' to postmodernist architecture, literature, music and philosophising.[2] It may be that Rorty gives up too soon, and at the very end I shall suggest that a central feature of the postmodernist attitude towards philosophy is at least analogous to one characteristic of postmodernist cultural trends at large. Until then, however, I shall not be concerned with these larger dimensions of culture. It is possible, I believe, to discern the main contours of what, for better or worse, is dubbed postmodernist philosophising without becoming too taxed by its connections with the architecture of Venturi or the photography of Sherry Levine.[3]

Pronouncing the end or death of philosophy is nothing new. During the last two centuries, three terminal scenarios have been especially popular. First, that of philosophy's apotheosis. Philosophy comes to a glorious end by achieving its end or *telos*. Thus, in the related versions of Hegel and Marx, philosophy's goal is the overcoming of alienation – Spirit's recognition of, or Man's creation of, a world to be 'at home' in, 'at one' with. Once this is achieved, whether in Hegel's *Encyclopaedia* or in the victory of the proletariat, philosophy is left with nothing more to do.

Second, what could be called the 'Balkan' scenario. Philosophy, like many a Balkan state, comes to an end when the various territories it embraces break away and, not without a rearguard struggle, achieve autonomy. Philosophy, to switch metaphors, is the amateur precursor of later disciplines, notably the sciences. With professionalisation, Natural Philosophy becomes Natural Science, Mental Philosophy becomes Cognitive Psychology, and (so futurologists predict) that last bastion of the amateur, Philosophy of Language, becomes Linguistics or Semiotics.

Finally, the suicide scenario. An honest philosophical reflection, so it goes, is forced to concede that, by its own lights, the enterprise of philosophy is impossible, nonsensical even – so the far, far better thing to do is to depart from the scene. An early version of this scenario is sometimes attributed to Nietzsche, but the best-known one was furnished, sixty years ago, by the Logical Positivists. Once it is recognised that the only meaningful statements, beyond those of mathematics and logic, are the empirically verifiable ones of common sense or the sciences, then traditional philosophy ('metaphysics') goes down the same tube as theology and mysticism.

There are apparent echoes, certainly, of these scenarios among some postmodernists and their heroes. For instance, when Heidegger writes that 'the unfolding of philosophy into the autonomous . . . sciences is the legitimate completion of philosophy',[4] he is seemingly endorsing a combination of the apotheosis and 'Balkan' verdicts. Philosophy achieves its proper end by dissolving into the sciences. Derrida, it seems, is offering a version of the suicide scenario when claiming that philosophical reflection on language destroys various distinctions on which philosophy relies, such as that between literal and figurative uses of words.[5]

It soon becomes clear, however, that these verdicts are more radical, more devastating, one might say, than the earlier ones. Thus there is no Hegelian triumphalism about Heidegger's version of philosophy's self-completion which, on the contrary, is the final chapter in a sorry story shaped by Plato's unfortunate preface. And while the dissolution of philosophy into technology and cybernetics may mark the victory of professionalisation, that is nothing to celebrate but, rather, a distinguishing aspect of this, our age of 'destitution'. For Derrida, unlike the Logical Positivists, the self-destruction of philosophy is not an event to be welcomed because it permits the sciences to pursue their ambitions unmolested: since the assumptions and distinctions, now 'exploded', on which philosophy has rested are the ones on which the traditional ambitions of science have also relied. For neither author, therefore, has philosophy ceded its place in favour of some more privileged and secure form of knowledge.

A closer look at Heidegger's account will help bring out the 'devastating' character of postmodernist pronouncements of the end of philosophy. Heidegger offers us a 'history of Being' which, roughly, recounts the dominant categories in terms of which successive ages have conceived of Being – from Plato's Forms to Nietzsche's Will to Power and the technological understanding of the twentieth century. The history is one of an inevitable development, for the latest stages constitute the 'most extreme possibilities' of the programme initiated by Plato. Nietzsche's and technology's understanding of Being is 'Platonism inverted', and exhausts the directions philosophy might take.

Heidegger's reasoning is this. With Plato, philosophy became metaphysics: the attempt to explain existence and justify knowledge on the basis of some underlying 'ground', perspicuously representable by and to the properly trained and functioning intellect. Examples of such 'grounds', in chronological order, would be Plato's Forms, God, Spinozan Substance, Kant's transcendental categories, and Hegel's *Geist*. What the chronology of this list reveals is that the 'ground' of Being and knowledge gets increasingly conceived as something interior to thought or consciousness, thereby reflecting the increasing conviction that all we can represent to ourselves with certainty are constituents of ourselves, of 'subjectivity'. Kant's categories are structures, not of reality (which is unknowable), but of consciousness; and knowledge of Being, for Hegel, is Spirit's understanding of *itself*. The story closes with the further realisation that, in Rorty's words, 'the only thing we can be certain about is what we want . . . our own desires . . . The only cosmology we can affirm with the certainty Plato recommended is our own . . . world picture, our own way of setting things up for manipulation, the way dictated by our desires'.[6]

Heidegger's 'history of Being', then, is one of massive irony. The Platonic, metaphysical search for 'grounds' issues in the recognition that there are none – or, what comes to the same thing, the only 'ground' for a representation of reality is a human will which invents pictures or world-views that help to achieve its utilitarian goals. The search for truth, for a correct representation that mirrors reality leads, inexorably, to the denial of the need for and possibility of truth – or, what comes to the same thing for Heidegger, truth is finally measured only by 'results'. 'Scientific truth becomes equated with efficiency of results.'[7]

The reason this is more lethal than earlier 'end of philosophy' scenarios is that it entirely lacks their message of 'The king is dead. Long live the king!' Philosophy cannot deliver the 'grounds' and certainties of truth which were its original ambition, but nor can the disciplines which succeed it. For, when honestly perceived, these have abandoned such notions in favour of mere technical efficiency.

It is surely an attitude like this towards 'grounds' and truth which pervades and is distinctive of postmodernist philosophising, despite remarks by some postmodernists that might suggest a less radical outlook. Let me illustrate.

The most quoted observation on philosophy and postmodernism is Lyotard's. Having defined philosophy – 'modern' philosophy, at least – as the attempt to 'legitimate' discourses by an 'appeal to some grand narrative', or 'metanarrative', he then defines the postmodernist attitude as one of 'incredulity towards metanarratives'.[8] His list of such 'meta-narratives' includes 'the dialectic of Spirit . . . the emancipation of the rational or working subject, [and] the creation of wealth'. But if these are a representative sample of 'metanarratives', few philosophers in this, or indeed any, century would see themselves as 'modern' rather than 'postmodern' in Lyotard's sense. For most of them would share his 'incredulity' towards 'legitimating' scientific discourse, say, by appeal to Hegelian dialectic, Marxist emancipation, and the like.

But there are other passages in Lyotard where a more radical and contentious message is apparent. For instance, those where he describes the sciences as so many 'games', the 'rules' of which, being 'specific to each particular kind of knowledge', cannot be used to legitimate other 'games' nor, except in a bootstrap operation, by way of self-legitimation. Again, he writes that statements are only 'judged to be "good" because they conform to the relevant criterion . . . accepted in the social circle of the "knower's" interlocutors'.[9] It is clearly remarks like these, which imply abandonment of any discourse's pretension to objective legitima-tion and truth – and not, simply, 'incredulity' towards Hegelian dialectic et al. – which Lyotard needs to substantiate if his reduction of philo-sophy to 'the study of systems of logic or history of ideas' is to be plausible.[10]

Richard Rorty, too, occasionally sounds less radical than he really is. For example, while his hostility to truth as correspondence with reality is unequivocal, there are places where he seems to be redeeming the notion of truth by analysing it in terms of 'intersubjective agreement'. And there are, of course, many passages with dithyrambs to science, the 'exemplary' human activity, which might suggest a greater epistemolo-gical faith in science than Heidegger's. But appearances are deceptive. 'There is nothing', Rorty writes, 'to be said about . . . truth . . . apart from descriptions of the familiar procedures of justification which . . . [our] society . . . uses in one or another area of enquiry.'[11] This, he insists, is not to offer a new, redeeming theory of truth, but to deny there is anything for there to be a theory of. 'True' is simply a word each of us uses to 'commend . . . these beliefs which he or she finds good to believe'.[12] Here 'good' is to be taken ethically, not epistemologically, and it is for ethical reasons – confessedly 'ethnocentric' ones, at that – that science is superior to, say, magic or mysticism. 'The only sense in which science is exemplary is that it is a model of human solidarity'[13] – of that free, democratic, co-operative spirit which Rorty admires. Moral preference or prejudice aside, then, Rorty's verdicts on philosophy as determining the grounds of truth, and on science as furnishing the truths thus grounded, are every bit as harsh as Heidegger's and Lyotard's.

Can we, then, say that the radicalism of the postmodernist outlook resides in its global denial of the importance and possibility of truth? Not quite, for even this does not capture how 'devastating' that outlook is. To see this, we need to introduce a complication, one which will muddy the distinction between that outlook and some rival ones.

Let me introduce this via a brief glance at a dispute which divides interpreters of Nietzsche. For some of these, Nietzsche is 'the first postmodernist', the prototype deconstructor of knowledge and truth.[14] For others, however, the correct assessment of Nietzsche is Heidegger's: he was 'the last metaphysician', the author of one more 'Platonism', albeit an 'inverted' one.

Now everyone is agreed that Nietzsche dismisses the possibility of truth or knowledge as correspondence to reality. But whereas the first group of interpreters focus on remarks like 'Truth is a mobile army of metaphors' which happen to have caught on, the second group emphasise his apparent proposal that the degree of *power* conferred by beliefs and values provides a universal criterion for deciding which to accept. In the one case, the focus is on passages which seem to mock the notion of truth *tout court*; in the other, Nietzsche is deemed to operate with a notion sufficiently *like* truth, in crucial respects, to place him inside, not outside, the metaphysical tradition.

The moral of this is that for Nietzsche or anyone else to count as a postmodern, he must not only deny that truth is a necessary, desirable, or even possible objective of enquiry, but must also deny all this of any objective which is recognisably truth-*like*. Postponing for the moment the question of what makes a notion 'recognisably truth-like', my claim can be illustrated and elaborated by reflecting on the much reported disagreement between Lyotard and Habermas over 'universal con-sensus' as the ideal goal of serious discourse. The point at issue is not whether truth *tout court* is an ideal goal, since Habermas does not suppose that universal consensus is *evidence* for a correct depiction of objective reality. Like Lyotard, he is hostile to the Enlightenment vision of knowledge transparent to detached rational subjects, and emphasises the context-bound, historically situated character of all enquiry. But while, because of this, universal consensus does not entail truth, it does play several of the roles traditionally served by the ideal, albeit chimerical, of truth.

To begin with, consensus, like truth, is a desideratum: it is that towards which enquiry and 'communicative action' are 'orientated'. Second, just as the rational subject of tradition makes his beliefs answerable to truth, so the rational social agent, for Habermas, is willing to submit his beliefs to the universal criteria which would be furnished by an ideal consensus. Finally, Habermas holds that speakers are necessarily understood to 'raise validity claims with their speech acts' and so to aspire to a 'validity . . . distinguished from the social currency of a *de facto* . . . practice'.[15] ('Universal validity breaks every provinciality asunder'.[16]) This is his analogue to the familiar Kantian view that we could not understand one another's words unless we took each other to be trying, for the most part, to speak the truth – the difference being that 'validity' is defined in terms of an ideal consensus.

It is because this consensus plays roles traditionally served by truth that we may speak of it as a truth-*like* notion. And it is in denying the need for and desirability of a notion serving these roles that Lyotard displays his postmodernist colours, his dismissal not only of truth but of truth-likeness. Working towards consensus is not nice even if you can get it: for it would impose a kind of epistemological 'terror', stifling further experiments of thought. It is 'paralogy' – dissension, plurality, incommensurability – which should be the goal of enquiry. Anyway, this consensus is a pipe-dream. No criteria can be 'universally valid for language-games, when it is clear that language-games are . . . subject to heterogenous sets of pragmatic rules'.[17] And he would doubtless endorse Rorty's point that anyone's conception of the 'ideal situation' which is supposed to yield an ideal consensus will reflect the prejudices of his place and time.[18] The conception of a twentieth-century left-wing social democrat like Habermas will hardly be that of a medieval theologian. What would be regarded as a fair and legitimate contribution to open debate by the one might be regarded as a symptom of Satanic possession by the other.

This rehearsal of the Habermas–Lyotard debate confirms, then, the radicalism of the postmodernist position: it is pitted not only against truth, but against any notion playing the same, or closely analogous, roles to that of truth. The postmodernist's rivals are all those – old-style objectivists, Peircean pragmatists, Habermasian advocates of social reason, and so on – who insist that we do need, should want, and can deploy a notion with these roles.

On a not implausible characterisation of philosophy, its fate – whether it ends or survives – is a simple corollary of the outcome of the issue just described. For if philosophy is the attempt to elucidate the proper goal of all enquiry, the general conditions which warrant statements and theories, and the presuppositions of intelligible discourse, then it will survive only if Lyotard et al. are wrong and there really is something here to elucidate.

But there is, without a further refinement, an element of imbalance in this diagnosis of the issue between postmodernists and their opponents. It is indeed *typical* for these opponents to insist on a notion – truth itself or something truth-like – playing the three roles mentioned. Yet the third of these roles has, I think, a centrality that the others lack. Thus, to begin with, it is possible, if unusual, to hold that truth is both available and ascertainable, but to deny that it ought to be an important goal of enquiry: to insist, for example, that it is a prosaic thing, an obsession for which stand, in the way of the pursuit of what really matters – the accumulation, say, of Pater's 'delicious sensations', or contented submission to the 'beautiful illusions' of myth. At any rate, Nietzsche's question 'Suppose we want truth: why not rather untruth?' is not an *absurd* one.[19]

Second, it is both possible, and not that unusual these days, to hold that truth (or the truth-like) is available, but to deny that it furnishes *universally* binding constraints. This is *relativism* which, despite the elasticity of the terms, is worth distinguishing from postmodernism. The relativist wants to preserve the notion of truth (or the truth-like), but to relativise it to cultures, world-views or whatever. He does so because he believes that, within a culture or world-view, truth plays an essential role in enabling intelligible discourse. Whilst he proscribes invidious comparisons between the claims which are integral to different cultures or world-views, he accuses the postmodernist of blindness to the necessity felt by people who share a given culture or view to regard these claims as transcending any merely local currency.[20]

The refinement, then, is this: if postmodernism is to be distinguished, not only from its more familiar rivals, but from the positions just sketched, its crux must be the denial that discourse requires a basis of the kind which truth has traditionally been thought to provide. At any rate, the issue I want to address in the remainder of this talk is whether discourse (scientific or everyday) is imaginable among participants who are blithely indifferent to, or with no conception of, truth (or any recognisable surrogate).

It is not my ambition to settle that issue, but I would, by considering the replies the postmodernist might make to some critical queries, like to suggest that his position is not as hopeless as his critics imply. It will be convenient to present the debate in the form of a dialogue.

Q. Are you seriously suggesting that speakers could and should give up employing 'true' and 'false' in appraisal of one another's assertions?

A. Not, certainly, that they should. These terms are extremely useful, enabling speakers to endorse the statements of others without having to repeat them. Imagine having to recite the Bible or *Das Kapital* in order to express one's agreement with its statements. Still, they are *redundant* devices, employed by ordinary speakers only for convenience and carry no ineliminable commitment to anything about correspondence with reality and the like.

Q. But don't speakers need – at any rate don't we, as theorists of their linguistic and cognitive practices, need – a concept of truth (or the truth-like) in order to explain essential features of their practices? These include the *progress* which hardly anyone denies that science has made over the years, and more important still, the fact that speakers understand the meanings of what they say and hear. Progress is surely towards truth, and understanding utterances is a matter, primarily, of grasping the conditions under which they would be true.

A. You beg several questions here. Quite a few people deny that science progresses and plenty more hold that, though it may, this is to be understood in a pragmatic sense – the making of safer predictions, bridges, medicines etc. – not closer approximation to truth, ideal consensus, or whatever. Again several writers, like Derrida, would deny that utterances enjoy the stability and discreteness of meaning which would permit pairing them off with truth-conditions. And even if this hostility towards stable meanings is exaggerated, it is not obvious that meanings are best characterised in terms of such conditions. Moves in a game, or passages of music, after all, have meaning, but not truth-conditions. And recall, here, Wittgenstein's dictum that 'understanding a sentence is much more akin to understanding a theme in music than one may think'.[21]

Q. When people make statements, it is part of their self-understanding that they stand to be *corrected*, that (*pace* Protagoras) judgements are not guaranteed by the making of them. So isn't the notion of falsity, and therefore that of truth, implicit in people's understanding of their linguistic practice?

A. Speakers are indeed prepared to accept that their judgements may not be ones which, on reflection, could be endorsed in the framework within which they are made, and so may be corrected and called 'false'. But such falsity is as immanent to the framework as is a 'false move' to the game in which it occurs. What we deny, and what the concept of truth or the truth-like requires, is that the framework itself can be corrected and falsified. To cite Wittgenstein again, 'I did not get my picture of the world by satisfying myself of its correctness', and one should not ask of this picture 'is it true or false?', since 'it is the substratum of my enquiry and asserting'.[22]

Q. But what, on your view, *is* it to assert something? To assert that *P* is surely to claim that *P* is true, and this is how speakers take one another's assertions.

A. To be sure, one cannot assert *P* and then deny it is true since, as already noted, to call an assertion 'true' is to endorse it. But the triviality of this means that no light is cast on the nature of assertion by saying that one asserts things as being true. Anyone puzzled as to what it is to assert that *P* will be just as puzzled as to what it is to assert it as true. We don't deny there are difficulties in elucidating the practice of assertion, only that it is any resolution of these to haul in a notion of truth. What we need is to *locate* assertion within a wider context of behaviour, a 'stream of life'; to describe, for instance, how asserting *P* connects up with behaviour in ways that merely mouthing the words, or speaking them ironically, does not – ways that will make plain why someone asserting *P* cannot, generally, remain sanguine when someone else asserts Not-*P*.

The manner of these responses prompts a rather different characterisation of the postmodernist verdict on philosophy, one that may better illuminate its relation to the wider culture of postmodernism.

The responses indicate that the postmodernist target is not merely the notion of truth (or the truth-like) but a wider tendency of which that notion is one important manifestation. It might be called 'the craving for depth', which we have already encountered in several of its forms: Habermas' insistence that our speech-acts are more than they seem, since they implicitly make validity claims which transcend the warrant of our current practice; the many 'onto-theological grounds', as Heidegger calls them, which metaphysicians have variously held responsible for the beings we encounter; the 'metanarratives' of Progress, Dialectic etc. which have purported to reveal the processes underlying the history of thought; or the idea that linguistic understanding is explained by speakers' having internalised a truth-conditional theory of meaning for their language.

In each case, the postmodernist reaction is less to criticise the 'deep' explanations offered than to deny the need for such explanations. We don't *do* with our words more than what is apparent on the surface; beings don't require 'grounding' in the quasi-causal creatures of metaphysics; changes in scientific thought are discontinuous, *ad hoc*, and reflect no underlying process; linguistic understanding comes with training and socialisation, and calls for no intermediary in the shape of speakers' 'theory of meaning'.

The phenomena which have apparently prompted searches for depth call either for explanation in familiar (and 'immanent') empirical terms or for no explanation at all, but for perspicuous descriptions which afford an overview of their place within a wider setting.

The slogan of postmodernism might then be Wittgenstein's dictum, 'Nothing is hidden', or perhaps Heidegger's similarly intended exhortation to 'let things be' and not inflict upon them a theoretical reduction to something 'deeper'. It is the suspicion of these two men towards 'the craving for depth' which makes them heroes of postmodernist writers. That Heidegger finally rejected the label 'philosophy' for his thinking, whereas Wittgenstein described himself as 'doing philosophy', is unimportant. For Wittgenstein was as aware as Heidegger that he was doing something radically different from philosophy as traditionally pursued. In particular, he was not offering better theories than his predecessors, but assembling reminders and descriptions which, by inducing a way of seeing things for what they are, obviate the need for theory.

It is here that a link is forged with postmodern culture, whose products, according to Fredric Jameson, are distinguished by their 'depthlessness'.[23] The neo-realist painter portrays faces as they look, and not as the configurations of cubes, dots or whatever with which 'modernists' thought to reveal the underlying structures beneath the appearances. In the 'contrived depthlessness' of postmodernist architecture, the façade of a building is just that, a façade: designed to please the eye, not as an integral component in the 'real' function of the building as, say, 'a machine for living' – to quote Le Corbusier's famous definition of a house. Even the conservative political theories sometimes dubbed 'postmodernist' emphasise the surface of political life. Thus, it is not the sense of a deeply buried 'social contract', beloved of 'modern' theories, but the overt symbols of, say, crown, flag, and ceremony which bind men and women together in a polity. Commenting more widely on the break between modernism and postmodernism, David Harvey recalls that for many modernists, too, 'understanding had to be constructed through the exploration of multiple perspectives'. These constructions, however, were conducted with an optimism, quite absent among the postmodernists, that they would 'reveal . . . the true nature of a unified, though complex, underlying reality'.[24]

As this brief survey doubtless indicates, different kinds of depth – depth, perhaps, in different senses – are under the postmodernists' attack. Nevertheless, if my diagnosis of their pronouncements on the end of philosophy is sound, they share in the spirit which imbues the general culture of postmodernism.

NOTES

1 Habermas (1987).
2 Rorty (1991).
3 For a good general survey of postmodernist culture, see Harvey (1989).
4 Heidegger (1976).
5 See especially 'White mythology' in his *Margins of Philosophy* (1982).
6 'Heidegger, contingency, and pragmatism', in Rorty (1991), p. 29.
7 Heidegger (1976), p. 64.
8 Lyotard (1979), pp. xxiii–xxiv.
9 Ibid., p. 19.
10 Ibid., p. 41.
11 'Science as solidarity', in Lawson and Appignanesi (1989).
12 Ibid., p. 11.
13 Ibid., p. 15.
14 See, for example, Deleuze (1986).
15 Habermas (1987), p. 322.
16 Ibid., p. 322.
17 Lyotard (1979), p. 65.
18 'Habermas and Lyotard on postmodernity', in Rorty (1991), p. 168.
19 *Beyond Good and Evil*, I, 1.
20 On the relation between relativism and postmodernism see Margolis (1991).
21 Wittgenstein (1969a), Section 527.
22 Wittgenstein (1969b), pp. 94 and 162.
23 Jameson (1984).
24 Harvey, (1989), p. 30.

BIBLIOGRAPHY

Deleuze, G. (1986) *Nietzsche and Philosophy.* London: Athlone.
Derrida, J. (1982) *Margins of Philosophy.* Chicago: University of Chicago Press.
Habermas, J. (1987) *The Philosophical Discourse of Modernity.* Cambridge: Polity Press.
Harvey, D. (1989) *The Condition of Postmodernity.* Oxford: Blackwell.
Heidegger, M. (1976) 'Das Ende der Philosophie und die Aufgabe des Denkens', in *Zur Sache des Denkens*, Niemayer (translated in Heidegger, *Basic Writings*, Harper & Row).
Jameson, F. (1984) 'Postmodernism, or the Cultural Logic of Late Capitalism', *New Left Review*, 146.
Lawson, H. and Appignanesi, L. (eds.) (1989) *Dismantling Truth: Reality in the Postmodern World.* New York: St. Martin's Press.

Lyotard, J.-F. (1979) *The Postmodern Condition*. Manchester: Manchester University Press.

Margolis, J. (1991) *The Truth about Relativism*. Oxford: Blackwell.

Nietzsche, F. (1966) *Beyond Good and Evil*. Trans. W. Kaufmann. New York: Vintage Books.

Rorty, R. (1991) *Essays on Heidegger and Others*. Cambridge: Cambridge University Press.

Wittgenstein, L. (1969a) *Philosophical Investigations*. Oxford: Blackwell.

(1969b) *On Certainty*. Oxford: Blackwell.

Part II

The critique of modernist political thought

Historically, political theorists have sought out the foundations of political principles in various areas: theism, the idea of a natural order, philosophy of history, a conception of human nature and a theory of the self, and the undiscoverable laws of reason. In the opening chapter of this section Raymond Plant lays out the basis of modernist political theory and political philosophy showing how problems internal to its own development result in antinomies and paradoxes which have made the general undertaking difficult to sustain. He explores the logics of communitarianism and liberalism and their unassimilable counterclaims, and does this by employing a wide range of resources but particularly those of Wittgenstein and Lyotard.

In Plant's final focus on the the self, as treated in the discussions of communitarian and liberal theorists, he notes how communitarians reject the liberal theory of the encumbered self on the grounds that it is both sociologically false; and also, in Wittgensteinian terms, philosophically false. On the other hand, Plant shows that communitarians themselves are pretty unclear about the relation between the self and its values and ends, in part because they make claims about universal features of the self.

In the end Plant espouses a left Hegelian position which sees a role for theorising universal features of human life and reasons for action based upon them, while allowing that what fills in these universal features must depend on contexts and social meanings. As with Habermas, Plant sees a role for both the general and the particular in a revitalised political theory.

In contrast Diana Coole shows how one particular strand of the clientele supposedly benefiting from modernist political thought in its various forms – whether libertarian and liberal, or communitarian and collectivist – has sought through gender politics a new kind of voice and a significant reframing and appropriation of the intellectual resources required to implement the promise of the Enlightenment which seems to have been forgotten within patriarchal interpretations of this movement.

Coole, taking note of Lyotard's discrediting of the grand narratives of modernity, argues that it is the emancipatory grand narrative with which feminism has been aligned. Linking Lyotard's critique with feminist and critical theorists' analysis of modernity, Coole offers a Foucauldian account of the linkage between modernity and women's oppression. Since grand narratives are also master-masculine projects, and since too they define modernity, it is clear that there is no space here for women's emancipation. Feminism appears then to be both a resolutely modern discourse, and to have its goals precluded by the very material and cultural structures of modernity itself.

She suggests that feminists can escape this impasse only by using postmodern strategies. These are explored under three heads: theorising the game – Lyotard's and Foucault's agonistics; playing the game – a politics of representation; and exploding the game – Lyotard's sublime and Kristeva's semiotic appeal to an unnameable which would transgress and subvert the oppositions on which modernity builds. Ultimately, Coole ends by arguing that a radical politics is compatible with postmodernism and, implicitly, with feminist objectives.

Closely following on from Coole's exposition, Judith Squires observes that the recent turn to culture that characterises postmodern theorising can be seen either as a turning away from politics or as a reconceptualisation of the political. Whereas modernist conceptions of the political are located within the state, civil society, or personal realms of life, postmodern perspectives have highlighted discursive, linguistic, psychological and performative moments of political action. The political is thus seen as neither procedural, hermeneutic, nor expressive but as aesthetic.

For Squires it is significant that under the rubric of 'the cultural politics of difference' there is a distinct attempt to hold on to the ontological and epistemological insights of postmodernism, whilst addressing the more conventional political issues of institutional access and representation. This renewed interest in the procedural aspects of the political emerges out of the ubiquitous postmodern concern with 'difference' and the compulsion to 'recognise difference' publicly. Insofar as aestheticist politics engages with the question of justice at all, it is concerned with justice as recognition rather than as (re)distribution, which more conventionally characterised various modernist forms of political perspective. Yet there is a tension between constituting political procedures and celebrating the fluidity of heterogeneous difference. In attempting to negotiate a synthesis of aestheticist politics with mechanisms of just recognition one is faced with an ethical question that will not go away: which differences are to be inscribed within political structures and why?

Squires claims that in the attempt to resolve this dilemma, many theorists are currently engaging critically with the model of deliberative democracy developed by Jürgen Habermas. This chapter goes on to explore several critical readings of deliberative democracy which variously undertake the task of integrating the insights of an aestheticist politics into the more traditional political concerns of the nature of institutional mechanisms for securing just recognition.

6   Antinomies of modernist political thought: reasoning, context and community

Raymond Plant

. . .we are here as on a darkling plain
Swept with confused alarms of struggle and flight,
Where ignorant armies clash by night.

> Matthew Arnold, 'Dover Beach'

At the foundation of well-founded belief lies belief that is not founded.

> Wittgenstein, *On Certainty*

That a society needs some kind of moral foundation, a set of beliefs which either do or might hold it together, is a general assumption of political philosophy. Indeed many political theorists have held the view that some kind of transcendental sanction is necessary for morality and for moral and political ties. Locke, for example, argued in his *Letter on Toleration* that: 'Promises, covenants and oaths, which are the bond of human society, can have no hold or sanctity for the atheist, for the taking away of God, even if only in thought, dissolves all.'[1]

On the other hand, if morality is subjective then we need a set of principles which will provide a foundation for political accommodation between subjective standpoints. This idea has its roots in Plato in his critique of the Sophists who argued that man is the measure of all things, of what is true and what is false, of what is right and what is wrong. On this view politics was turned into a criterionless matter of persuasion and rhetoric rather than truth and rightness. With Plato's assumption that there is a clear distinction to be drawn between knowledge and belief he argued that the claim to authority of the ruler must be based upon his claim to possess such knowledge. The claim that practical reason must have a secure philosophical basis is a continuing theme, one repeated by Jürgen Habermas when he argues that:

If philosophical ethics and political theory can know nothing more than what is anyhow contained in the everyday norm of consciousness of different populations, and if it cannot know this in a different way, it cannot distinguish legitimate from illegitimate domination . . . If, on the other hand, philosophical

76

ethics and political theory are supposed to disclose the moral core of the general consciousness and to reconstruct it as a normative concept of the moral, then they must specify criteria and provide reasons; they must that is produce theoretical knowledge.[2]

This is a significant passage in that it shows Habermas haunted by the spectre of relativism. Without a clear basis for moral judgement we can make no transculturally binding judgements and we are left very much with Protagorean relativism. Habermas rubs the point home with reference to National Socialism which embodied a shared form of moral consciousness. Without some external standard of right or wrong how could it have been challenged? One of the tasks of philosophy is the cognitive validation of such an external standpoint.

However, there are major difficulties in trying to determine the cognitive basis on which such a philosophical ethics could in fact be founded. Given that such a theory is likely to include a conception of the good, or a conception of human flourishing which in turn would involve either normative or empirical assumptions about human nature, then as the positivists argued, such a view becomes enmeshed in deep philosophical difficulty. We have no clear idea how conceptions of the good can be rationally grounded and we have no clear view about how the empirical aspects of an account of human nature would support a theory of human flourishing, nor how the normative aspects of any account of human nature could be supported rationally. The fact/value distinction makes such arguments deeply problematic – a feature which has not really disappeared with the collapse of the overall positivist programme.

The problem of the subjectivity of value, then, poses deep issues for political theory and part of the liberal project in political theory once it has gone beyond seeing liberalism and political neutrality as merely a response to moral nihilism and fragmentation, has been to try to determine whether there are any rationally compelling rules which could underpin practical political reasoning in a world in which first-order moral agreement has become fragmented.

The problematic nature of the good is central in all discussions in this realm. This is clearly the case in three approaches characteristic of modern political theory: the utilitarian, which seeks principles of practical reason on the basis of certain limited assumptions about human desires; the theory of needs; and accounts of human rights. All such theories seem to require some conception of the good.

In the utilitarian case, the idea that there could be purely procedural ways of discounting some types of preference must be considered dubious. In the case of needs, in order to specify needs in any detail it is necessary to appeal to rather specific cultural norms. In the case of rights, if a basis for rights is to be found and if priorities between rights claims are to be adjudicated, then again it seems as though some reference has to be made to substantive theories of human flourishing and some account of the ordering of human needs: but where are the resources to come from to support such a theory? It is a central dilemma of liberal political thought that it recognises the fact of moral autonomy and moral individualism, while at the same time refusing to take its stand on the subjectivity or the incommensurability of values.

If it is true that the project of a liberal political theory, neutral between competing, subjective conceptions of the good, fails, because such theories always involve substantive accounts of human flourishing, then we seem to arrive at a fundamental problem, namely whether conceptions of the good, so central to practical reason, are capable of being rationally grounded; or whether, indeed, this is to pose the wrong question. Perhaps, however, there is an alternative approach which eschews the delineation of a philosophical foundation for ethics. What I want to discuss here is precisely the alternatives to such foundational approaches.

The first approach has come to be called communitarian and rather crudely, at this stage of the argument, may be taken as saying that political goods cannot be determined by abstract reasoning, nor are they freely chosen by atomised moral agents, but rather arise out of and are implicit in the ways of life of particular communities. The second answer is that the search for external rational foundations for practical reasoning is misconceived because even if, *per impossible*, they could be found, they would in fact be inert in relation to practical dilemmas. We do not need theoretical foundations for a way of life and to conceive the political philosopher's task in this way is misconceived. Practical reason is not about *sophia* (wisdom), justified claims to objective knowledge, but rather *phronesis* (judgement), the capacity for practical deliberative judgement in particular situations. These two views tend to coalesce in the communitarian/interpretive approach to the discipline.

The communitarian approach in political philosophy, which has come to be associated with Michael Sandel, Michael Walzer and Charles Taylor, arose in part as a reaction to the work of liberal theorists such as Rawls and Dworkin, as the title of Sandel's book *Liberalism and the Limits of Justice* suggests. However, it is important to recognise that the idea of community has frequently been invoked over the past 200 years as an attempt to correct what has been seen as the individualism, the subjectivism, the atomism, the alienation, the instrumentalism, the contract-based and market-oriented character of liberalism. Hegel,

T. H. Green, Bosanquet, Tawney, Raymond Williams and Robert Paul Wolff have all in different ways invoked the ideal of community as a way of trying to combat these baneful features of liberal society. So modern communitarian thought is not really new. Indeed, in Britain the Idealist movement, influenced more by Hegel than by Kant's emphasis on universal rules, saw the community as the source of political values and conceded a large and central place for groups in a liberal society in which one learned to acquire an identity. However, these critics appealed to the idea of community as an inescapable ideal which individualistic liberalism found it impossible to accommodate, whereas the role of community in the work of modern critics of the liberal project is in fact multifaceted and it has at least both a normative and an epistemological role. Since these aspects play a central part in under-pinning the ideal role which community also plays in their theories, I want to outline these different roles and their importance for the liberal project because they are often run together in the work of communitarian political theorists.

However, before going on to discuss these two issues in detail I will attempt a broad sketch of some of the central themes of communitarian political theory which will show its importance, the ways in which it challenges some of the assumptions of liberal political thought, and the role which the normative and epistemological aspects of the theory play within it.

The epistemological role played by the idea of community relates to the points made earlier in the chapter about conceptions of the good. Communitarians reject the idea that we can develop cogent views of the good by abstract philosophical reasoning, nor are they the product of individual preference or emotional attitude. Rather they are embodied in the ways of life of particular communities. The philosopher cannot give them any external rational foundation. They are given, however implicitly, in particular forms of life and the task of the philosopher is to bring them fully to consciousness and, as it were, reclaim them. He is not creating them, however; they are implicit in particular ways of life. In a sense the community is the basis of practical reason and political judgement, but these bases are not universal in scope nor indubitable as the foundational assumptions of many political theorists seem to imply. This does not mean, however, that they are arbitrary. They are only arbitrary in the sense that they could have been different, but given they are as they are they enter into and constitute the way of life of the particular society in question. They are restricted and local but this is to be expected. Practical reason has to speak to the situatedness of human life.

Here there is a big difference between the aims of communitarian thought and at least the programmatic aspirations of liberalism. Rawls, for example, argues on the final page of *A Theory of Justice*:

Thus to see our place in society from the perspective of this position is to see it *sub specie aeternitatis*: it is to regard the human condition not only from all social but also from all temporal points of view. The perspective of eternity is not a perspective from a certain place beyond the world, nor the point of view of a transcendent being; rather it is a form of thought and feeling that rational persons can adopt within the world. And having done so, they can, whatever their generation, bring together in one scheme all individual perspectives and arrive together at regulative principles that can be affirmed by everyone as he lives by them, each from his own point of view.[3]

This passage makes strongly universalist and foundational claims which, as we shall see later, Rawls modifies, claims which are criticised not so much in detail, but as a project by the communitarians. The same point is made more exactly although more prosaically by Dworkin when he argues as follows:

In the end, political theory can make no contribution to how we govern ourselves except by struggling, against all the impulses that drag us back to our own culture, toward generality and some reflective basis for deciding which of our traditional distinctions and discriminations are genuine and which spurious, which contribute to the flourishing of the ideals we want, after reflection, to embrace.[4]

Is the project of political theory to provide some universal values as a foundation for practical reasoning in politics, or is it to bring to a fuller consciousness the values which are implicit in the communities of which we are a part? Are the reasons universal, or part of a complex set of reasons which are implicit in a specific way of life? The answers given to these questions clearly determine the scope of political theory and the vocation of the political philosopher.

This brings me on to the second aspect of the communitarian case which might be termed ontological. Communitarians criticise the ontology and in particular the theory of the self put forward by liberal theorists and the conception of the human condition which follows from this. This involves making the case for arguing that the self at least in part is constituted by the values of the community within which the person finds him or her self and therefore that choosing values in some kind of abstract way as envisaged by liberal theory just embodies a false moral ontology.[5]

There is another strong theme in communitarian writing too, namely that the liberal project, or perhaps more comprehensively the Enlightenment project of providing universal principles of political morality, whether based upon rights or justice, is misconceived, not only because such theories cannot be given a rational foundation but because they mistake the relationship between theory and practice. The flourishing of society cannot be secured by agreement on abstract principle, but rather has to trade on values which are implicit in the way of life in society as it exists.

Certainly the idea that knowledge and understanding can only be gained by leaving the everyday world behind has a long history as an image in Western thought, as in Plato's philosopher leaving the cave of everyday life for the sunlight of the Forms. Or more prosaically, as in Rawls' Original Position, in which the rational contractors discount all the specific knowledge of themselves and their interests and thus of their specific identities; in Dworkin's insurance game; or most bizarrely by Ackerman who imagines a perfect technology of justice in which on a spacecraft (to separate us wholly from the world of interests) we reason about the distribution of manna (a resource without any specific qualities other than being capable of being transformed into 'any of the familiar material objects in our own world').

However, Walzer, perhaps the most self-conscious communitarian, argues in *Spheres of Justice* that this approach cannot provide the foundation for practical reasoning about values which those who have exemplified it have thought. On the contrary, while justice

and equality can conceivably be worked out as philosophical artifacts . . . a just or egalitarian society cannot be. If such a society isn't already here – hidden as it were, in our concepts and categories – we shall never know it concretely or realise it in fact.[6]

Do we need a universal ethics to sustain our society or do we need an ethos, a set of values implicit within society which the philosopher can play a role in bringing to the surface?

The issues at stake here have been well described by Rorty,[7] when he rejects, following Lyotard, meta-narratives[8] in which the philosopher seeks to describe or predict the activities of such entities as the noumenal self (Kant), Absolute Spirit (Hegel), or the proletariat (Marx), or Ideas or Forms (Plato). These meta-narratives are stories about metaphysical entities which, in Rorty's view, purport to justify loyalty to or in some cases breaks with contemporary communities. These meta-narratives purport to provide a rational basis for political action and judgement. Again this is an old argument about the whole Enlightenment project of a set of universal principles compared with what Justus Moser, the eighteenth-century German thinker, called Local Knowledge: an understanding of the values implicit in a specific and localised way of life.

So what is at stake here is political philosophy's current relationship with the rationalising, cosmopolitan assumptions of the Enlightenment: 'the truth of generality versus the truth of specificity, that is, truth at the level of abstract principles, versus truth embedded in immediate circumstances'.[9]

The final aspect of the communitarian case in a sense builds upon these other points. If the community is the source of values and is constitutive of the self then the idea of community becomes of normative significance and community itself is something to be valued, as opposed to the typical political values expressed by liberal individualism. Given that the locus of the good and the sources of personal identity are to be found in community, then community should be sustained as the necessary environment for human flourishing.

Reasoning and community

The epistemological basis of communitarian thought can perhaps best be seen in relation to the later philosophy of Wittgenstein. This is not because Wittgenstein is much referred to by communitarians and interpretivists, except Rorty, but rather because his fundamental work on the philosophy of language provided a background in modern thought from which communitarians could draw.

First of all, Wittgenstein rejects his earlier foundational understanding of language. Rather as Peter Winch elegantly puts it: 'Reality is not what gives language sense, but what is real and unreal shows itself in the sense which language has.'[10] A word does not derive its meaning from its link to some unmediated external reality as opposed to its use within a stream of life. If this is true it follows then that philosophical reflection on religious and political language cannot take place in a vacuum; rather we have to be concerned with those traditions, practices, language games and contexts in which words have a home. Philosophical reflection on political language cannot take place in formal or abstract terms employing formal devices such as the appeal to logical consistency or the law of non-contradiction. We have rather to look at the meaning of moral and political concepts within specific moral traditions and contexts. Insofar as they have such a place within a particular moral practice, they are going to have close relationships with other terms within that practice. So philosophical reflection cannot ultimately be pursued in a piecemeal way but has to involve trying to become clear about interrelationships between ideas in a rich social context. Philosophy is therefore inherently contextual, but struggling for a clear view of the context.

A second theme in Wittgenstein's philosophy which is central to an understanding of its impact upon modern political thought is the rejection of essentialism: the view that there must be a common element to all uses of a term and the view that there is a strict set of necessary and sufficient conditions governing the use of a term. Here, the stalking horse is primarily Plato, but Wittgenstein's rejection of this model has important implications across the range of political theory, not just those of a Platonist sort. In many of his dialogues, for example the *Theatetus* (147), *Meno* (70–4), *Euthyphro* (6–7), *Republic* (507), Plato depicts Socrates as becoming exasperated with his discussants when in response to a question such as what is justice or what is knowledge, they go on to give examples. In the *Euthyphro*, for example, Plato argues that there is a need for a general account (*logos*) of a concept or a principle. Secure moral judgement, and by extension, political judgement, depends upon a philosophical theory which will give an account of the terms used in the judgement. Without this, as Plato says in the *Republic*, 'the many are seen but not known'. Therefore, giving examples misses the point. We need rather an account, a *logos*, of what makes these cases of justice or knowledge.

Wittgenstein rejects this approach. In *The Blue Book*, for example, he argues that: 'The idea that in order to get clear about the meaning of a general term one had to find the common element in all its applications has shackled philosophical investigation.'[11] This tendency to look for a common element Wittgenstein links to a craving for generality[12] which he sees as infecting philosophy. Instead of recognising the multifaceted nature of language and its relation to social practices which inevitably means a good deal of particularity, the craving for generality leads us to develop these complex metaphysical theories in which, as Wittgenstein says, 'language goes on holiday'. It becomes detached from the contexts in which it naturally functions and becomes part of a complex theory which just because it abstracts from particularity, then really fails to shed light on that particularity. Objectivity too is internal to context and there is no context-free standpoint from which we can evaluate the world and social practices. We cannot look to metaphysical theories and certainty to provide us with a basis for a secure way of life.

If I have exhausted the justifications I have reached bedrock and my spade is turned. Then I am inclined to say: 'This is simply what I do.'[13]

What has to be accepted, the given, is forms of life.[14]

There are no a priori reasons for action, no a priori principles of practical reasoning which can be identified independently of the particularities of context and practice. The principles by which we live do not depict the world or some kind of antecedent moral order, so much as embody the commitments by which we live.

The general thesis might seem to imply that the practices and language games in question are arbitrary. They are certainly arbitrary in that they could have been different. Language games are not arbitrary, however, in the sense that whole ways of life embody them and that within these ways of life things have meaning and significance. They are not arbitrary in the sense that they cannot be changed at will because such a change would involve a massive change in our lives. If we are interested in ideas of justification, of right, of truth, then we shall have to understand them in this contextual way. There can be no a priori theory of right and justification. Language games do not get refuted by metaphysical argument, they get forgotten because they lose their point and purpose in a particular social context.

It would be a mistake to think, however, that the context of a particular social practice or community is itself a foundation for thinking and reasoning. Wittgenstein wants to move us away from the idea of foundations altogether. It is not that we are replacing metaphysical foundations with communitarian or contextual ones, rather that:

Giving grounds, however, justifying the evidence, comes to an end; but the end is not certain propositions' striking us immediately as true, i.e. it is not a kind of seeing on our part, it is our acting which lies at the bottom of the language game.[15]

Again the insistence is that it is commitment to a practice which is the basis for reasoning and for practical reasoning, not some pure attempt to argue for the incorrigibility of a particular set of propositions as a universal foundation for practical judgement.

That words do not have common elements or essential definitions clearly has implications for any attempt at a general political theory in which, abstracted from context, the terms in the theory must be used in an exact way. However, we may try to fix the meanings of words in everyday life for practical reasons. In setting up the terms of practice for a game such as noughts and crosses, we are aware that we have not given an exhaustive definition of 'game', but equally we can fix the boundary of the concept in question for this particular purpose.

However, when we move to political theory the position is by no means as clear-cut. For here a particular definition may well itself embody a political standpoint. For example, whether justice can include social justice in the distribution of resources as social democrats believe, or whether it should be restricted as neo-liberals think; whether commu-

nities of interest are genuine communities as liberals argue they are, or
not as communitarians of both the right and the left deny; whether
rights are social and economic or only civil and political; in each case we
have to accept that drawing the boundary in one place rather than
another implicitly involves making a political decision, or at least a
decision with political consequences.

These decisions do not reflect the way the world is or some necessary
order which the mind has to follow, but rather reflect more generally our
needs, interests and purposes. Some philosophers, such as Habermas in
his book *Knowledge and Human Interests*,[16] have linked knowledge to a
set of human interests and then tried to give a transcendental deduction
of a particular set of basic human interests. This latter point relates
particularly to the foundationalist approach in political theory in the
sense that a good deal of such theorising has had to do with devising
frameworks for ranking the importance of human interests according to
some metaphysical scale of value. The problem for the foundationalist
now is where the metaphysical resources for such a deduction are to
come from.

This brings us back to the traditional concern of political philosophers
with theories of human nature which are supposed to fulfil this function.
This depends, however, upon our being able to formulate some kind of
universal theory of the self, and a sense of the fundamental interests
which all persons have in common. However, Wittgenstein's arguments
about the nature of the human mind to which we now turn have been
thought to deal a death blow to the idea that we can in philosophy
determine in an asocial way what the fundamental purposes and
interests of human beings are.

The point at issue here is what might be seen as Wittgenstein's
commitment to the view that there is a non-contingent link between the
self and the social context of which it is a part. This insistence on the
link between self and society relates centrally to one theme which critics
of the liberal project have frequently invoked, namely the extent to
which the self in liberal theory is seen as atomised, asocial, solitary. It
has led one critic of liberalism to argue that central to liberalism is the
attempt to solve the problem which arises when 'essentially solitary
individuals'[17] come together in civil society.

If this is indeed a fair characterisation of liberalism, then since on
Wittgensteinian terms there can be no logical separation of self from
context, it follows that a central element of the liberal position is
defective. The idea that self and context can be separated received its
most paradigmatic statement in the work of Descartes, who argued in
the *Meditations* that it was possible to doubt the existence of the

external world, the existence of other human beings and the existence of one's own body; but not the existence and the contents of one's own mind.

The argument for the denial of this position is found in *Philosophical Investigations* and is concerned with what would have to be the case for us to possess the whole range of mental concepts in the absence of other people and relationships. The relevance of Wittgenstein's point to the very heart of political philosophy, follows from the claim that it is not possible to derive a set of values about human flourishing, or the nature of human needs and desires, without looking at the social context which makes that account of flourishing or needs intelligible and provides a justification for it. A typical example is the debate over needs and wants which has been much discussed in philosophy during the past twenty years, particularly through the utilitarian emphasis upon desire.

Language is inseparable from rule following and one cannot follow a private rule because one cannot discriminate in a purely private way whether one is following the rule or not. Justification for the use of a term means, as Wittgenstein says, 'appealing to something independent', whereas a private check on rule following is like a person who buys 'several copies of the same morning paper to assure himself that what it said was true'. Similarly the language in terms of which we describe our states of consciousness, such as desires, wants, needs and so forth, are words in 'our common language' not just 'intelligible to me alone' and this follows from the nature of rule following.

Given the claim that ideas such as rationality, justification and explanation are internal to particular language games and the social practices of which they are a part and the ways in which these differ in potentially incommensurable ways so that there can be no supra or a priori substantive standards of rationality, it follows that the intelligibility of action has a non-contingent link with a common language and its norms, and also that justification for action takes place within such a context too. There can therefore be no a priori or metaphysical theory of reasons for action just because such theories are not internal to specific practices, but equally there can be no account of reasons for action which derives them from some Cartesian psyche separate from the world of common language and common norms.

We can now see how this Wittgensteinian framework provides something of an intellectual background to communitarian and interpretative political philosophy. It is possible to see arguments of the sort we have been considering as forming a backcloth to these more directly political arguments. Indeed Richard Rorty acknowledges this as a central theme in his book *Contingency, Irony and Solidarity*.[18]

The appeal to community

Most of the themes of communitarian political theory are implicit in the Wittgensteinian perspective on language. First of all is the idea of the internal relation of reasons to particular practices and the way in which ideas such as a reason for action have to be linked to a common understanding and a common vocabulary. Most of these themes are found, for example, in the programmatic statements in Walzer's *Spheres of Justice*, where he identifies a number of ways in which his approach differs from what he takes to be the more universalistic and a priori road of other modern political theorists.

The first element is that of particularity and the social context. In the case of a *A Theory of Justice*, Rawls seems[19] to develop an a priori and universalistic view of the moral reasoning of individuals in a situation which discounted everything specific about them when they are behind the veil of ignorance, or in the Original Position. Instead of asking the Rawlsian question 'What would rational individuals choose under universalising conditions of such and such a sort?', we should rather concentrate on the more specific questions 'What would individuals like us choose, who are situated as we are, who share a culture and are determined to go on sharing it? What choices have we already made in the course of our common life? What understandings do we already share?' Questions of political philosophy are questions about specific societies with particular values. Justification, argumentation has to take place within such contexts and not external to them.

Secondly, the kinds of goods which concern political theory such as office, economic goods, membership, desert, leisure, and so forth are social goods in the sense that they do not have a neutral meaning which is uncontaminated by specific cultural identities. There can be no thin theory of goods, no substantive theory of primary goods. We can make a universal list of goods incorporated into a priori theories of practical reasoning only if 'they are abstracted from every particular meaning – hence for all practical purposes meaningless'.[20] It is what Wollheim calls a 'bleached'[21] theory. In this sense, there can be no a priori theory of reasons for acting or for political judgement. In these terms modern political philosophy can be seen as a rerun of the debate between Kant and Hegel. The big difference between modern communitarians and Hegel is that the moderns reject Hegel's attempt to link specific forms of society and the different accounts of the nature of the self and its ends together into some metaphysical theory which saw them as progressing towards more and more adequate forms of human fulfilment in world history.[22] This meta-narrative of legitimation has now to be rejected.[23]

Modern communitarian theorists, however, do agree with Hegel that social meanings are historical, they change over time and present meanings have to be understood in terms of their historical development. This means that as there cannot be a universal political philosophy, so there cannot be a transhistorical one. What count as the relevant reasons for action depend not upon some essentialist or transcultural or transhistorical theory but upon the contingent circumstances of particular cultures. It is in the rejection of a transhistorical meta-theory that they differ sharply from Hegel's own account of the link between self, good and society.[24]

Getting a clear view of a practice has to be an internal exercise and is much more like developing an adequate understanding of a literary text than it is producing a representation which is clearly true or false in the sense that it depicts an independent reality, as Charles Taylor says in discussing this problem: 'We have to think of man as a self interpreting animal. He is necessarily so, for there is no such thing as the structure of meanings for him independently of his interpretation of them.'[25] If an interpretation is contested, as is likely, then all we can do, as Taylor argues, is:

to show him through the reading of other expressions why [the contested expression] must be read in the way we suppose. But success here requires that he should follow us in these readings and so on, it would seem potentially for ever. We cannot escape an ultimate appeal to a common understanding of the expression, of the 'language' involved.[26]

There are two further but final themes which emerge from this Wittgensteinian background. The first has to do with the nature of the self; the second with the role of philosophy. As we have seen Wittgenstein provides strong reasons for thinking that the self cannot be understood independently of society because of the non-contingent link between language, the characterisation of inner experience and social standards. This provides the background for the communitarian claim that the self cannot be considered in an unencumbered way.

On the contrary, communitarians want to argue for situated selves in which the self is socially constituted and the reasons for action available to the self are those which are available as the common stock in the community. Lyotard draws the conclusion from this to which we shall return that: 'the social subject itself seems to dissolve in this dissemination of language games'. Liberal political theory insofar as it seeks to derive some universal reasons for action from the idea of the unencumbered self, agency, a thin theory of the good, all done in abstraction from any particular social practice, is sending language and thought on holiday.

The second implication of Wittgenstein's thought which might be held to support a communitarian approach in political philosophy is a claim that philosophy is inert in attempting to provide foundations for a way of life or set of beliefs. Philosophy cannot give to society or to particular practices within society any particular foundation. What Lyotard has called meta-narratives, philosophical theories which hold practices together in some kind of total outlook, whether it is as with Plato participating in the Form of the Good, with Hobbes' mechanistic and geometrical understanding of human nature with a complete naturalistic framework, or Hegel's account of the role of particular aspects or moments of human nature in the movement of *Geist*, have collapsed and we should not be looking for alternative philosophical foundations of a totalising sort.

The grand narratives of the good, the noumenal self, the proletariat in history or *Geist* do not in fact hold societies together, they are dislocated from the societies whose beliefs they are thought to sustain and legitimise. What gives a practice cohesion and legitimacy is internal to it. It is a matter of ethos[27] rather than grounds or foundations. Loyalty to institutions, belief in their value, is not grounded in anything other than the fact that, as Rorty argues, they overlap with lots of other members of the group with which we identify for purposes of moral or political deliberation and the fact that these beliefs, values and loyalties are distinctive of the group and it is through these that it builds up its self-image and its sense of worth.

This approach refocuses the nature of political philosophy. It is interpretive, bringing to light the values, principles and the reasons which count in a particular context for action. Political philosophy and political judgement are linked much more to Aristotle's idea of *phronesis* rather than Plato's *sophia*; more to practical deliberation weighing the factors which count in a given context rather than some general theory about what would ground political judgement *sub specie aeternitatis*. On this kind of approach philosophical ethics 'does not propose any new ethics, but rather clarifies and concretises given normative contents'.[28] This also means that philosophy does not necessarily play any kind of privileged role in this clarification process. It can, as both Gadamer and Rorty argue, be achieved just as effectively by other means, such as art or literature, by narrative and story telling as much as by 'theory'. The arts in Rorty's view may well bring a community's self-consciousness to life because they 'serve to develop and modify a group's self image by, for example apotheosising its heroes, diabolising its enemies, mounting dialogue among its members and refocussing attention'.[29]

It would follow from this argument that if the focus of ethical judgement is the ethos of a society or the set of values and norms which give reasons for action in that particular society, then if an ethos has become degenerate and no longer gives guidance, it cannot be restored by philosophy. A new ethics can only emerge from the fragments of the old, it cannot be derived from some universal form of abstract reasoning, nor from some meta-narrative about the role of *Geist* or the Good.

Liberal thought and community

We need now to turn to the contrast between communitarian and liberal political thought to see how sharp the methodological disagreements in fact are. The alleged contrasts are between: universality and particularity; foundations and interpretation; the relationship of philosophy and praxis; and the understanding of the role of the Western tradition in political thought and particularly its contemporary deontological form. In some ways these polarities can be put in terms of Aristotle versus Kant. Many communitarians look to Aristotle for inspiration since his thought in both the *Ethics* and the *Politics* seems to be concerned not so much with universalistic claims but rather reflection on the aspirations, values and ethos of citizens in the Athenian polis of his day. He was concerned with reflecting on the circumstances and the values of the polis and trying to put into some theoretically self-conscious way the links with and differences between values so that they could illuminate *phronesis* – practical judgement in particular circumstances. Aristotle's distinction between *sophia* and *phronesis* is taken as pre-figuring the current concern with the inert nature of theoretical and universalistic reason in the context of practical judgement about ethics and politics within a particular society. Kant, on the other hand, seems to be the founder of modern deontological theories. He claims that his account of moral judgement is independent of any psychological theory about human nature, or any particular assumptions about human desires and interests drawn from a particular society. He claims to be able to produce a general theory about the requirements for moral action. Moral and political judgement is detached from particular ends and purposes in a particular community. It is formal, abstract and universal but for the very same reason, inert. So we need to consider how sharp these contrasts actually are and this is crucial because what is at stake is the nature and ambition of political theory and also the vocation of the political theorist.

Let us begin with the contrast between foundational claims and interpretive strategies. A good deal of the history of political thought and almost all of contemporary deontological liberal thought is considered by communitarian critics to be concerned with providing foundations for judgements, practices and institutions and to be neglectful of circumstance, particularity and locality. Certainly some figures in the history of political thought can be read in this foundationalist way and perhaps Plato is the best example. However, there are dangers in looking at the history of political thought as if it does embody this sharp distinction.

The assumption is that metaphysics and epistemology are at the heart of philosophy and the foundationalist is concerned to draw out the ethical and political implications of his foundational metaphysical and epistemological assumptions. This assumption, however, can involve a misreading of a good deal of political philosophy. The reason why this may be a misreading has been well stated by Alasdair MacIntyre:

There is an important, although common misreading of the structures of ancient and medieval thought which projects back on to that thought an essentially modern view of the ordering of philosophical and scientific enquiries. On this modern view, ethics and politics are peripheral modes of enquiry, dependent in key part on what is established by epistemology and the natural sciences . . . But in ancient and medieval thought, ethics and politics afford light onto other disciplines as much as vice versa. Hence from that standpoint, which I share, it is not the case that I first must decide whether some theory of human nature or cosmology is true and only secondly pass a verdict upon an account of the virtues which is based upon it.[30]

If this is a correct interpretation of at least some of the history of political thought, then the contrast between communitarian and interpretive models is overdrawn in that figures such as Aristotle and Hegel were not just deriving political conclusions as remote consequences from metaphysical first principles and conceptions of human nature. Rather, as MacIntyre argues elsewhere:

I cannot look to human nature as a neutral standard, asking what forms of social and moral life would give it the most adequate expression. For each form of life carries with it its own picture of human nature. The choice of a form of life and a choice of a view of human nature go together.[31]

Whether this is a plausible view of the history of political thought is an issue which we cannot really discuss in detail here, but if, for example, the work of Aristotle or Hegel[32] is considered, it is certainly not clear that how they think about politics fits into the foundationalist model. Indeed in the case of Hegel it would be odd if this were so, in that his thought is all about the transformation of human nature and our understanding of ourselves in complex historical circumstances. As he argues in his work on human nature in *The Philosophy of Subjective Spirit*:

The Ego is by itself only formal identity. Consciousness appears differently modified according to the difference of the given object and the gradual specification of consciousness appears as a variation in the characteristics of the objects.[33]

Certainly Hegel's argument that self-consciousness is not a given but an achievement which develops of necessity in relationships of mutual recognition provides as strong a link between self and others as Wittgenstein's argument about private languages and it could not be argued that he sees human nature in a static way to which correspond appropriate forms of social and political life.

It is not just that the contrast between foundational and communitarian approaches is a mistaken account of a good deal of the history of political philosophy, it also fails to do justice to recent developments in the subject, particularly relating to the work of John Rawls, who can be credited with the revival of liberal deontological political theory which seems to have the universalist overtones which communitarians reject. *A Theory of Justice* does appear to have such universalist tendencies and certainly the book has been read in that way and for good reason, particularly if one considers the whole argument in relation to the eloquent summary on the final page of the book. Even within the book, however, there are features which give pause for thought and more particularly in Rawls' subsequent interpretation of the scope and nature of his enterprise in his essay 'Justice as Fairness: Political not Metaphysical'.[34]

In the book itself Rawls makes two points which are of the utmost importance in seeing how he thinks that his very abstract arguments apply to understanding political judgement in particular societies. The first is the early analogy which Rawls draws between theorising about justice and grammatical theory, which leads him on to his account of what he calls reflective equilibrium. In Section 9 of the book he argues that it is possible to draw an analogy between moral theory, of which the theory of justice is a part, and the theory of grammar. In a grammatical theory we begin with the fact that people have the capacity to speak a language and to recognise well-formed sentences within that language. Clearly the ability to do this on the part of a native speaker requires some implicit knowledge of grammar which may reach various degrees of sophistication and articulation. However, the theory, if there is one, which will account for all of these capacities will be very complex if it is to be systematic and coherent and will 'require theoretical constructions that far outrun the *ad hoc* precepts of our explicit grammatical knowledge'. Similarly, moral theory does not operate in a vacuum. It is concerned with a coherent conceptual grasp of our everyday moral judgements, and he goes on to argue that this will 'certainly involve principles and theoretical constructions which go beyond the norms and standards cited in everyday life'. In particular in Rawls' view it will require the contract theory and the mathematics associated with the maximin theory. However, the important point for the moment is that the theory, however complex it becomes, is an attempt to set out in a coherent and systematic way the principles and values which inform first-order moral judgements. In this sense it is not a priori or metaphysical. It is a theoretical attempt to understand the connections or lack of them between our deep-seated moral judgements. In this sense therefore part of the communitarian criticism of Rawls becomes muted because he is not trying as he sees it to produce a metaphysical theory (despite what he implies intermittently in the book with its talk of Archimedean points and a conception of justice *sub specie aeternitatis*) but a coherent theory of our first-order moral judgement. In this sense he starts where the communitarian starts, with the moral judgements of a particular community, and as Rawls sees it in his later work, those judgements to do with liberty and equality which are characteristic of a liberal democratic society.

This point is further reinforced when he discusses the device of reflective equilibrium in the book. The attempt to produce a coherent account of moral judgement is a two-way process. Moral theory has to start with existing moral judgements but equally, as the process of theorising gets under way, some of these judgements may have to be modified in the light of what their implications for other judgements are seen to be in the light of trying to achieve a coherent picture. In this theoretical attempt we are trying to do justice to those moral judgements which we accept in a considered way; those which we arrive at when we are not frightened or upset, those which we arrive at when we are not excessively concentrating on our own interests and when we do not expect to gain from making the judgement in one way rather than another. In trying to arrive at such a theory we shall move to higher levels of abstraction but these abstractions, such as the contract theory, the device of the Original Position and the like, are ways in which we try to shed light on some of the basic moral intuitions of a liberal society such as that all citizens are free and equal and that they have some capacity for autonomy in relation to their moral values. The important point, however, is that as in the theory of grammar our theories can be brought into some illuminating and explanatory relationship with our ordinary judgements.

I have said already that moral theory as Rawls sees it is a two-way process: the theory completes and renders coherent first-order moral judgements while at the same time the theoretical construction is constrained by this first-order moral data in the same way as the theory of grammar is constrained by the features of our being able to speak a language. At the same time, the demand for a coherent theory may well require some revision of first-order judgements if that turns out to be so. It is essentially a two-way process. Given this, the problem clearly arises as to which judgements might be displaced by the demands of theoretical coherence. Are there any moral judgements which are so fundamental that they can never be displaced by theoretical considerations?

Given that Rawls now accepts explicitly that the moral judgements which philosophy has to theorise are specific to a particular way of life which cannot be given any metaphysical foundation, they are thrown up by history and tradition, he sees two roles for political philosophy. In a society without much disagreement, the task of political philosophy would be that of reflecting 'upon and getting a clear view of the political life expressed in that culture'. Political philosophy would seek a kind of 'public self-understanding'. This would be quite like what Wittgenstein called a perspicuous representation of a way of life. However, in a society in which there are cleavages between considered judgements, for example between liberty and equality,[35] the task of political philosophy would be to consider ways in which these values can be reconciled by drawing upon the underlying values of the culture particularly those of freedom and autonomy:

Thus the real task is to discover and formulate the deeper basis of agreement which one hopes is embedded in common sense . . . In addressing the public culture of a democratic society, Kantian constructivism hopes to invoke a conception of a person implicitly affirmed by that culture, or at least one that would prove acceptable to citizens if it was properly presented and explained.[36]

Indeed, this is the only way political philosophy could work in a society characterised by liberal democracy, which is the kind of society Rawls regards himself as theorising. It has to work with the values implicit in the culture, not by attempting to draw upon some kind of metaphysical view of morality which Rawls, like Walzer, regards as inert in a democratic society marked by different conceptions of the good, and of human flourishing: 'Thus the essential agreement in judgements arises not from the recognition of a prior and independent moral order, but from everyone's affirmation of the same social perspective.'[37] In this sense, therefore, Rawls assumes that a liberal democratic society does have a community of meaning and this has to be drawn out, rendered perspicuous and made coherent by political philosophy.

Nevertheless it is still important to consider the general theoretical differences between foundationalists and communitarian/interpretive political philosophers and to get as clear as we can about the precise issues at stake between them. We therefore turn to a more explicit examination of how communitarians operate with the concept of human nature and the idea of basic interests and needs, powers and capacities of the human mind which have been central to the foundationalist approach to political theory. The basic question is whether communitarians can in fact get along without universalistic values of their own.

Some communitarians are concerned by what appear to be the deeply relativistic consequences of something like Wittgenstein's philosophy in the sense that if we have no external standards of evaluation then it might be that not only can we not give a way of life any foundation, but we may not in fact be able to understand at the end the values, principles and concepts which are part of a way of life which we do not share. In some cases this has led back to a concern with human nature in the sense that we have to appeal to some limiting features of human life as a standard in terms of which we make other societies comprehensible, leaving aside the question for the moment of an evaluation of such ways of life and practices. This point is made very well by Peter Winch in his famous essay 'Understanding a Primitive Society':

I wish to point out that the very conception of human life involves certain fundamental notions – which I shall call limiting notions – which have an obvious ethical dimension, and which indeed in a sense determine the ethical space within which the possibilities of good and evil in human life can be exercised. The notions which I shall discuss very briefly here correspond closely to those which Vico made the foundation of his idea of natural law, on which he thought the possibility of understanding of human history rested: birth, death, sexual relations.[38]

Such limiting conditions which are, as he says, of a universal nature, might link up with the foundationalist's argument that political values and moral principles could in fact be grounded in such limiting conditions of human nature. It is certainly arguable that communitarian political philosophers do in fact appeal to similar limiting features of human life within which their own communitarian thought is conducted. If they do operate with a notion of some universal features of human life and with evaluative principles which follow from these, then it might be held that the difference between communitarian and foundational political thought in the context of arguments about the role of ideas about human nature in political philosophy is in fact not so marked as protagonists on each side might want to contend.

These issues come out most clearly again in Walzer's arguments in *Spheres of Justice*. The first way in which Walzer invokes some idea of human nature, or at least certain fundamental concerns from which he draws evaluative conclusions, is in terms of his argument about the nature of human beings as culture-producing creatures. He says this in *Spheres of Justice*:

We are all culture producing creatures; we make and inhabit meaningful worlds. Since there is no way to rank and order these worlds with their understanding of social goods, we do justice to actual men and women by respecting their particular creations . . . Justice is rooted in distinct understandings of places, honours, jobs, things of all sorts that contribute to a shared way of life. To override these understandings is (always) to act unjustly.[39]

Here the moral principle that we should not invade self-understandings and accepted cultural and political values is rooted in a universalistic claim that in fact human beings are culture-producing creatures and thus presumably have a fundamental concern with the status and integrity of what they have produced. This feature of human life provides both a limiting condition of political theory, namely that we should respect the cultural productions of people, and of political practice, namely that an invasive society which overrides the values which groups within a society have produced is a less just polity than one which grants autonomy to cultural groups and what they have produced. Whether this is a foundational claim or not (and given the ethical consequences which follow from it it is difficult to see why it is not), it is certainly a universalistic one.

In a more recent work, *Interpretation and Social Criticism*, Walzer goes further and argues that we can, in fact, think in terms of there being some transcultural, minimal morality. All societies have prohibitions on 'murder, deception, betrayal, gross cruelty'. Again these are, to use his own words, 'a kind of minimal and universal moral code'.[40] In this case, however, he wants to see them not as discovered, or invented by philosophers so much as emerging out of 'many years of trial and error of failed, partial, and insecure understandings' and he goes on to argue 'that these universal prohibitions barely begin to determine the shape of a fully developed or livable morality. They provide the framework for any possible (moral) life, but only a framework . . . One cannot simply deduce a moral culture or for that matter a legal system from the minimal code.'[41] These would on the contrary be filled in by the understandings implicit in different ways of life which cannot be put into any overall framework of adequacy or inadequacy. These 'variations are necessarily plural in character'. Walzer wants to preserve his pluralism within a universalistic framework, a framework which is not based upon some kind of philosophically discovered framework so much as a set of limits which emerge from the general circumstances of human life. For our purposes, however, we can see that even the most fully developed communitarian theory makes some ineliminable reference to universal features of human life and morality and therefore that the contrast between foundational and communitarian approaches is not so clearly demarcated as protagonists would like to think.

This point comes out in two other ways too. The first of these is the idea that the basis of political judgement has to be the social meanings internal to particular practices, communities and cultures. We shall not get illumination through some kind of universalistic approach in which we try to develop some general theory to account for the concept we use. Equally, we cannot give a concept a philosophical justification outside the language game of which it is a part. However, this assumes that we do have a clear idea of what is the appropriate context in terms of which the concept can both be rendered intelligible and some justification for its use found. Wittgenstein seems to regard this as relatively unproblematic, but we can question whether this is in fact so. Use, as much as ostensive definition, can be variously interpreted and this issue can arise in two ways.

First of all, we might have a genuine puzzle about the appropriate home for a term. What is the appropriate linguistic context to illuminate what we mean by it? To put the point in a way which might make its salience to political philosophy more obvious, what community of discourse is the appropriate one for our understanding the term? There is no clear-cut answer to this question in many cases. The boundaries of the context may be very obscure, as Wittgenstein's own reflections on essentialism make clear. In the *Philosophical Investigations* he uses very simplified examples, for example, people building a house in which words like 'slab' and 'building block' are used. In these cases the individuation of the language games is a comparatively easy matter. But for many terms and perhaps for those which most interest the philosopher this may not be the case. There may be acute boundary problems which may not be solved by closer inspection. This point is in fact made in passing by Winch when he argues that while the criteria of logic differ from language game to language game, for instance science and religion, he goes on to say, 'This is, of course, an over simplification, in that it does not allow for the overlapping character of different modes of social life.'[42] This is obviously the case, but then it is not clear how we determine the appropriate context for locating a concept and therefore the conditions which will make the concept intelligible and its use justified by the basic assumptions of that context or language game.

We might therefore have to look for external reasons of a philosophical sort for placing the concept in one place rather than another. Again it may not be possible to avoid a need to consider external reasons of precisely the sort that the Wittgensteinian approach was determined to avoid. A particular example of this might be the use of the idea of obligation by moral and political philosophers. Alasdair MacIntyre has argued very forcibly that the notion of obligation has a sense only within the context of a society in which people have very clear roles and that deontological theories in which the idea of duty and obligation are central make sense only within that kind of context which has now effectively broken down. Whether this argument is plausible is not our main concern here; what matters is how such an argument about the appropriateness of context is to be resolved and it is at least arguable that resolving it will not be achieved by following the Wittgensteinian argument to look rather than to think. Again, what is the context of use, intelligibility and justification cannot be determined without considering external reasons.

This issue comes up in a more specific way in relation to communitarian political thought. The context of justification is the community with its shared social meanings. But following from the arguments above we have to ask the question, what is the community in question?

Here there are at least two problems. One of the deep paradoxes of communitarian approaches to political theory is that we are not really offered a theory of community, as Nancy Rosenblum has argued.[43] Communitarians will have to reply that we do not need a theory of community, just because this will look like a foundational or universalist theory of the sort they want to disavow. However, it is clear that they cannot do without such a theory. The first reason is that in Walzer at least the assumption seems to be that the moral community, with its shared understandings, is coextensive with the legal, juridical, national or political community; that, as Galston argues, 'the community of shared meaning is in fact the nation state'.[44] The communitarian project is to interpret and reclaim the sense of shared meanings in Rosenblum's words 'latent' in the nation-state. However, it is not clear why community should be understood in this way. There may be nation-states with a strong sense of community – Iran and Japan might be examples which spring to mind. Equally, however, the opposite seems to be the case with regard to other states in which there are substantial cleavages: Spain with the Basques, Sri Lanka with the Tamils, Britain with its problems of Northern Ireland and its Muslim community, Nigeria with its deep cleavages between Ibo, Yoruba and Hausa Fulani groups are just a few examples. There may be deep communitarian cleavages within a society which forms a juridical whole. Do these jurisdictions possess a latent community which the communitarian can reclaim as a basis for understanding and justifying political practices? Certainly the problem caused within British society by the publication of Salman Rushdie's *The Satanic*

Verses leads one to think that there are in fact deep cleavages here which may not be resolvable by appealing to shared understandings. The publication of the book offended the religious sensibilities of Muslims; liberals, however, argued that in a secular society religious beliefs should not be made immune from criticism which involves irony and ridicule. This issue also relates to Rawls, who as we have seen has to trade upon the idea of an implicit community of values in a liberal society.

The second point is that other forms of community may well transcend nation-states and again Islam might be a good example here. The sense of identity may well be linked to shared meanings which transcend national frontiers and may not in fact be found within national frontiers, as again the British example of the Salman Rushdie affair in relation to its own Islamic community may show, or the fact that people are killed in the Punjab as the result of a book published outside that society. In this sense the assumption that the appeal to community as the source of values as opposed to any kind of external reasons of a universal and foundational sort may appear to be optimistic. As Rosenblum argues, the communitarian appeal to the latent community which is supposed to be found at a deep level within the procedural republic of Western liberal societies may not respect the deep disagreements which such societies embody: 'What these shared meanings are, how widely they are shared, and what degree of conflict is permissible without the loss of latent community remains an open question.'[45] Without some general theory of community, which would transcend the appeal to particular communities, the communitarians' approach seems to be flawed. They cannot accept that the typical values of a liberal society – mutual toleration, some degree of distributive justice and the free market economy – are sufficient for an account of community just because the values involved here are of a procedural sort. For there to be a community there have to be shared meanings, shared goals and purposes for the society, but there is little account of how these things are latent within liberal societies.

For Dworkin, the idea of justice is our critic, not our mirror as Walzer implies. He writes that: 'We need to argue for any theory of justice of that kind, by finding and defending critical principles of the appropriate sort.'[46] This point is made even more forcefully by Gewirth when he argues in very similar circumstances:

Hence there still remains a need . . . to adjudicate rationally among different competing moralities, for each of which supreme moral authoritativeness is claimed and each of which propounds different answers to the distributive and substantive questions about whose interests and which interests should be considered in the various possible ways of life and society.[47]

In doing this we shall be committed to a liberalism of the deontological sort which recognises moral diversity and tries to formulate a set of general principles of right conduct which will be neutral between different conceptions of the good. However, Rorty comes back on precisely this point in 'Post Modernist Bourgeois Liberalism', in which he argues that it is precisely by reference to historical data and anecdote that we can deal with these cleavages, rather than by an appeal to general principle.

This leads to a further point at issue between the communitarian and Dworkin's approach, namely the role of the political philosopher in a democratic society. Walzer is rather worried about the general claims of political philosophy and the role of the political philosopher in a democratic society. On Walzer's view this approach leading to the formulation of general, critical principles would undermine democracy in the sense that when 'we have discovered them, or once they have been announced to us, we ought to incorporate them into our everyday moral life'.[48]

He rejects this approach, partly for all the reasons given; he does not believe that they can be found in the abstract way Dworkin insists upon. If we can hit upon the right principles they are 'only there because they are really here, features of ordinary life'. We can only come across such principles and regard them as morally binding because they are really linked with the social meanings of the community. However, his objection is not just to the epistemological problems involved in 'discovering' or 'finding' principles which do not already draw upon what is implicit in our way of life, but also to the conflict which would then exist between the role of the philosopher and the democratic attempt to negotiate a society in which there are deep cleavages between social meanings.

Rights, entitlements, distributive justice, needs – their nature and what is required for their satisfaction – have to be negotiated democratically by 'temporary coalition of interests or a majority of voters'. However, Dworkin regards such democratic attempts to resolve such problems in a situation in which there are no shared meanings, unguided by general principles, 'only a selfish struggle'.[49] Thus behind this debate about communitarian and foundational approaches lie different views about the nature of political philosophy's role in a democratic society.

Self and society

I now want to turn to the final aspect of disagreement between communitarians and liberal foundationalists, namely the theory of the self. It will be recalled that the communitarian critic regarded the liberal foundationalist as operating with a notion of an unencumbered self, a self which in Sandel's argument is prior to the ends which it espouses. This is necessary if we are to arrive at a general and foundational set of reasons for action. Of necessity this requires us to reason with an abstract theory of the self and with a very abstract set of goods such as primary goods. The communitarian rejects this assumption for two reasons. The first is that it is sociologically false for the reason that our identities are created out of our participating in shared ways of life and a politics that relies on theories which arise out of abstracts from these identities cannot move us. As Lyotard says in the passage quoted earlier, the social self becomes disseminated in a range of language games. Secondly, it is philosophically false for the reasons given by Wittgenstein about the necessarily social character of the self. The impossibility of a private language means that we cannot identify our experience except through concepts which are part of a common stock of experience. The idea of the unencumbered self is incoherent and cannot serve as the basis of shared political judgements and commitments.

When we look in detail at the communitarian political theorists, however, they are in fact very inexplicit about what in fact is the relationship between the self and its values and ends. While they believe in what Sandel calls the situatedness of the self, situated that is in a nexus of values and the social practices of which they are a part, they do not appear to want to say that the self is wholly constituted by such practices. This is partly for reasons which we have already seen in relation to Winch and Walzer, namely they do regard the self as having certain universal features which must be part of any recognisable form of human life even if what these mean in any society is going to be filled in with reference to the social meanings embodied in that way of life. However, this leaves the nature of these universal features of the self very inexplicit. Either these universal features are going to be so filled in by the plural meanings in particular societies that we can say nothing of substance about the actual contents of these universal features, or alternatively, we can say something meaningful about these universal features in which case the contrast with the unencumbered selves of the liberal foundationalists is overdrawn. This is no doubt why, as Rosenblum argues, communitarians are very ambiguous when it comes to specifying the relationship between self and society, qualifying these formulations in crucial ways. Take the following examples: 'Our experience is what it is, shaped in part by the way we interpret it; and this has a lot to do with the terms which are available in our culture. . .'[50] and Michael Sandel's argument in 'Morality and the Liberal Ideal' that we are partly defined by the communities which we inhabit.

These are crucial although realistic qualifications to any theory which regards the nature of the self as wholly constituted by the community of which the individual is a part. As Rosenblum comments, this is a very modest thesis as it stands and thus not all the qualities of the person are in any sense intrinsically social and inalienable. We then need some account of what is not constituted by society because without it the liberal foundationalist can come back and say that it is precisely these unconstituted parts of the self on which he or she wishes to draw in working out some more universalistic theory of action. Again it would appear that the contrast at stake here is not all that clear-cut. However, it is a crucial contrast for the communitarian to maintain, in the sense that many contrary thinkers have argued that it is precisely our ability to stand back, as it were, from the roles, the values, the practices of which we are a part that constitutes the basis of human freedom. This is certainly so with Kant, who has influenced the liberals so much. It is just because our actions are not determined by our heteronomous or situated nature, that we are ultimately autonomous agents able to act for universal reasons not determined by our situated nature. The same point is also made by Hegel, who is usually seen as being on the communitarian side of this argument, when he sees freedom as part of the 'infinite negativity of spirit, able to abstract from the particular situation of the self'. While no doubt our ability to act and choose always has to be based upon the weighing up of particular claims arising from our situation there is as Kymlicka argues 'nothing empty or self defeating in the idea that these communal values should be subject to individual evaluation and possible rejection'.[51] This evaluation may be with reference to standards which are independent of the particular situation of which we are a part, for example the criterion of universalisability which is crucial to Kant's notion of the categorical imperative. This would also fit with Rawls' idea that we always have the liberty to revise our ends however situated we are just because we are not wholly determined by them, a point which even communitarians adopt given the careful way they qualify the argument that the self is situated. Indeed, it is at least arguable that Lyotard accepts the same view, as in the passage quoted he talks only about the disseminated nature of the social self, while leaving it open as to whether there are other aspects of the self not susceptible to his analysis.

There is also little in Wittgenstein's argument about the social situatedness of the self to support the communitarian position here. The fact that we are not able to identify our experience except in ways that presuppose a common stock of terms to refer to inner experiences does not entail that once these terms have been learned from the common stock, they cannot be used in new and innovative ways, as A. J. Ayer pointed out in his essay 'The Concept of a Person'.[52] This could only be true if we took the rather implausible view that words and concepts are totally tied to the sorts of conditions under which they were learned. The argument does not entail that we cannot stand back from the common stock and evaluate that common stock of descriptions once we have learned that language.

Overall therefore, the contrasts of a methodological sort at stake between communitarians and foundationalists are not clear-cut. This argument still has a long way to go but I would imagine that we may move towards what might be called a left Hegelian position, in which we see a role for theorising about universal features of human life and reasons for action based upon them while allowing as the communitarians have taught us that what fills in these universal features is going to depend a great deal upon context and social meanings. It is a left Hegelian position in that we do not think any longer that we can give a metaphysical basis of the sort that Hegel himself gave to the place of these universal features of human life, nor do we feel that we can put different social meanings of needs, justice and entitlement into some kind of architectonic framework of the sort that Hegel looked to a metaphysical philosophy of history to give. The pluralists are right in agreeing with Hegel that 'the shapes which the concept assumes in the course of its actualisation are indispensable to the knowledge of the concept itself',[53] but they go wrong in thinking that it is not possible to say anything of a transcommunitarian sort about what are the fundamental interests of persons and indeed their own practice belies this. Rawls' own development, which in *A Theory of Justice* was Kantian, has gradually moved in a Hegelian direction in his more recent writings, but he has not lost sight of the need for a general theory in which the disputes about the social meanings within a society and between societies have to be mediated. There is, therefore, scope for both the general and the particular in political theory, as Hegel saw very clearly in his account of concrete universals, and any full theory is going to have to do justice to both.

NOTES

1 Locke (1968), p. 133.
2 Habermas (1979), pp. 202–3.
3 Rawls (1972), p. 587.
4 Dworkin (1985), p. 219.
5 See Taylor (1985a).
6 Walzer (1983) p. xv.

7 Rorty (1983), p. 585.
8 Lyotard (1984).
9 Beiner (1989). I am indebted to this paper for the formulation of some of the issues in what follows.
10 Winch (1972), p. 12.
11 Wittgenstein (1969a), p. 19.
12 Ibid., passim.
13 Wittgenstein (1958), para. 217.
14 Ibid., p. 226e.
15 Wittgenstein (1969b), para. 204.
16 Habermas (1971), p. 313.
17 Jaggar (1983), p. 40.
18 Rorty (1989).
19 I say 'seems' because of the subsequent discussion of Rawls later in the chapter.
20 Walzer (1983), p. 8.
21 Wollheim (1984), p. 202.
22 See Taylor (1979), pp. 166ff.
23 See Rorty (1983).
24 See Taylor (1979), passim.
25 Taylor (1985b), p. 17.
26 Ibid.
27 Beiner (1989).
28 Ibid.
29 Rorty (1983), p. 587.
30 MacIntyre (1984).
31 MacIntyre (1967), p. 268.
32 But again see the account given of Aristotle in chapter 2 of Plant (1991). Hegel does make some central assumptions about human nature, see Plant (1983), passim.
33 G. W. F. Hegel, in H. Glockner (1927–30), p. 259.
34 Rawls (1985).
35 Ibid., p. 519.
36 Ibid., particularly the second section.
37 Ibid., p. 518.
38 Winch (1972), p. 42.
39 Walzer (1983), p. 314.
40 Walzer (1987), p. 24.
41 Ibid., pp. 24–5.
42 Winch (1958), p. 101.
43 Rosenblum (1987), chapter 7.
44 Galston (1989), p. 121. My discussion here is indebted to Galston.
45 Rosenblum (1987), p. 166.
46 Dworkin (1985), p. 219.
47 Gewirth (1978), p. 10.
48 Walzer (1987), p. 6.
49 Dworkin (1985), p. 217.
50 Taylor (1979), p. 87. See Sandel (1984), p. 17, for similar qualifications.

51 Kymlicka (1989), p. 51.
52 Ayer (1963), p. 101.
53 Hegel (1932).

BIBLIOGRAPHY

Ayer, A. J. (1963) *The Concept of a Person and Other Essays*. London: Macmillan.
Beiner, R. (1989) 'Do We Need a Philosophical Ethics? Theory, Prudence and the Primacy of Ethos', *Philosophical Forum*, 20, 3.
Dworkin, R. (1985) *A Matter of Principle*. Cambridge, MA: Harvard University Press.
Galston, W. A. (1989) 'Community, Democracy, Philosophy: The Political Thought of Michael Walzer', *Political Theory*, 17, 1.
Gewirth, A. (1978) *Reason and Morality*. Chicago: Chicago University Press.
Habermas, J. (1971) *Knowledge and Human Interests*. Trans. J. J. Shapiro. London: Heinemann.
    (1979) 'Legitimation Problems in the Modern State', in *Communication and the Evolution of Society*. Trans. T. McCarthy. Boston: Beacon Press.
Hegel, G. W. F. (1927–30) in H. Glockner, *Samtliche Werke*. Vol. X. Stuttgart: Fromman Verlag.
    (1932) *The Philosophy of Right*. Trans. T. M. Knox. Oxford: Clarendon Press.
Jaggar, A. (1983) *Feminist Politics and Human Nature*. Totowa, NJ: Rowman and Allenheld.
Kymlicka, W. (1989) *Liberalism, Community and Culture*. Oxford: Clarendon Press.
Locke, J. (1968) *Epistola de Tolerantia*. Ed. and trans. R. Kilbansky and J. Gough. Oxford: Clarendon Press.
Lyotard, J.-F. (1984) *The Postmodern Condition*. Trans. G. Bennington and B. Massumi. Manchester: Manchester University Press.
MacIntyre, A. (1967) *A Short History of Ethics*. London: Routledge.
    (1984) 'Bernstein's Distorting Mirrors', *Soundings*, 67, 1.
Plant, R. (1983) *Hegel*. 2nd edn. Oxford: Blackwell.
    (1991) *Modern Political Thought*. Oxford: Blackwell.
Rawls, J. (1972) *A Theory of Justice*. Oxford: Clarendon Press.
    (1985) 'Justice as Fairness: Political not Metaphysical', *Philosophy and Public Affairs*, 14: 223–51.
Rorty, R. (1983) 'Post Modernist Bourgeois Liberalism', *Journal of Philosophy*, 80: 583–89.
    (1989) *Contingency, Irony and Solidarity*. Cambridge: Cambridge University Press.
Rosenblum, N. (1987) *Another Liberalism*. Cambridge, MA: Harvard University Press.
Sandel, M. (1984) 'Morality and the Liberal Ideal', *The New Republic*, 7 May 1984.
Taylor, C. (1979) *Hegel and Modern Society*. Cambridge: Cambridge University Press.
    (1985a) 'Atomism', in *Philosophy and the Human Sciences: Philosophical Papers*. Vol. II. Cambridge: Cambridge University Press.

(1985b) 'Interpretation and the Sciences of Man', in *Philosophy and the Human Sciences*.

Walzer, M. (1983) *Spheres of Justice*. Oxford: Martin Robertson.

(1987) *Interpretation and Social Criticism*. Cambridge, MA: Harvard University Press.

Winch, P. (1958) *The Idea of a Social Science*. London: Routledge.

(1972) 'Understanding a Primitive Society', in *Ethics and Action*. London: Routledge.

Wittgenstein, L. (1958) *Philosophical Investigations*. Oxford: Blackwell.

(1969a) *The Blue and Brown Books*. Oxford: Blackwell.

(1969b) *On Certainty*. Oxford: Blackwell.

Wollheim, R. (1984) *The Thread of Life*. Cambridge: Cambridge University Press.

7   Master narratives and feminist subversions

Diana Coole

Over recent years, a number of articles entitled 'Feminism and Post-modernism' have appeared.[1] This is indeed a title I might have myself used, were it not for two misgivings. These are first, that such a formula is reminiscent of those which abounded in the days when feminism still saw its theoretical quest in terms of some yet unachieved grand synthesis, as in the influential 'Unhappy Marriage of Marxism and Feminism.'[2] This quest, as feminists and postmodernists would now agree, is no longer on the agenda.

My second misgiving with such a formulation is that feminism and postmodernism are not commensurable as, for example, feminism and Marxism, or feminism and liberalism, were. In those cases, two explicitly political and modern ideologies, sharing interests in emancipation, liberation and justice, were being brought together. They could agree that one purpose of theory was to incite and guide political practice via the rational disclosure of certain truths about inequality or oppression, which might then be challenged. Neither a political ideology, nor claiming any critical insight into structures of stratification, postmodernism actually rules these out as politically suspect and theoretically illegitimate. It evokes only a mood, style or condition of contemporary culture, which it finds immune to representation. Thus feminism and postmodernism are quite different types of discourse, or language game, and the usual concern behind the titles conjoining them has actually been whether a feminism so thoroughly identified with modernity can survive its assault by postmodernists.

This implies a beleaguered feminism whose exponents would be well advised simply to dismiss postmodernism as anti-feminist and to insist upon its modernist credentials – a position which has indeed been widely endorsed.[3] Yet this antagonistic formulation will not do either, because postmodernism is not something that has assaulted a previously untroubled feminism from without. The latter has already, in my opinion, been driven down the postmodern road due to its own internal logic. The idea of a universal feminist theory and political practice had already had to be abandoned due to recognitions of *differences* between women which defined conflation. Charges of racism, ethnocentrism, ageism, heterosexism and so on already suggested that any totalising theory of women's oppression was imperialist, an illegitimate exercise of power by those whose perspective tacitly marginalised some women as deviant or backward, while privileging their own ideas as true. At the same time, feminists were questioning the Enlightenment discourses in which their own emancipatory project was grounded. Their suspicion that these spoke with a masculine voice, and that *any* theory which claimed mastery or truth necessarily did the same, committed them to questioning the philosophical foundations of modernity in a very post-modern way. To put it differently: this scepticism towards universal theories and projects is central to what we *mean* by postmodernism, such that feminism had already become, in significant ways, post-modern. I do not then believe it is possible to return to an earlier confidence, nor do I think that in responding to postmodernism, feminism reacts to something alien or external. Where relations of either synthesis or opposition become untenable, feminists must invent a new strategy for themselves.

What I want specifically to address in my chapter, is that point at which considerations of feminism and postmodernism locate their greatest tension, and it is this which my title, 'Master narratives and feminist subversions', is intended to convey. What has attracted feminists to postmodernism is that it questions the foundations of Enlightenment reason which they denounce as gender-biased, while suggesting strategies for their subversion. What has alarmed them is that the relativism implied by postmodernism seems to rule out any privileged critique or vision offered by women and therefore to reduce their expressions to one choice among many. In other words, grand narratives *including* feminism are discredited, and the crucial question as I see it, is whether postmodern strategies can nevertheless yield a radical politics of gender. I will say at the outset, that I believe they can.

The Postmodern Condition

Because of the complexities of the postmodern debate, and because he has been most explicitly associated with the delegitimation of grand narratives, I intend to hang parts of my discussion on Lyotard's *The Postmodern Condition*. By using Lyotard, rather than, for example, the more pessimistic Baudrillard, I am intentionally biasing my account towards a more optimistic and revolutionary reading of postmodernism, aware that, as Habermas says of such versions, it 'could be that they are merely cloaking their complicity with the venerable tradition of counter-Enlightenment in the garb of post-Enlightenment'.[4]

Lyotard's explicit concern is with knowledge, whose foundations are alleged to have lost their legitimacy in a postmodern age. On the one hand, he agrees with Rorty that epistemological realism, where science would be seen as a faithful mirror, or representation, of nature, is no longer tenable (a judgement with which many feminists would today wish to concur). On the other hand, the myths on which science relied in order to justify its quest are also claimed to have lost legitimacy, and it is to these that Lyotard is referring when he defines postmodernism as 'incredulity towards metanarratives'.[5] By grand, or meta-, narratives, he means the sort of stories which emerged during the Enlightenment, and which have made sense of modern Western people's epistemological and political adventures in terms of a vision of history as progressing relentlessly towards a rational outcome. Within this context they have defined the rules of the game by which truth or justice are evaluated. Grand narratives also therefore serve as political myths, and it is in this sense that they have been most important to feminism.

Although they are not the only ones, Lyotard identifies two dominant grand narratives of modernity. These are not, as critics sometimes claim, Marxist versus liberal, but an idealist 'speculative narrative' versus the humanist 'narrative of emancipation': Hegel versus Kant.[6] Marxism might fall into either camp, for example in its Stalinist versus its Frankfurt School guises. Like other French thinkers, Lyotard's hostility is most obviously directed at the speculative and dialectical narrative, since it is here that a project of totalisation, which would realise all meaning within a closed system, is most evident.

Now, this idealist version has always been attacked by feminists, because the system it presents is explicitly hierarchical and exclusionary in terms of gender. Woman, Hegel makes clear, has a natural and ontological affinity with irrationality, emotion, particularity, passivity, immaturity, non-reflectiveness and caprice. Her entry into reason remains precarious and mediated by men and she thereby threatens the very progress which history enacts.[7] It is then rather with the metanarrative of emancipation that feminism has had intimate, if increasingly ambivalent, ties. Here it is the people who legitimate laws and norms; the pursuit and dissemination of rational, and especially scientific, knowledge, is legitimised as functional for their emancipation. It is in its name that feminists have until recently issued their demands for equality and justice.

However, it becomes evident as Lyotard's account unfolds, that this apparently emancipatory project increasingly comes to share the penchant for totalising, closure and homogeneity that is to be found in its speculative counterpart. For the instrumental role it grants to knowledge not only leads to the suppression of inefficacious non-scientific knowledges (such as story-telling, which is now deemed 'fit only for women and children').[8] It also results in a triumph of performativity: a merely technical language game whose concern is no longer with truth or justice, but with efficiency and power. The liberal democratic cultures which were inspired by the emancipatory myth are thus left, Lyotard contends, with 'the ideology of "the system" with its pretensions to totality'.[9] He calls this silencing of other knowledges 'terror', and although this is undertheorised here, it is underwritten by a history which in many ways resembles Horkheimer and Adorno's *Dialectic of Enlightenment*. Here the quest for freedom through instrumental reason and the domination of nature, concludes with a system that can only keep reproducing its own sterile formulae. Locked into a closed totality of homogeneous meanings which has repressed all otherness, uncritical reason can make no appeal to any unrecouped dimension which might inspire creative development or enrichment, nor to any narrative that might legitimise it.[10] From this critical theory perspective, modernity reaches a dead end, but Lyotard's view is that this apparently closed totality can yet be opened up by postmodern strategies. However, before moving on to this, I want first to see where feminism stands on this alleged degeneration of the emancipatory project.

The specific claim that feminism advances here, is that the grand narratives of Enlightenment are better described as master narratives, where the term mastery has two related meanings. First, master narratives are those in which the subject adopts a position of mastery in relation to its objects. This might be the sort of conceptual mastery claimed by reason over material, natural or historical phenomena, or the sort of technological mastery of nature which such knowledge facilitates. In either case, the position adopted by subjects is one of domination and distance, rather than for example one of reciprocity, wonder, interrogation or playful engagement. Owens usefully reminds us here of Heidegger's definition of modernity as the age of representation for the purpose of mastery[11]: a definition which corresponds with Marx's notion of commodification, Weber's purposive rationality, critical theorists' instrumental reason and Lyotard's performativity. It is also echoed in Derrida's claim that the whole Western metaphysics of presence is predicated on a will to representational mastery.

But secondly, mastery suggests a specifically gendered position, in which the subject adopts a masculine stance and where that which is to be mastered is in some sense feminine. Insofar as mastery of the former type is associated with domination over the non-rational, and the non-rational has consistently been associated with the feminine, the two senses of mastery are closely related. The argument advanced by feminists is therefore that the false universalisations and imperialistic totalisations; the representational closures and will to dominate; the disengaged subject position – all these orientations which critics of modernity attack, are marked by masculinity and are thus quite gender-specific.

Women and modernity

The assertion of some intrinsic relationship between modernity and masculinity has indeed become so familiar that its rationale is rarely rehearsed today. I do not have time to discuss or criticise it in any detail either, but I do think it is important to be aware that such claims are advanced from a variety of different positions, not all of them unproblematic.

The crux of the relation for recent feminists has lain in an association between masculinity and rationality. The irony, and danger, of this equation is that it appears to assert the very association which patriarchy always insisted on anyway, when it claimed that men are *naturally* more adept at abstract thinking while women are *naturally* more practical and emotional. In order to distinguish their *critical* position and to give it political potential, feminists must therefore avoid such naturalistic or essentialist claims. The best way of doing this, I believe, lies in insisting that reason has become gendered, rather than being a property of men, and that gender has a contingent and historically defined content which evolves within relations of power.

Three different lines of argument equating rationality with masculinity, might be identified in recent feminist work. First there is the influential object-relations approach, which hovers on the border between sociology and psychoanalysis. Here it is suggested that because it is always women who have mothered, gendered personalities result from the asymmetry of family relations. Boys and girls evince masculine or feminine ways of knowing and behaving, because of their respective difference from, or identity with, their primary carer. The ways we call masculine are the ones males typically adopt and these have acquired privileged status in the form of objectivity and impartiality.[12]

Secondly, there are those theories which find sexual difference at the heart of subjectivity and define all culture as phallocentric. Psychoanalytic followers of Lacan argue that the symbolic is under the law of the father and that to become a subject is to accept his prohibitions, which are structured into language. Its orderly syntax and illusion of communicative mastery leave us with experiences devoid of pleasure, yet vulnerable to irruptions of a pre-Oedipal ecstasy whose repressed voice the phallocentric symbolic calls feminine. Nevertheless, the woman who would be a subject and communicate rationally, rather than babbling psychotically, must adopt a masculine identification and speak that language which is guaranteed by the phallus.

Finally, there are more cultural approaches. These may overlap with the preceding category, insofar as they tend to agree that culture relies on series of binary and hierarchical oppositions, where the feminine is consistently associated with the inferior and that which is to be excluded, while masculinity is identified with reason and culture. However, some exponents of this view are critical of the Lacanians for allegedly instituting a new, and seemingly insurmountable, dualism of sexual difference. Gender is more likely in this third account to be a historical construct although femininity still emerges as culture's other, where masculinity is associated with both desirable character traits and mastery of its unruly opposite.[13]

While this last argument seems to be the least vulnerable to accusations of essentialism, one difficulty with them all is that they tend to speak of Western culture generally and can only suggest that things have become worse in modernity. The blame for this degeneration then usually falls on the Cartesian–Kantian subject, who became foundational for the Enlightenment and whose rationality emanates from a disembodied and unified ego severed from the materiality and contingency of its milieu. This subject then lies at the heart of feminist and postmodern attacks on modernity since it allegedly encapsulates the orientation to masculinity and mastery which they reject.[14]

Still, this is all rather abstract and it seems to me that one might wish to link its equations more closely to actual women's fate within modernity as well as to the more specifically instrumental reason whose quest it was to dominate nature. Then one might also invoke the Hobbesian subject, who appeared in the seventeenth century and whose rationality was explicitly defined as an aggressive mode of calculation designed to satisfy an appetite for power and commodious living. Although Hobbes described this human nature as universal and ungendered, subsequent political theorists made it clear that such motivation and behaviour were appropriate only in men and in the public realm. By looking to the Hobbesian–Cartesian–Kantian subject as foundational, we can therefore find one that is behaviourally as well as epistemologically masculine, and I think this permits a fuller and less idealist indictment of modernity than feminists have recently favoured. It will also allow us to be more specific about the requirements and possibilities of modernity's postmodern subversion.

In this context, I would emphasise how much feminism was a constituent part of modernity, which provided both the conditions and the theoretical foundations that were needed for its emergence. In other words, I do not think that feminism as we understand it, could have arisen in any other context and perhaps it cannot survive outside it. On the other hand, I also want to suggest that modernity is intrinsically immune to the goals that feminism pursued and that this realisation, which has been gathering strength over the last two decades, has now thrown feminism itself into a state of crisis.

Modernity suggests a complex yet coherent configuration, in which philosophical Enlightenment corresponded with modernisation processes, where the former's faith in reason accompanied the latter's progress in rationalisation. For women, modernisation meant a much clearer differentiation of sex roles and this worked to their disadvantage, where wealth and power were now associated with the public realm from which they were excluded. At the same time, men were gaining the civil and political rights that went along with their more public presence, and so women's lot degenerated relative to that of men, permitting them to recognise themselves as a distinct but oppressed class. Enlightenment thought then provided an apparently gender-neutral vocabulary with which to articulate this recognition, as well as an emancipatory vision of a just and equal society where rights and freedoms would accrue to all individuals regardless of their sex. In this sense, first-wave feminists did not develop any metanarrative of their own, but rather relied upon liberal and Marxist versions of progress.

In fact, as feminism emerged, it took over all the foundational ideas of modernity. Most significantly, it enthusiastically seized upon its universalist ethical and political demands, asking only that these be applied consistently. These demands were underpinned by the Enlightenment's building blocks of naturally free individuals, whose emancipation consisted of removing obstacles to self-determination and the full development of the rational faculties. The primary demand was thus one of equality, where feminism was an oppositional movement defined in terms of its attack on certain exclusions. However, as these exclusions from citizenship were rectified, it became obvious that more profound levels of inequality were at work and so feminists found themselves driven into increasingly more complex analyses of what oppressed women. The form these analyses took was again typically modern insofar as they used a hermeneutical, or depth, approach. That is, one of feminism's tasks became an unmasking and demystifying process. Prejudices and irrational ideas about sexual hierarchy were subjected to rational critique at the same time that systematic operations of patriarchy were disclosed operating beneath the debris of individual misery. Feminism did not then present itself as simply composing a story, or moral vision, about women which might inspire them to unite, but claimed to be telling the truth about a universal form of power and stratification in which all women were victims of a ubiquitous patriarchy. It was only at this stage, reached by radical feminists like Shulamith Firestone in the early 1970s, I would suggest, that feminism became a grand narrative in its own right, although in fact its model here was that of Marxism, which inspired it to seek the origins, as well as a mono-causal account, of oppression.[15]

This particular totalising approach was soon discredited because, as I said earlier, it could not accommodate the variety of oppressions and differences among women. To some extent it was also a victim of its own success, because like critics of capitalist modernity, feminists managed to describe a system of (patriarchal) power that was so total, it became extremely difficult to see how change might occur. But in any case, my contention is that feminism was already destined to turn against modernity once the implications of gender difference, inadequately dealt with by the earlier equality-based theories, became clear. It is therefore necessary to look more critically at the modernist foundations that an earlier feminism had appropriated.

One sense in which feminism was typically modern was in pitting itself against tradition. Women's exclusion from citizenship was generally attributed to the endurance of traditional theories and values concerning natural hierarchy, and it was this legacy that early feminists hoped to dispel by appealing to enlightened reason. Indeed, I think that in this sense modernity *does* remain an unfinished project for women. However, what this anti-tradition stance failed to recognise, was that modernity was itself *creating* and *reproducing* sex roles and gender identities that were inimical to sexual equality. Worse, by a Foucauldian-type of reversal, women's pursuit of emancipation was actually strengthening the grip of patriarchy over them.

How had this come about? I think it would be mistaken to seek one cause or agency here. Rather, a variety of new discourses and technologies happened to combine in the complex yet rigid patriarchal system we know as modernity. Modernisation meant the proliferation of a novel series of oppositions. Its spatial division between home and work corresponded with distinctions between reproduction and production, private and public. Modernity created a domestic environment at the same time as it engendered a public realm and thanks to its sexually based division of labour, it was men who entered the latter. The point is, that these distinct realms did not pre-exist modernity and then find women and men differentially ascribed to them; rather they were an integral and crucial development of modernity itself, such that their norms were evolved contemporaneously with the new sex roles and gender identities. It was the public realm, of state and civil society, that was associated with modernisation and rationalisation, while the private sphere was excluded as its other, where traditional and naturalistic norms still operated to compensate for the austerity and harshness of public life. From this point of view, the private sphere was *necessarily* excluded from the values of modernity, but within the bifurcations that modernity had engendered, women became an integral part of this pre-modern space. For gender identities were being *reconstructed* in accordance with the new public/private split.

The men who operated publicly had also to be constructed into appropriate kinds of subject with strong ego boundaries, self-control and unified identities. Assertive individualism and instrumental rationality in the economy were to combine with a capacity for abstract thought and impartiality in science and politics. These Hobbesian–Cartesian–Kantian qualities were precisely those which were now presented as natural, normal, rational and human, i.e. as the very precondition and definition of emancipation. But of course, they were only normal for men, and even they had to be disciplined accordingly. As Hegel says, manhood is 'attained only by the stress of thought and much technical exertion'.[16] To be altruistic, poetic, passionate, or motivated by partiality towards one's family, was rightly seen as antithetical to the logic of this new public space. But of course these were the very qualities that were now being redefined as feminine and as appropriate to the private world. Not only were women being ideologically exhorted to evince such femininity, they were also being disciplined to construct themselves according to its norms, thanks to new kinds of discourse and techniques of power that were becoming available. Female bodies and feminine desires were not, according to this Foucauldian interpretation, imposed upon reluctant ungendered subjects, but constructed those subjects as already gendered and in accordance with exclusions that were right at the heart of modernity. From this perspective then, the denial of citizenship to women was not just a question of inconsistency or injustice, and men's insistence on their incapacity to participate in public life was not just a rationalisation of privilege. Women really had been constructed in such a way that their domestic roles and feminine identities became antithetical to modernity, enlightenment, reason and politics. In most cases they did become that which had to be excluded if these were to exist, such that the so-called human project of emancipation and the so-called human capacity for reason had already been defined as synonymous with masculinity, while masculinity was construed as precisely that project which would render subjects fit for freedom by excising all traces of femininity. The problem was not then one of justice, but of modernity's foundations, and the more women demanded justice, the more they entrenched those foundations.

Because early feminists accepted modernity's linkage of femininity and irrationality, they had to rely on contesting instead the link between sex and gender. Thus both Wollstonecraft and Mill agreed that femininity was a progress-threatening narrow-mindedness, but insisted that it was imposed by a combination of patriarchal culture, inadequate education and the poverty of domestic experience. In other words, femininity was an artificial and inauthentic identity from which the emancipated woman must escape into her humanity. Wollstonecraft is quite explicit that women's emancipation means their accession to masculinity when she writes: 'I would presume that *rational* men will excuse me for endeavouring to persuade them [women] to become more masculine and respectable.'[17] The problem with this move is, however, that sex and gender were *not* contingently linked within modernity; in fact it is in the very rigidity of their coupling, where sex roles and gender identities are indissolubly intertwined, that I would locate the particular oppressiveness of modernity for women. What was aspired to was therefore inclusion in a public world, where male roles and masculine identities were inscribed as part of an indissoluble package. Insofar as women *succeeded* in entering this realm then, they were perceived as abnormal, and indeed they were deviant, divided selves, in the terms that modernity had set for them. For they were obliged to collude in modernity's exclusion of all that it defined as feminine, while finding that patriarchy would recognise no other identity for them.

Only one alternative strategy presented itself. This was the far more radical contestation of the linkage between masculinity and modernity which was exemplified by utopian socialism and radical feminism. Here we do find some sort of feminine grand narrative. Yet from the way I have defined modernity, this cannot be a narrative of *modernity*, since there is no image of a non-patriarchal, non-masculine modernity available. Modernity, on this reading, *means* differentiated roles and identities, where there is no space for contingency or radical change to slip into the tight alignment between public life, masculinity, rationality and emancipation. The equality discourses feminists used only reinforced this union, yet the more radical feminists insisted on women's difference, the more they reinforced their exclusion. In other words, modernity left no way for women to find emancipation there, and if they would look outside to a counter-, or postmodernity, then it is contradictory for them to use the modernist language of sexual identity and emancipation or the modernist strategy of totalising theory or metanarrative. For feminism itself emerged, or was even engendered, only as the other of modern patriarchy, and it can only step outside its orbit by defining itself quite differently. It is then this logic which drives feminism towards postmodernity in spite of itself.

Despite their focus on gender, it would then seem that feminists are confronted by similar political questions to modernity's male critics. Namely, are its closures and exclusions so total that opposition is impossible, or at least immediately assimilated and made harmless? If it is possible, must we look inside the system for some subversive force there, or should we search outside for some as yet uncolonised agent of change? And finally, if this endlessly assimilating totality is associated with (instrumental or masculine) reason, would it be necessary to look to reason's other – i.e. to that realm which Western culture encodes as feminine, but which critics of modernity have also called Being, nature, the unconscious, the sublime, the aesthetic, the Dionysian, the primordial?[18]

Despite the attractions of this last position for some feminists, two problems might immediately be identified. First, as Habermas and others have pointed out, it makes paradoxical the critical position of its exponents, who generally rely on the very reason they condemn. For feminists, it would deny the critical engagement with patriarchal discourses that has been so fruitful for them. And secondly, it continues, and merely revalorises, the equation betwen femininity and nonreason that patriarchy has always insisted on. It still uses the binary oppositions of masculine/feminine and reason/nonreason which have structured Western thought to women's disadvantage and uses an oppositional model structured in terms of either/or. In particular, there is the danger of essentialising femininity as some inherently subversive force waiting in the wings of history, and thus formulating a new grand narrative. It is with such problems in mind then, that I will recommend postmodern strategies in my concluding section.

Feminism and postmodernism

One reason for the decline of grand narratives and totalising theories is that as we enter a postmodern age, they lose their historical referent. For insofar as postmodernism is used as a periodising concept, it suggests an age whose fragmentation, technology and global scale defy cognitive mapping. That is, we are unable to represent the new social formation in any coherent way. There is no longer a sense of a social system or history that would be more than the sum of their parts, and our roles and identities assume a correspondingly fractured and mobile form.

There is general agreement among postmodernists that such changes relate to a new dominance of culture, where we become anaesthetised against meaning due to an excess of media images, simulations, information, communications, signs and free-floating signifiers. This cultural bric-à-brac makes no pretence at mirroring any reality; it appeals to no consensus or grand narrative, merely circulating as fiction, spectacle, and fascination. It is this fluid culture which itself constructs a profusion of meanings, surrendering the pretence that these are grounded in any objective referent.

It is not then surprising that the primary site of political struggle should have shifted to the cultural sphere, where discourses, identities and subjectivities are engendered. Power is now discerned in processes of privileging, excluding, marginalising, constructing and distorting on the level of meaning. For feminists, this has moved political interest away from more traditional conceptions of power as being exercised by certain recognisable agents over others, where the focus was on a sex war, and towards questions of representation and gender. Academically we can see this in a shift of interest away from the social sciences and towards literary criticism and cultural studies. Politically it has meant emphasis on a politics of the subject, rather than on the more material and structural questions of equal jobs, pay and citizenship.

It is then this sense of modernity's fissuring which facilitates, and corresponds with, a postmodern politics as subversion from within. In particular, the rigid binary system on which modernity is founded begins to look vulnerable. For example, although feminists have not so far paid much attention to the sociology of postmodernity, developments like the feminisation of the workforce, or new technologies which make redundant modernity's home/work split, would appear to threaten the very linkages and oppositions at the heart of modernity, which I blamed for women's oppression there – namely, the rigid association of sex roles and gender identities; the disparaging and exclusionary definition of femininity; and the uncompromising alignment of biological sex with gender. These are further threatened by an excess of media images which multiply, transgress and implode such distinctions. My point is not of course that patriarchy is self-destructing, but that its foundations are shifting in a way that opens it to a different kind of feminist politics. Such a politics is, however, inseparable, I would suggest, from more general postmodern strategies that would subvert the foundations of modernity, and even of Western culture itself.

What, then, are these postmodern strategies? I will suggest three levels on which they simultaneously operate, and I will call these theorising the game, playing the game and exploding the game.

By *theorising the game*, I mean a postmodern way of describing power and conflict which makes a postmodern mode of politics conceivable. Modern theories are typically dualistic and oppositional here: two parties, two classes, two sexes. Where the power of one side appears total, the effect is politically paralysing. But this is doubly so because the opposition is structured by its antagonist and thus unwittingly colludes with it. Thus as I argued earlier, feminism was the mirror image of patriarchy, defined only negatively by its exclusions. Such binary theories, built on notions of inside/outside, inclusion /exclusion, centre/ margin, thus keep opposition within a circle of closure.

Postmodernism avoids these aporias by thinking strategically and by substituting shifting, plural differences for fixed, binary difference. Language as a free play of signifiers, rather than the dialectic, is its model. Such thinking is well exemplified by Lyotard, who describes the social bond in terms of language games. In the postmodern condition where information circulates, he argues that each self exists in a complex and mobile fabric of relations.[19] Individuals find themselves caught in a variety of language games, where each move shifts meanings and incites counter-moves, such that no one is wholly powerless, and where an unexpected or imaginative move might cause disorientation or even change the rules.

In this context, Lyotard identifies two different modes. One is terror, which is actually beyond the game because its efficacy lies in threats to eliminate opposing players and games.[20] Instrumental reason operates thus. The other mode is agonistics, a sort of jousting which involves both power and the 'sheer pleasure' of invention. This is the usual form social exchanges take, where playing defies closure and where a politics of the symbolic takes place, since 'to speak is to fight, in the sense of playing'.[21] Agonistic language games thus move beyond stratified binary power, towards a more mobile form where everyone intervenes and has effects. In this sense they resemble Foucault's description of a circulatory and capillary power, 'a network of relations always in tension', where we are all both vehicles and victims. Foucault also speaks of agonism, as 'a relationship which is at the same time reciprocal incitation and struggle; less of a face-to-face confrontation which paralyzes both sides than a permanent provocation'.[22]

This postmodern way of thinking thus avoids the impasse of modernist critique, by opening up spaces within the system for its internal transformation and for everyday strategies of subversion, imagination and resistance. It is especially conducive to feminism, because it can accommodate a politics of the personal. It empowers individual women to the extent that even the most trivial domestic negotiations are situated within the interminable process of redefining and shifting representations of gender. Indeed, it is perhaps on this level that contemporary feminism has enjoyed its greatest success, even if the results are not spectacular in a grand narrative sense.

If we do think of women's struggles in this way, then it might make sense to think of patriarchy exercising a reign of terror until, say, the First World War, in that it excluded women from citizenship and high culture, thus effectively silencing them. Demands for equality would be demands for the right to become players, to participate in certain language games, and postmodern feminism might then be construed as women's gaming. Here the stakes are both shifting definitions and images of gender, and changing the rules of games themselves, by challenging what counts as a legitimate and meaningful expression. For example body languages, languages of pleasure, narratives – games which are suppressed as feminine or invalid – might now take place alongside the rational and scientific discourses of modernity. Similarly in the arts, the appearance of women as major players opens the door to previously devalued forms and genres. It is not sufficient, however, merely to add on games defined as feminine, since this leaves untouched the dominant game which is one of gender. This then is where the stakes are highest, when we play at the level of meaning's gendered and binary foundations.

It is then this ongoing strategy of negotiation and subversion that postmodern accounts of society and power recommend, and this brings me to the level of *playing the game*, where we find the most recognisably feminist postmodernism in the form of a politics of representation. One aim here is to resist the narrow way in which women's roles and identities are defined by modernity. Feminist work in the cinema and literary and visual arts has been especially fecund in this regard, confusing and transgressing the usual gender distinctions.[23] In this sense, postmodern feminism might be associated with a new avant-garde, although a certain caution is needed here. For as Huyssen reminds us, in 'relation to gender and sexuality . . . the historical avant-garde was by and large as patriarchal, misogynist, and masculinist as the major trends of modernism'. For intent on distancing itself from the banalities of everyday, and especially domestic, life, its practitioners still adopted a stance of distance and mastery, even as they claimed to speak with a feminine voice.[24] It is, then, the mastery assumed by the masculine subject or the male gaze, which is most crucially to be subverted. A politics on this level must displace the subject-mode that is assumed in the production of totalising theories or realist images; that is, its target is not just the *content* of representation, but the gendered nature of the process itself.

Feminists' aim here, like that of poststructuralists generally, is therefore to clarify and displace these processes of representation by showing the power which operates within them. To achieve this, they use a variety of cultural strategies. Humour, pastiche, parody, (mis)quotation, decontextualisation, bizarre juxtapositions, excess, syntactical chaos and invention, decentre and recode dominant representations to render them relative, provisional, laughable, unnatural, unworkable. This is then no opposing feminist counter-culture which would rival masculine forms, but a subversion of the latter from within which forces them into an open and contestable position.

Deconstruction operates similarly in philosophy, where it discloses the contingent and unstable nature of meaning. It thereby undercuts the mastery assumed by those who would dominate it by rendering it total and transparent. It shows that closure is always premature and suppressive of the mobility and fluidity on which meaning floats. It demonstrates the irreducibility and non-assimilability of difference and plays up the otherness and heterogeneity which defy absorption into the rational. It would not then glorify or entrench the irrational, but invokes it in order to decentre reason and its project of mastery.

This brings me to *exploding the game*, and I think this allows us to see why postmodern subversions which focus on gender are the most significant and the most beneficial to women, even if they are not legitimised by a feminist grand narrative. Modernity's critics, from romantics through critical theorists to poststructuralists, agree that the main problem is its rationalistic closure. By attempting to capture the real in a totalising discourse of reason and linguistic transparency, its subjects claim cognitive mastery. But this mastery has been recognised – and indeed recognises itself – as a gendered project. The sort of subjectivity and character traits required for such rationality are defined as masculine and valued as a male norm. Psychoanalysis is even more insistent here: a masculine identification with the father is the precondition of entering subjecthood or language at all.

If this closure is to be effaced then, it seems that the gendered foundations of modernity, and perhaps of Western culture itself, must be tackled, and this is why the feminist concern with gender is the most radical assault on modernity's foundations. For as psychoanalysis and critical theory make clear, all subjects suffer from repressions and sacrifices which suppress the feminine side of individuals and the nonrational but inexhaustible sources of meaning that are encoded as feminine. A 'feminine subject-position' (if this is not a contradiction in terms) suggests a more open, playful, engaged and decentred orientation, which is both more creative and more pleasurable, because it evokes the heterogeneous and the nonrational in knowing and laying down meaning.

Postmodernism would thus elude modernity's closure by evoking the unrepresentable. Lyotard calls this the sublime, and Kristeva, the semiotic, but it is precisely the unrepresentable which Western culture has consistently encoded as feminine and feared as the ruin of its will conceptually to dominate nature and banish contingency. Indeed, it is just this ruination which its postmodern invocation is designed to achieve.

In this context, Lyotard distinguishes between modern and post-modern art. While the former recognises the unrepresentable but remains nostalgic for the lost omniscient subject, the latter rejoices in such loss, emphasising instead 'the increase of being and the jubilation which result from the invention of new rules of the game'. He concludes: 'Let us wage a war on totality; let us be witness to the unpresentable; let us activate the differences and save the honour of the name.'[25]

Similarly, Julia Kristeva writes: 'Let us say that postmodernism is that literature which writes itself with the more or less conscious intention of expanding the signifiable and thus human realm.' Such writing aims 'to blaze a trail amidst the unnameable'.[26] Kristeva is, however, more explicit in her recognition that the unnameable is marginalised and repressed in phallocentric culture, as feminine. In her psychoanalytic terms, this is the semiotic realm, an order preceding the Oedipal phase when subjectivity will be assumed alongside a gendered identity and entry into the symbolic. It is therefore feminine insofar as it is non-phallic and prior to the imposition of the father's law, the incest taboo which tears apart the mother–child dyad. Kristeva does not essentialise this distinction: men and women might both speak with a feminine voice by evoking the disruptive semiotic, whose rhythms destabilise the apparently transparent symbolic by inscribing an economy of pleasure and logic of nonreason there. But they thereby become gender-complex, or 'subjects-in-process' as she puts it, transgressing the boundaries between conscious and unconscious, symbolic and semiotic, rational and irrational, masculine and feminine. In so doing, they also subvert the binary oppositions which order the symbolic, and so they undercut the dualistic oppositions of gender on which culture insists.

To the extent that postmodern and avant-garde transgressions succeed, then, they undermine the repressive subject-positions demanded by Western culture; they unhook gender identifications from sexual referents, and they resist the either/or of gender identity which forbids our being masculine and feminine, rational and nonrational in a complex, unique and unstable way. The result would therefore benefit all subjects, but I believe that women would be disproportionately privileged, since it is they who have been most repressed, divided and marginalised by patriarchal alignments. It is in this sense, then, that so-called feminine expressions force open the closures of Western culture and the rigidities of modernity, even while their goal is to deconstruct the gendered codings and exclusions which label such expressions as feminine.

In subverting narratives of mastery, feminists might render obsolete their own grand narrative. But it is nevertheless their postmodern strategy of deconstructing gendered oppositions, that lies at the heart of radical assaults on modernity.

NOTES

1 For example S. Suleiman, 'Feminism and Postmodernism. A question of Politics', in I. Hoesterey (ed.), *Zeitgeist in Bebel. The Post-Modernist Controversy* (Bloomington & Indianapolis: Indiana University Press, 1991); S. Lovibond, 'Feminism and Postmodernism', in R. Boyne and A. Rattansi (eds.), *Postmodernism and Society* (London: Macmillan, 1990). Or subtitled, e.g. B. Creed, 'From Here to Modernity: Feminism and Postmodernism', *Screen* 28, 2 (1987). I think that *Feminism/Postmodernism*, ed. L. Nicholson (New York and London: Routledge 1990) is more appropriate, although I would prefer to see both words pluralised.

2 H. Hartmann, 'The Unhappy Marriage of Marxism and Feminism: Towards a more progressive Union', *Capital and Class*, 8 (1979).

3 For example by Lovibond, 'Feminism and Postmodernism'; by most of the authors (although more ambivalently) in the *Feminism/Postmodernism* volume; by M. Zalewski, 'The Debauching of Feminist Theory/The Penetration of the Postmodern', *Politics*, 11, 1 (April 1991); by M. Barrett, 'The Concept of "Difference"', *Feminist Review*, 1987. For an enthusiastic endorsement of postmodernism for feminists see S. Hekman, *Gender and Knowledge* (Cambridge: Polity Press, 1991). Very broadly speaking, feminists in the social sciences have remained sceptical regarding the virtues of postmodernism, whereas those involved in literary criticism or cultural studies have been more convinced of its radical potential – probably unsurprisingly, since it is here that a politics of representation is being waged.

4 J. Habermas, *The Philosophical Discourse of Modernity*, Trans. F. G. Lawrence (Oxford: Polity Press, 1987), p. 5.

5 J.-F. Lyotard, *The Postmodern Condition* (Manchester: Manchester University Press, 1984), p. xxiv.
6 Lyotard, *The Postmodern Condition*, pp. 37, 64. In this form, the two major metanarratives resemble Merleau-Ponty's politics of reason and of understanding, respectively, where these were similarly associated with terror. See *Humanism and Terror* (Boston: Beacon Press, 1969).
7 See D. Coole, *Women in Political Theory* (Brighton: Wheatsheaf-Harvester, 1993), ch. 8.
8 Lyotard, *The Postmodern Condition*, p. 27.
9 Ibid., p. 65.
10 M. Horkheimer and T. Adorno, *Dialectic of Enlightenment* (New York: Seabury Press, 1972). See also Husserl's *The Crisis of European Sciences* (Evanston: Northwestern University Press, 1970).
11 C. Owens, 'The Discourse of Others: Feminists and Postmodernism', in H. Foster (ed.), *Postmodern Culture* (London: Pluto Press, 1985), p. 80 note 32.
12 This is the kind of argument advanced by N. Chodorow, D. Dinnerstein and C. Gilligan. For postmodern criticism of it, see N. Fraser and L. Nicholson, 'Social Criticism without Philosophy', in L. Nicholson (ed.), *Feminism/Postmodernism*, pp. 29–33.
13 See for example G. Lloyd, *The Man of Reason* (London: Methuen, 1984).
14 See for example S. Bordo, 'The Cartesian Masculinization of Thought', *Signs*, 11, 3 (1986); S. Harding, *The Science Question in Feminism* (Milton Keynes: Open University Press, 1986); C. Gilligan, *In a Different Voice* (Cambridge, MA: Harvard University Press, 1983).
15 S. Firestone, *The Dialectic of Sex* (London: Women's Press, 1979).
16 Hegel, *The Philosophy of Right*, Trans. T. M. Knox (Oxford: Oxford University Press, 1967), p. 264.
17 M. Wollstonecraft, *A Vindication of the Rights of Woman* (London: Everyman, 1929), p. 7.
18 See J. Habermas, *Philosophical Discourse of Modernity*, especially Lecture IV; A. Jardine, *Gynesis. Configurations of Woman and Modernity* (Ithaca and London: Cornell University Press, 1985).
19 Lyotard, *The Postmodern Condition*, p. 15.
20 Ibid., pp. 46, 63f
21 Ibid., p. 10.
22 M. Foucault, 'The Subject and Power' in Dreyfus and Rabinow, *Michel Foucault: Beyond Structuralism and Hermeneutics* (Brighton: Harvester 1982), p. 222.
23 For discussions of such subversive and transgressive practices, see for example: J. Wolff, 'Postmodern Theory and Feminist Art Practice', in R. Boyne and A. Rattansi (eds.), *Postmodernism and Society* (London: Macmillan, 1980); L. Hutcheon, *The Politics of Postmodernism* (London and New York: Routledge, 1989), ch. 6; C. Owens, 'The Discourse of Others'; S. Suleiman, 'Feminism and Postmodernism'; L. Mulvey, 'Visual Pleasure and Narrative Cinema', *Screen*, 16, 3 (Autumn 1975); B. Creed, 'From Here to Modernity: Feminism and Postmodernism', *Screen*, 28, 2 (1987); J. Barry and S. Flitterman, 'Textual Strategies: The Politics of Art-Making',

Screen, 21, 1 (1980); R. Lee, 'Resisting Amnesia: Feminism, Painting and Postmodernism', *Feminist Review*, 26 (July 1987).

24 A. Huyssen, *After the Great Divide* (London: Macmillan, 1986), pp. 59, 61.
R. Williams also notes the connection in *The Politics of Modernism* (London: Verso, 1989), ch. 3.
25 Lyotard, *The Postmodern Condition*, p. 82.
26 J. Kristeva, 'Postmodernism?', *Bucknell Review*, 25, 2 (1980), pp. 137, 141.

8   In different voices: deliberative democracy and aestheticist politics

Judith Squires

> In the past ten years we have seen an extensive 'turn to culture' . . .
> Within this general shift we can see a marked interest in analysing
> processes of symbolization and representation – the field of 'culture' –
> and attempts to develop a better understanding of subjectivity, the
> psyche and the self.
>
> Michèle Barrett, *Words and Things*

Introduction

The 'turn to culture' which characterises recent postmodern theorising
has had important ramifications for political theory and practice. For
many, it has represented a turn away from politics, for others a
reconceptualisation of the political. The nature of 'the political' has long
been subject to dispute within political theory. Yet the disputes have
tended to take place within a topographical framework, evaluating
competing conceptions of the political as located within the state,
civil society or the personal realms of life. In contrast, postmodern
perspectives on the political have tended to adopt non-topographical
conceptions which are dynamic and fluid. Rather than focusing on
institutions, these perspectives have highlighted discursive, linguistic,
psychological and performative moments of political action. On this
schema, the political is neither procedural, hermeneutic nor expressive,
it is aesthetic.

These aesthetic conceptions of the political have offered significant
insights into contemporary society. For instance, contemplating the fact
that lesbian and gay politics, long before it called itself queer, incorporated an aesthetic of performance and display, and one which centrally
emphasises the body, Elizabeth Wilson asks: 'why is it that some forms
of political protest appear more effective when couched in aesthetic
terms? Why are there periods, like now . . . when politics seems to have
to be expressed in aesthetic terms?' (Wilson, 1993: 115). Whilst
traditional political perspectives offer few theoretical tools to engage

with such questions, the more aestheticist perspectives have brought a wealth of theoretical insights to bear. Yet the exclusive focus on the aesthetic has also proved to have its limitations. Aestheticist politics, characterised by acts of transgression and defiance offer only a tenuous basis for addressing issues of group emancipation and social justice.

In this context it is significant that there has been a recent and noticeable tendency amongst those theorists working within the post-modern or aestheticist framework towards a consideration of questions of justice and a contemplation of issues of institutional politics. Under the broad title of 'the cultural politics of difference' there is currently a distinct attempt to hold on to the ontological and epistemological insights of postmodernism, whilst addressing the more conventional political issues of institutional access and representation. This renewed interest in the procedural aspects of the political emerges out of the ubiquitous postmodern concern with 'difference' and the compulsion to 'recognise difference' publicly. As Nancy Fraser notes: 'The "struggle for recognition" has become the paradigmatic form of political conflict in the late twentieth century' (Fraser, 1995: 1). Schematically, one might argue that insofar as aestheticist politics engages with the question of justice at all, it is concerned with justice as recognition rather than as (re)distribution, which more conventionally characterised various modernist forms of political perspective. Demands for recognition of cultural difference require, minimally, that formal mechanisms of inclusion within the polity be secured. For this one needs procedures, perhaps even constitutional guarantees. Yet there is a tension between constituting political procedures (which inevitably posit some stability of identity and require exclusions of certain differences) and celebrating the fluidity of heterogeneous difference. In attempting to negotiate a synthesis of aestheticist politics with mechanisms of just recognition one is faced with an ethical question that will not go away: which differences do we want to inscribe within our political structures and why?

It is my claim that in the attempt to resolve this dilemma, many theorists are currently engaging critically with the model of deliberative democracy developed by Jürgen Habermas. For this framework seems to offer a possibility of negotiating the issues of justice and difference through an account of deliberative decision-making. I intend to explore the scope for critical readings of deliberative democracy which might undertake the task of integrating the insights of an aestheticist politics into the more traditional political concerns of the nature of institutional mechanisms for securing just recognition.

Feminist voices and the 'turn to culture'

Whilst many social theorists have represented the current predominance of the cultural as itself a logic of late capitalism (and therefore to some extent determined by the economic and to be viewed with cynicism), reflections upon recent feminist practices reveal the extent to which the turn to culture can also be viewed as a result of multifarious forms of active political struggle (and hence to be viewed more positively as a form of resistance to dominant power relations). Focusing on the latter perspective, I shall briefly survey recent developments within feminist politics to indicate the context in which the cultural politics of difference emerges. For developments within feminist theories and practices have to a large extent paved the way for theorising an extensive, non-institutional conception of the political, focusing on questions of sub-jectivity as of central political importance and engaging with the aesthetic as an essential component of the political. Many of the shifts now commonly characterised as postmodern emerged through earlier feminist debates and forms of activism. Nonetheless, the central distin-guishing feature between some forms of early second-wave feminism and current forms of a cultural politics of difference is the former's focus on an essential category of identity (in this case 'woman') and the latter's adoption of a performative conception of heterogeneous identities. Accordingly, assertions of difference become plural rather than dichot-omous and one discerns a movement away from contemplation of 'a different voice' towards consideration of recognition of 'different voices'. This move, characterised by one theorist of the politics of difference as a process of *pluralisation*, requires that we rethink the *pluralist* imagination: 'the dissonant relation between pluralism and pluralisation' is 'the constitutive tension of pluralist politics itself' (Connolly, 1995: xiv). In other words the emergent claims to positive recognition of identity among constituencies whose previous identifica-tions (along lines of gender, sexuality, nationality, class, race or religion) were experienced as injurious or degrading, coupled with contemporary theories of identity, require that we develop new forms of pluralism, new procedural mechanisms which might ensure justice through political recognition. As Tariq Modood comments: that many leading political theorists 'come to place diversity, pluralism and multiculturalism at the centre of their theorising, with the emphasis being on the justness of cultural rather than economic transactions, is . . . determined by changes in the political world; by the challenges of feminism, the growing recognition that most Western societies are, partly because of movements of populations, increasingly multi-ethnic and multi-racial, and the growing questioning of whether the pursuit of a universal theory of justice may not itself be an example of a Western cultural imperialism' (Modood, 1996: 177).

In this context, I shall briefly survey the 'challenges of feminism' which helped to bring the cultural turn about. Contemporary feminist discourses are characterised by two dominant schools of thought: the maternalist/radical and the postmodern. These schools of thought focus primarily upon the notions of 'caring' and 'alterity' respectively and adopt correlative expressive and aesthetic conceptions of the political. These approaches (though frequently at odds with one another) share a critique of the liberal or procedural conception of the political. The caring perspective of expressive politics emphasises particularity and contextuality; the alterity perspective of aesthetic politics emphasises the semiotic and the pre-discursive. Both issue a direct challenge to the conception of the political which assumes abstract individuals with pre-formed preferences which they seek to articulate within and realise through institutional mechanisms. In order to emphasise this commonality, it is perhaps worth contextualising this claim within an account of the ongoing dichotomy between informal and institutional conceptions of the political at work within feminist practices and discourses. For I shall be assuming that the 'turn to culture' has taken place not only within feminist theory and within the academy, but in feminist practice and contemporary cultural articulations of political activism.

Debates about women's political participation have purposefully not only focused upon questions of why and in what ways women have been excluded from full participation in the formal institutions of politics, but also explored the extent to which women have nonetheless been active in informal, movement-based politics. The juxtaposition of these two concerns raises the conceptual issue of the scope of 'the political' itself and the forms of action deemed political. The slogan 'the personal is political', which arose to challenge orthodox definitions of the political, acted as a rallying cry for a whole generation of feminists and is often perceived to be the key statement of second-wave feminism. The claim implicit in this statement is that women *are* political actors, where the political is held to include all power-structured relations from the interpersonal to the international. Historically women have been excluded from participation in the formal institutions of politics by states limiting citizenship in various ways which privilege the hegemonic form of masculinity at that time. Thus at differing periods the performance of military duty, property ownership and the capacity for rationality have all been deemed preconditions for the granting of full participation rights. Under these conditions most women have been structurally excluded from formal political participation (Brown, 1988).

In response to this state of affairs feminist campaigns have taken a variety of forms ranging from the pursuit of increased women's participation within those formal institutional politics as currently exist to the extension of the definition of the political in such a way as to reveal and valorise women's extensive existing forms of political participation outside the formal institutions. The former strand was prominent in the campaigns for women's right to vote, the latter during the 1960s and 1970s when this right had been secured, but women's status little improved (Millett, 1970; Morgan, 1970). Nineteenth-century feminists campaigned for the right to vote and also the right to stand in elections. In so doing, they concentrated upon formal equality before the law within the institutions of mainstream party politics. These goals are now largely realised within Western liberal democracies (women securing the franchise between 1906 in Finland and 1975 in Portugal).

However, to concentrate on these forms of political participation alone is felt by many feminists to reproduce those masculine assumptions which have worked to blind us to much of women's political participation for centuries. Many women typically organise outside of state structures in such things as women's peace movements and ecology movements (Mies and Shiva, 1993). Many of their activities are concentrated below the level of the state and are often geared towards agitating against oppressive state structures and policies. Women have also tended to be involved in issues and movements that cut across state boundaries (Peterson and Runyan, 1993). During the peak of the second-wave movements there were a large number of protest strategies adopted, including spontaneous action, well-organised campaigns of sit-ins, marches and demonstrations, such as the 'Reclaim the Night' actions in England and West Germany in 1977, in Italy in 1978. Yet perhaps the most common form of protest at this time were actions of the written word. The prolific number of journals, news-sheets, magazines and books of women's issues is an important manifestation of women's political participation over this period.

All these forms of political protest were 'movement events', working outside the formal mechanisms of procedural politics. The political participation which was advocated during this period by many within the women's movement was direct participation in women's autonomous organisations. These organisation aspired to be open to all, non-hierarchical and informal. Issues of participatory democracy became central, with great attention paid to organisational practice (Pateman, 1970). However, for many the experiences of the radical participatory democracy of the women's movement became paradoxical (see Phillips, 1991). Although claiming to be open to all, women's groups were largely unrepresentative. The absence of formal structures often worked to create an insularity which left many women feeling excluded and silenced. The emphasis on participation was too demanding for those who were juggling many other demands on their time, and the lack of representative structures raised serious questions of accountability. Perhaps because of these developments, there has been a notable shift of focus back towards the more conventional forms of political participation for many women. By the 1980s many feminists became again more centrally concerned with the importance of mainstream politics, working to increase the numbers of women present within parties and legislatures, and to pursue policies in the interests of women.

Various strategies have been adopted for increasing the number of women in the legislature: ranging from the purely rhetorical encouragement of women to enter into the system as it is, through positive action such as training, to positive discrimination and the adoption of quotas (Lovenduski and Norris, 1993). Party reforms, including new systems of candidate selection, new means of policy-making, and the establishment of new structures of government (such as ministries for women) have all been adopted. It has been shown that the most significant factor influencing women's success in entering national politics is the electoral system itself, specifically the operation of proportional representation, multi-member constituencies and party lists (Norris, 1995).

However, a concern with a more extensive notion of the political has not diminished with the waning of the cohesive women's movement. Rather, it has transmogrified into new, contemporary forms, which I label expressive and aesthetic, and which might be located within the 'radical/cultural' and 'postmodern' schools of thought respectively. Despite the hostility between the 'expressive' and 'aesthetic' camps, they share a tendency to extend the boundaries of the political beyond the institutions of the state, or indeed of civil association.

Expressive and aesthetic conceptions of the political

The expressive conception of the political draws most explicitly on the work of Carol Gilligan, whose claim that women's experience of interconnection shapes their moral domain and gives rise to a different moral voice (Gilligan, 1982: 151–76) has been widely used as a basis for feminist politics. In criticising Lawrence Kohlberg's research into moral development on the basis that it privileged an 'ethic of justice' over an 'ethic of caring', Gilligan offers feminists a framework within which they might critique the individualism and universalism of liberal political institutions. As Benhabib notes, 'Gilligan's critique of Kohlberg radically questions the "juridical" or "justice bias" of universalist moral theories' (Benhabib, 1992: 146). Contra Kohlberg, whose model of moral development assumed that the highest level of moral development involves the ability to abstract and universalise moral rules, Gilligan argued that we can distinguish between two ethical orientations: that of justice and rights on the one hand and that of care and responsibility on the other. The latter requires a contextuality, narrativity and specificity not valued in the former. Gilligan made the further claim that women were more likely to manifest the latter than were men, giving them a different – but not inferior – moral sense.

This claim is echoed in the writings of the 'maternalists' who argue for a feminised version of citizenship (Ruddick, 1980; Elshtain, 1981) and articulate a female political consciousness that is grounded in the virtues of women's private sphere – primarily mothering. This is an expressive politics. Social justice, it is asserted, is not sufficient to generate a morally acceptable polity, we also need to adopt the maternal mode of caring as a basis for public interactions. The claim is that women's experiences as mothers within the private sphere provide them with certain insights and concerns which are valuable to the public sphere but currently absent from it. Articulated in this form, I find the expressive conception of the political largely unappealing. The illusion of cohesion and unity, of consensus and collectivity can all too easily become dangerous rhetorics which seek to repress fragmentation and difference (Dietz, 1992; Mouffe, 1992a). Yet one might nonetheless seek to attend to the call of the 'different voice' represented by the caring perspective, in one's formulation of the political without endorsing this 'maternalist' vision. Notably, Benhabib has advocated that we modify the deliberative model developed by Habermas to take account of both the 'concrete and the generalised other' (Benhabib, 1992). What this might mean in terms of state mechanisms for policy formation is far from clear as yet. The practical challenge for those convinced by the theoretical pertinence of the caring perspective is to conceive of procedural mechanisms of political inclusion which allow for contextualised rather than formal–abstract perspectives.

In contrast to the expressive, the aesthetic conception of the political draws most explicitly on the work of Judith Butler. It too offers feminists a framework within which they might critique the individualism and universalism of liberal political institutions, but from a very different basis. Rather than claiming a distinct female identity and ethic, Butler's aesthetic approach questions the notion of a stable identity *per se*: 'there are those,' she argues, 'who seek recourse to Gilligan and others who establish a feminine specificity that makes itself clear in women's communities or ways of knowing. But every time that specificity is articulated, there is resistance and factionalization within the very constituency that is supposed to be *unified* by the articulation of its common element' (Butler, 1995: 49). The recognition of this resistance, leading to a political emphasis upon plural rather than dichotomous differences, arises from a performative notion of identity. 'A performative act is one which brings into being or enacts that which it names, and so marks the constitutive or productive power of discourse' (Butler, 1995: 134). The subject is 'performatively' constituted, in other words constituted by language, produced within a given network of power/ discourse. Rather than doing away with the 'doer' behind the 'deed' as many have believed, Butler argues that the 'doer' 'will be the uncertain working of the discursive possibilities by which it itself is worked' (Butler, 1995: 135). This approach emphasises the subject's historicity and susceptibility to change thereby allowing for the possibility of disruption of constricting identities.

It is from this perspective that writers such as Elizabeth Wilson have expressed concern that politics and liberatory practices come to be conceived of as acts of transgression, as the 'single fragmented act of defiance, unencumbered by any overarching theory or coherent world view, offering only a tenuous basis for addressing issues of group emancipation and social justice' (Wilson, 1993: 114). Similarly, Fraser notes that 'at the deepest level [Butler] understands women's liberation as liberation *from* identity, since she views identity as inherently oppressive' (Fraser, 1995: 71). Fraser's concern, like Wilson's, is that this conception of liberation is inadequate, privileging deconstructive over reconstructive critique as the mode of feminist theorising. 'Moreover, it is arguable that the current proliferation of identity-dereifying, fungible, commodified images and significations constitutes as great a threat to women's liberation as do fixed, fundamentalist identities' (Fraser, 1995: 71). Accordingly, the tension within current feminist discourse is played out between essentialist and social constructivist perspectives, leading to maternalist/expressive or postmodern/aesthetic politics.

Yet, one might note that Butler herself acknowledges that: 'within feminism, it seems as if there is some political necessity to speak as and for *women*, and I would not contest that necessity. Surely, that is the way in which representational politics operates' (Butler, 1995: 49). Whilst feminist perspectives regarding subjectivity are frequently characterised as being either essentialist or social constructivist, in theory and in practice, most feminists are both essentialists and constructivists.

Within theoretical debates some have constructed schemas that label radical feminists as essentialists and postmodern feminists as constructivists, but detailed reading reveals much more ambivalent affiliations than this allows. Luce Irigaray, for example, is a poststructuralist who might be considered essentialist, whilst Monique Wittig might be categorised as either radical or Marxist feminist (depending on one's definitional categories) but explicitly endorses social constructivism. Others, such as Gayatri Spivak, have argued for a strategic essentialism as the most effective political stance open to contingent clusters of fluctuating identities.

In this focus on the ontological questions of subjectivity we witness a rearticulation, in its most contemporary manifestation, of the long-running dialectic within feminism between informal and institutional notions of the political, between difference and identity, deconstruction and reconstruction. Rather than signalling weakness and confusion within feminisms these continuing dialogues attest to one of feminism's central strengths: its ongoing attempts to question/deconstruct/reconstruct aspects of life and categories of meaning that have been systematically differentiated and demarcated within mainstream modernist practices. I want to focus here, not on this debate between the expressive and aesthetic perspectives, but on the fact that *both* perspectives have conventionally been located as outwith the legitimate remit of the political in modernist discourses. In this context, the attempt to contemplate the integration of the expressive and/or the aesthetic *and the procedural* within the political realm seems to me to be one further positive significant development currently emerging from within feminist writings and practices. The scope for such an integration lies at the very heart of current debates about the cultural politics of difference and the possible mechanisms for reconfiguring procedural politics such that it might realise cultural justice. I hope to have indicated above that the tension between the expressive and the aesthetic formulations of the cultural turn will inform the paradoxes witnessed in current cultural politics of difference debates.

In short, within contemporary feminisms there is scepticism regarding engagement with the state and ambivalence towards policy formation based on a radical scepticism about the patriarchal/enlightenment discourses concerning justice, equity and emancipation and resulting in an expansive, informal understanding of politics. Yet, there is also a very real perceived need to integrate these perspectives into an institutional framework, to consider the scope for creating space for 'different voices' within the institutions of the state. Whilst the turn to culture, signalling an engagement with expressive and aesthetic issues, has been a productive one for feminists, perhaps the time has come to focus on retaining the insights of the expressive and/or the aesthetic whilst addressing institutional and material issues within the state.

Deliberative democracy and the aesthetic

In order to undertake the above task, I shall use the model of deliberative democracy developed by Jürgen Habermas as an exemplar of a procedural approach to the political. It is currently the most favoured form of procedural politics on offer and is gaining increasing interest from feminist and difference theorists (Benhabib, 1992; Meehan, 1995; McCarthy, 1991; Bernstein, 1991; Gutmann, 1994; Cohen and Rogers, 1995). It is the Habermassian political perspective which, more than any other, currently offers a rejection of and alternative to the trend towards embracing postmodern politics. It represents a clear attempt to articulate a defence of the unfinished project of modernity.

I argue that the procedural model of the political developed by advocates of deliberative democracy explicitly and necessarily excludes both the expressive and aesthetic, thereby specifically excluding those conceptions of the political which might be held to be distinctly feminist and also those which adopt a cultural politics of difference. Given this, one must question the adequacy of this deliberative model to the task more generally of recognising the distinctive contribution of feminist theories of political participation, or to the task of ensuring the institutional presence of those who are most closely associated with these more extensive cultural conceptions of the political.

Habermas seems to offer what many would like to believe possible: a critique of the metaphysical and individualistic aspects of Enlightenment thought, whilst providing a basis of universal morality and constitutional democracy. He takes a socially constructed notion of the self and yet derives a universal cognitive formalism from the structures of interaction, allowing us to critically evaluate existing moral and institutional practices from a universal standpoint. Although he rejects Kant's transcendental method his work shares Kant's formalism, cognitivism and universalism. By formalism, I mean the assertion that it is the form not content of moral judgement which is defining; by cognitivism, I mean that moral conflicts can be resolved through argument (a cognitive skill achieved through a developmental process); by universalism, the form of moral reasoning at a given stage in any culture is identical, i.e. the criteria for moral reasoning hold universally. These elements in Habermas' work lead to a commitment to proceduralism and deliberative democracy characterised as a response to the poverty of the liberal model and the 'ethical overload' of the republican conception of democracy. The liberal or Lockean view of the democratic process, Habermas claims, represents government as an apparatus of public administration and society as a market-structured network of interactions among private persons. 'Here', he argues, 'politics has the function of bundling together and pushing private interests against a government apparatus specialised in the administrative employment of political power for collective goals.' On the republican models on the other hand 'politics is conceived as the reflective form of substantial ethical life, namely as the medium in which the members of somehow solidary communities become aware of their dependence on one another and, acting with full deliberation as citizens, further shape and develop existing relations of reciprocal recognition into an association of free and equal consociates under law' (Habermas, 1996a: 21).

Habermas situates his own proceduralist model of democracy between these two models: 'the republican model as compared to the liberal one has the advantage that it preserves the original meaning of democracy in terms of the institutionalization of a public use of reason jointly exercised by autonomous citizens' but the republican model is wanting because 'politics may not be assimilated to a hermeneutical process of self-explication of a shared form of life or collective identity. Political questions may not be reduced to the type of ethical questions, where we, as members of a community, ask ourselves who we are and who we would like to be' (Habermas, 1996a: 23). Habermas' point is that discourses aimed at achieving self-understanding and clarification about the kind of society one wants to live in are 'a part of politics. But these questions are subordinate to moral questions and connected with pragmatic questions' (Habermas, 1996a: 24).

What then are 'moral questions'? 'Moral questions in the narrow sense of the Kantian tradition are questions of justice . . . The making of norms is primarily a justice issue and is gauged by principles that state what is equally good for all. And unlike ethical questions, questions of justice are not related from the outset to a special collective and its form of life. The politically enacted law of a concrete legal community must, if it is to be legitimate, at least be compatible with moral tenets that claim universal validity going beyond the legal community' (Habermas, 1996a: 25). So Habermas distinguishes his model of democratic politics from the liberal one in that it is characterised by public discourse, and further distinguishes it from the republican model in that it privileges justice rather than ethics. It is the question of this privileging of justice over ethics that interests me. If politics is about justice, not ethics, as defined by Habermas, then both the expressive and aesthetic politics of recent times are indeed post-politics, non-politics, lacking claims to universal validity, or in Wilson's phrase, emphasising the single fragmented act of defiance, unencumbered by any overarching theory or coherent world-view.

According to the Habermassian schema there are three distinct spheres of values:

Cognitive	Normative	Expressive
Objective	Social	Subjective
Natural world	Intersubjectively constituted world	Inner world
Strategic	Communicative	Aesthetic
Truth	Rightness	Sincerity

Politics, for those who adopt the deliberative democracy model, is properly characterised by the central column of values only. Yet, according to Habermas' narrative, the twin forces of modernist scientisation and pre-modernist mysticism have worked to engulf these values and rob us of a space for truly political deliberation. The Habermassian project is to carve out public spaces in which the central column of values might once again be adopted and articulated. In order to do so, one must challenge and repudiate both positivistic and 'postmodern' (or 'Young Conservative' in Habermas' lexicon) understandings of the political.

Habermas argues that new social movements are more symptomatic than emancipatory: they simply express identity disturbances caused by the colonisation of the life-world and try to resolve this colonisation process by the assertion of particularity, a retreat from political struggle into private communities. He therefore explicitly demarcates both the expressive and aesthetic politics of recent time as not properly political. Interestingly, Habermas does argue that the women's movements 'must be counted amongst those great mass movements which take up universal principles of equality. This does not apply', he continues, 'to other contemporary movements of protest' (Dews, 1986: 66). What then would Habermas make, are we to make, of the clear fact that gender politics has by and large shifted from pursuit of equality to assertions of difference? There is no 'great mass movement' seeking universal equality. There are a multitude of fleeting and fragmentary groupings asserting their identity and transgressing dominant norms frequently through expressive or aesthetic forms of politics: neither the radical/cultural nor the postmodern/aesthetic forms of feminist politics conform to the image of the women's movement that Habermas finds time to praise. Why might this be? Are we to bemoan this and encourage people to stop being frivolous and pursue a more considered democratic project? What are we to make of actions that 'simply express identity disturbances'?

By way of addressing this question one must critically explore the dependence of the deliberative democracy model upon an ethic of justice and its assertion of a communicative rationality, both of which are formalistic and universalistic. Adopting Habermas' own schema, an exploration of the third sphere of values – the expressive, subjective, inner, aesthetic and sincere – is central. Feminist theorists have above all else worked to establish the political significance of these values, challenging the modernist strategy of marginalising these values to a particular 'sphere'. Specifically, postmodern feminists have stressed that the aesthetic is not something which can be jettisoned from the political and located within religion and art alone, it pervades all actions and interactions. In writing the aesthetic off as a proper form of articulation for emancipatory struggle advocates of deliberative democracy not only fail to recognise this significant development made by gender theory, but also diminish their own understanding of what contemporary politics might encompass. Given the number of feminist theorists who now seem to be adopting precisely this deliberative democracy model (Benhabib, 1992; Meehan, 1995) this failure is of no small consequence.

For many commentators, the relation between the politics of modernity and of postmodernity renders the possibility of a synthesis between the procedural and the aesthetic fraught if not impossible. Specifically, it is claimed that Habermas, located as the key defender of the politics of modernity, 'adopts an uncompromisingly hostile approach towards post-structuralism/postmodernism . . . Habermas rejects postmodernism because in his view . . . it depends on an appeal to the Other. He is unable to attribute any emancipatory potential to alterity, or otherness, however because his basic ideas concerning communicative reason and an emancipatory project of modernity are predicated on its exclusion' (Coole, 1996: 221). Others are more optimistic about a progressive synthesis. Notably, Nancy Fraser contends that: 'feminists do not have to chose between Critical Theory and poststructuralism; instead, we might reconstruct each approach so as to reconcile it with the other' (Fraser 1995: 60).

The sceptic regarding synthesis would seem to have a strong case. It is a case made eloquently by Diana Coole in her response to Habermas' essay 'Modernity: An Unfinished Project' (Habermas, 1996b: 38–58). Coole reveals the extent to which Habermas depicts postmodernism in a manner fundamentally incompatible with his own project: locating its origins in Nietzsche, who is characterised as associating the aesthetic with non-discursive excitement and self-oblivion, 'aesthetically inspired anarchism', a frenzy of reason, ecstatic rather than self-conscious. Furthermore, Habermas depicts this Nietzschean tradition as one where 'the aesthetic overflows its boundaries to impose its particular validity claims on cognitive and moral reason, such that truth and value become matters of taste' (Coole, 1996: 222). Contemporary advocates of postmodernism are then accused by Habermas of making mystical appeal to something prior to reason and immune to it yet retrievable through transgressive experiences which would extinguish the rational subject. He characterises all as equating the Other with some prediscursive referent which precedes reason. The aesthetic then is equated by Habermas with 'some unspeakable and undifferentiated excitement which, he remarks, is now fashionably labelled feminine' (Coole, 1996: 223). Coole rightly points out that for Habermas, the effects of the aesthetic are resolutely non-emancipatory, and on this basis he condemns the postmoderns as 'young conservatives', retreating into antimodernism. On Coole's reading this is a mistaken stance, based upon a misunderstanding about the nature and location of the aesthetic itself. She is more sympathetic to Derrida's position: whereas Habermas claims that it is contingent distortions alone which impede the ideal of undistorted communication, Derrida claims that ordinary language is intrinsically riven by slippages, metaphors, absences, deferrals, desire and chance associations which mean that it always communicates both more and less than conversationalists intend. Coole's claim is that for Derrida recognition of alterity is not some mystical Other, but exists in the fault-lines and ruptures which structure language itself. To allow this undermines Habermas' discourse ethics: for to allow that even the most rational discourses will remain charged with alterity implies that to deny such alterity is to engage in a 'violent metaphysical project'. Habermas argues that in modernity the pre-discursive, mystical forces of alterity have been contained within religion and art, which are dismissed as apolitical. But what if alterity continues to circulate throughout the relations of modernity? Perhaps it is not simply a legacy of the premodern, but is a necessary aspect of modernity itself?

The aesthetic realm is cast by Habermas as transgressive, open to the unconscious, the mad, the feminine, the bodily. This realm is then defined as apolitical. Yet it is precisely the unconscious, the feminine, the bodily that have been the focus of so much feminist 'political' theory and practice. From a postmodern feminist perspective aesthetic questions are inherently political: the repression of the aesthetic articulations of everyday life is particularly damaging for women, who have long been associated with and defined by their relation to these articulations. Habermas' politics, formulated in the name of critical theory and an emancipatory project, excludes otherness and thereby particularly affects groups who are associated with it, or who forge their identities and life-forms along these lines: groups marginalised by pre-discursive processes. The central question, following Coole, is whether one can afford to turn one's back on this politics, since it affects, even constructs, the capacities and opportunities of actors who would participate in the free and equal manner that discursive democracy requires.

The problem, of course, is that even if one answers this question in the negative, it remains decidedly unclear as to how the endorsement of an aesthetic politics might square with the more prosaic concerns of policy formation. Once we allow the aesthetic as a valid mode of political articulation must we relinquish our appeal to the standards of reason and impartiality? And, if so, how would we avoid entropy and remain engaged in processes of transformation? Just how might acceptance of the importance of the body, desire, the semiotic, inform our construction of policy formation procedures?

Between an aestheticist politics and a politics of recognition

The extent to which the aesthetic can be incorporated within procedural notions of the political is a central one for those concerned with the politics of postmodernity. It is, I am arguing, a particularly knotty problem, to which no obvious resolution has yet been offered. Interestingly, the integration of the expressive into the procedural would seem to be much more easily accommodated. Those who advocate a politics of recognition based upon an expressive framework have found various means of synthesis available and have been drawn to the deliberative democracy perspective. To give but one example of this, consider the recent debate between Benhabib and Butler. Benhabib explictly modifies the Habermassian model of deliberative democracy by drawing upon the caring perspective of Gilligan, introducing the notion of the 'concrete' as well as 'generalized' other. Speaking of the work of Gilligan, Chodorow and Ruddick, she asks: 'as a project of an ethics which should guide us in the future are we able to offer a better vision than the synthesis of autonomous justice thinking and empathetic care?' (Benhabib, 1995: 30). This is a clear endorsement of the project of integrating the expressive and the procedural, and one which has been convincingly elaborated within Benhabib's writings. Butler, on the other hand, articulates an aesthetic politics which – as many have noted –

bears little clear relation to particular procedural forms of the political. She does, of course, nonetheless claim her concerns to be political (Butler, 1995: 36). Yet it is unclear, in terms of a procedural concern with just recognition, precisely what this aesthetic notion of the political might imply.

Fraser attempts to deal with this apparent problem by offering a synthetic reading of the two positions: 'we might,' she claims, 'develop a view of collective identities as at once discursively constructed and complex, enabling of collective action and amenable to mystification, in need of deconstruction and reconstruction. In sum, we might try to develop new paradigms of feminist theorizing that integrate the insights of Critical Theory with the insights of poststructuralism' (Fraser, 1995: 72). But Fraser's attempt to develop the 'weak postmodernism' discussed by Benhabib so as to make the latter's position more sympathetic to postmodern politics is rebutted by Benhabib who claims that the sort of commonsensical tailoring of theory to the tasks in hand proposed by Fraser is simply not postmodern: 'Fraser can reconcile her political commitments with a theoretical sympathy to postmodernism, only because in effect she has replaced "postmodern" by "neo-pragmatist" historiography and social research. As opposed to the pragmatic pluralism of methodological approaches guided by research interests, as advocated by Fraser, what postmodernist historiography displays is an "aesthetic" proliferation of styles which increasingly blurs the distinctions between history and literature, factual narrative and imaginary creation' (Benhabib, 1995: 112).

In other words, Fraser's proposed synthesis of these two perspectives is only viable in Benhabib's view because it *does not* draw upon the aesthetic perspective of postmodern politics. Were it to do so, as Coole indicated above it might, it would indeed remain antithetical to the unfinished modernist project of Critical Theory. The question of central interest then, is whether it is possible – contra Benhabib – to synthesise the aesthetic and the procedural conceptions of the political. One possible place to look is in recent articulations of the politics of recognition.

It is noteworthy that the numerous articulations of the cultural politics of difference currently on offer tend to involve calls for group representation (Gutmann, 1994; Kymlicka, 1995; Phillips, 1995; Young, 1990). Such proposals are inescapably more in keeping with expressive than aesthetic politics in that they tend to assume a version of what Charles Taylor calls 'the ideal of authenticity'. There is, he claims, a particularly modern notion of authenticity based upon the idea that understanding right and wrong 'was not a matter of dry calculation, but was anchored in our feeling. Morality has, in a sense, a voice within' (Taylor, 1994: 28). Modern culture, he claims, is characterised by a new form of inwardness, in which we come to think of ourselves as beings with inner depths. Being true to myself means being true to my own originality, and that is something only I can articulate. This ideal of authenticity leads directly to a politics of recognition in that original identity needs, and is vulnerable to, the recognition of others. In this context Taylor notes that 'not only contemporary feminism but also race relations and discussion of multiculturalism are undergirded by the premise that denied recognition can be a form of oppression' (Taylor, 1992: 50). It is, I think, evident that such a perspective is both compatible with the expressive politics discussed above and leads directly to a concern with mechanisms for group representation secured by procedural mechanisms of state politics. It is also evident that this notion of authenticity is not one commonly used within the postmodern lexicon. The performative notion of identity adopted within the aesthetic framework asserts that subjects are constituted *through exclusion,* not recognition.

As a result many who adopt a more performative notion of subjectivity are sceptical about the liberatory potential of group representation. For example, Chantal Mouffe rejects Iris Young's group representation model arguing that Young has an ultimately essentialist notion of 'group' which leaves her model – despite all her disclaimers – as not so different from the interest-group pluralism that she criticises (Mouffe, 1992b: 380). The only community which Mouffe allows as the basis for political action is a political community, a group 'bounded by their common identification with a given interpretation of a set of ethico-political values' (Mouffe, 1992b: 378). Arguing that all other communities are partial and exclusionary, the only notion of community which is acceptable as the basis for citizenship for Mouffe is an ethico-political community, that is a community which accepts the procedural mechanisms of democracy.

This critique is particularly interesting as Iris Young's *Justice and the Politics of Difference* is one of the few recent works within feminist political theory to address procedural, expressive *and* aesthetic conceptions of the political. She attempts to hold on to the commitment to both caring and alterity whilst negotiating issues of constitutional and procedural guarantees of participation within policy formation processes. As such her writings might be thought to offer a basis for attempting to find a resolution between these very different conceptions of the political.

Young draws on postmodern theories of alterity to develop a critique of impartiality as an ideal. She states: 'The ideal of impartial moral reason corresponds to the Enlightenment ideal of the public realm of politics as attaining the universality of a general will that leaves difference, particularity and the body behind in the private realms of family and civil society' (Young, 1990: 97). Contra this 'ideal' she argues that the meaning of the 'public' should be transformed to exhibit the positivity of group differences, passion and play. 'Modern ethics establishes impartiality as the hallmark of moral reason' (Young, 1990: 99). This ideal of impartiality underpins both the Kantian categorical imperative and the Hegelian account of the state as expressing universality as against the particularity of desire. So, by implication, both the liberal and the communitarian political models are subject to her critique. But what of the Habermassian model of deliberative democracy?

An alternative to moral theory founded on impartiality, argues Young, is communicative ethics: 'Habermas has gone further than any other contemporary thinker in elaborating the project of a moral reason that recognised the plurality of subjects' (Young, 1990: 106). As subjectivity, for Habermas, is conceived as a product of communicative interaction, moral rationality is dialogic. So Young is supportive this far, but: 'even Habermas seems unwilling to abandon a standpoint of universal normative reason that transcends particularist perspectives' (Young, 1990: 106). There is, she finds, a strain of Habermas' theory that relies on counterfactuals which build in an impartial standpoint in order to get universality out of the moral dialogue.

Now this is important. Habermas does want a justification for his political model based on impartiality: for him impartiality is dialogically secured via the ideal speech situation, it is procedural. Is this a problem? For Young and most feminist critics, the answer has been yes: 'Recent feminist analyses of the dichotomy between public and private in modern political theory imply that the ideal of the civic public as impartial and universal it itself suspect . . . the ideal of the civic public as expressing the general interest – the impartial point of view of reason – itself results in exclusion. By assuming that reason stands opposed to desire, affectivity and the body, this conception of the civic public excludes bodily and affective aspects of human existence' (Young, 1990: 109). It is precisely this scepticism about the public/private dichotomy and the definition of the public as 'impartial' that has led so many feminists to critique the public/private dichotomy and offer alternative visions of the political. Feminists have turned to expressive and aesthetic politics by way of endorsing the validity of particular, bodily expressions of desire, rather than universal, abstract statements of rationality. So it is that feminism comes to be characterised by expressions of desire rather than by claims of justice. But, assuming we do not want to give up on the emancipatory ideal, how might we now make the move from expressions of desire to claims of justice? And can we make this move without invoking some problematic appeal to impartiality that entails some exclusion of difference? How are we to arbitrate between competing and conflictual desires?

Young's response to the question of how interest seekers will be transformed into citizens who attend to the claims of others is sketchy. She addresses the dilemma in the following manner: she quotes a passage from Hanna Pitkin who argues that interest group competition draws us into politics because: 'we are forced to find or create a common language of purposes and aspirations . . . we are forced to transform "I want" into "I am entitled to", a claim that becomes negotiable by public standards' (Pitkin in Young, 1990: 107). Young then goes on to add: 'In this move from an expression of desire to a claim of justice, dialogue participants do not bracket their particular situations or adopt a universal and shared standpoint. They *only* move from self-regarding need to recognition of the claim of others' (Young, 1990: 107, italics added). But how precisely does this transformation occur? How does a cacophony of conflicting desires find resolution in just norms? Is mere presence enough? This question, which is at the heart of liberal, communitarian and deliberative political theory, is simply glossed over by Young. Appeal to transcendental Archimedean privileged positions, to embedded communal bonds, or to ethics which derive from the structure of undistorted communication, may all be problematic resolutions to the question in hand. But I think we ought to feel obliged to offer an alternative in their place.

This is the task facing theorists of the politics of difference. The focus on the aesthetic and the expressive offers great resources for reinvigorating political discourse and practice. The integration of the expressive into discourses about procedural politics has been notable within debate about the politics of recognition. There is a corresponding task, yet to be as fully developed, of integrating transgressive acts of aestheticist politics into the collective goals of democratic politics and to show how we might move from self-regarding need to recognition of the claims of others in a way which acknowledges epistemological, ontological and moral critiques of the impartiality and abstraction of the procedural model of political justice. Reflecting on the above, one might reasonably assume that the deliberative model of democracy is perhaps not the best procedural model of politics to adopt in these future negotiations of the procedural and the aesthetic. It is possible that other models, such as Mouffe's attempt to 'rescue political liberalism' in order to develop fully the potentialities of the liberal ideals of individual freedom and personal autonomy, offer a more productive way forward. This will involve breaking with rationalism and universalism and acknowledging the predominant role of the passions as moving forces of human conduct. Here politics is not about the recognition of all differences, but rather about the recognition of the inevitability of exclusion. In Mouffe's words: 'The specificity of pluralist democracy does not reside in the absence of domination and violence, but in the establishment of a set of institutions through which they can be limited and contested' (Mouffe, 1993: 146).

BIBLIOGRAPHY

Barrett, M. (1992) 'Word and Things', in A. Phillips and M. Barrett (eds.), *Destabilizing Theory*. Cambridge: Polity Press.

Benhabib, S. (1992) 'The Generalized and the Concrete Other', in *Situating the Self*. Cambridge: Polity Press, 148–77.

  (1995) 'Feminism and Postmodernism' and 'Subjectivity, Historiography and Politics', in S. Benhabib, J. Butler, D. Cornell and N. Fraser, *Feminist Contentions*. London and New York: Routledge.

Bernstein, R. (1991) *The New Constellation: The Ethical Horizons of Modernity/ Postmodernity*. Cambridge: Polity Press.

Brown, W. (1988) *Manhood and Politics*. Totowa, NJ: Rowman and Littlefield.

  (1995) 'The Mirror of Pornography', in *States of Injury: Power and Freedom in Late Modernity*. Princeton, NJ: Princeton University Press, 77–95.

Butler, J. (1995) 'Contingent Foundations' and 'For a Careful Reading', in S. Benhabib, J. Butler, D. Cornell and N. Fraser, *Feminist Contentions*. London and New York: Routledge.

Cohen, J. and Rogers, J. (1995) *Associations and Democracy*. London: Verso.

Connolly, W. (1995) *The Ethos of Pluralization*. Minneapolis: University of Minnesota Press.

Coole, D. (1996) 'Habermas and the Question of Alterity', in M. P. D'Entreves and S. Benhabib (eds.), *Habermas and the Unfinished Project of Modernity*. Cambridge: Polity Press.

Dahlerup, D. (ed.) (1986) *The New Women's Movement*. London: Sage.

Dews, P. (ed.) (1986) *Autonomy and Solidarity: Interviews with Jürgen Habermas*. London: Verso.

Dietz, M. (1992) 'Context is All: Feminism and Theories of Citizenship', in C. Mouffe (ed.), *Dimensions of Radical Democracy*. London: Verso.

Elshtain, J. B. (1981) *Public Man, Private Woman*. Oxford: Martin Robertson.

Fraser, N. (1995) 'False Anthithesis' and 'Pragmatism, Feminism and the Linguistic Turn', in Benhabib, Butler, Cornell and Fraser, *Feminist Contentions*. London and New York: Routledge.

Gilligan, C. (1982) *In a Different Voice*. Cambridge, MA: Harvard University Press, 1–22, 171–4.

Gutmann, A. (ed.) (1994) *Multiculturalism*. Princeton: Princeton University Press.

Habermas, J. (1996a) 'Three Normative Models of Democracy', in S. Benhabib (ed.), *Democracy and Difference*. Princeton, NJ: Princeton University Press.

(1996b) 'Modernity: An Unfinished Project', in M. P. D'Entreves and S. Benhabib (eds.), *Habermas and the Unfinished Project of Modernity*. Cambridge: Polity Press.

Kymlicka, W. (1995) *Multicultural Citizenship*. Oxford: Oxford University Press.

Lovenduski, J. and Norris, P. (1993) *Gender and Party Politics*. London: Sage.

McCarthy, T. (1991) *Ideals and Illusions: On Reconstruction and Deconstruction in Contemporary Critical Theory*. Cambridge, MA: MIT Press.

Meehan, J. (ed.) (1995) *Feminists Read Habermas*. London and New York: Routledge.

Mies, M. and Shiva, V. (1993) *Ecofeminism*. London: Zed Books.

Millett, K. (1970) *Sexual Politics*. London: Jonathan Cape.

Modood, T. (1996) 'Race in Britain and the Politics of Difference', in D. Archard (ed.), *Philosophy and Pluralism*. Cambridge, Cambridge University Press, 177–90.

Morgan, R. (ed.) (1970) *Sisterhood is Powerful: An Anthology of Writing from the Women's Liberation Movement*. New York: Random House.

Mouffe, C. (1992a) *Dimensions of Radical Democracy*. London: Verso.

(1992b) 'Feminism, Citizenship and Radical Democratic Politics', in J. Butler and J. Scott (eds.), *Feminists Theorize the Political*. London and New York: Routledge.

(1993) *The Return of the Political*. London: Verso.

Norris, P. (1995) *Political Recruitment: Gender, Race and Class in the British Parliament*. Cambridge: Cambridge University Press.

Pateman, C. (1970) *Participation and Democratic Theory*. Cambridge: Cambridge University Press.

Peterson, V. S. and Runyan, A. S. (1993) *Global Gender Issues*. Oxford: Westview Press.

Phillips, A. (1991) 'Paradoxes of Participation', in *Engendering Democracy*. Cambridge: Polity Press, 121–45.

(1995) *The Politics of Presence*. Cambridge: Polity Press.

Ruddick, S. (1980) 'Maternal Thinking', in *Feminist Studies* 6, 2 (Summer 1980).

Taylor, C. (1992) *The Ethics of Authenticity*. Cambridge, MA: Harvard University Press.

(1994) 'The Politics of Recognition', in A. Gutmann (ed.) *Multiculturalism*. Princeton, NJ: Princeton University Press.

Wilson, E. (1993) 'Is Transgression Transgressive?', in J. Bristow and A. Wilson (eds.), *Activating Theory: Lesbian, Gay and Bisexual Politics*. London: Lawrence and Wishart, 107–17.

Young, I. (1990) 'The Ideal of Impartiality and the Civic Public', in *Justice and the Politics of Difference*. Princeton, NJ: Princeton University Press, 96–121.

Part III

Technology and the politics of culture

Has politics a future? This question lies behind Herminio Martins' discriminating and perceptive account of the recent history of those thinkers who read their societies through the optic of technology as well as progress. Against the background of Francis Fukuyama's Hegelian end of history story, development and change have been perceived as enmeshed with those human products that are both science and technology, but particularly technology, the application of science to human well-being. Although as Martins cautions, well-being is not always the conscious goal of these thinkers. Here, resonating with Bauman's *The Holocaust and Modern Social Theory*, Martins brings out the Faustian side of Third Reich philosophies of technology where power and domination take pre-eminence over any bland bourgeois notions of do-gooding and improvement.

Martins follows the Saint-Simonian vision of the supercession of the political by the technological ('from the government of men to the administration of things') and its reception in Marxist, socialist and anarchist traditions, through its Promethean shape in the conquest of nature under state socialism and in its mid-twentieth-century version, 'Bernalism'. Eventually this vision embodies itself in Haraway's Cyborg, a feminist Gnosticism where flesh is restructured via the prosthetic. Martins contrasts this with the Faustian vision of the domination of nature, the idea of 'technology as destiny', a *Weltanschauung* which culminates in Heidegger's political ontology.

Martins sees the implications of information technologies for civil society and the public sphere as raising questions for the libertarian and communitarian options in political philosophy and their possible technological correlates. Given the relative autonomy of technological development as a major constraint on the politics of modernity, modern technologies can be seen as generators of ignorance and deep uncertainty. These engulfing aleatoric events may lead to the replacement of Faustian or Promethean models of the domination of nature by a shift to stewardship models in environmental politics and 'the government of things'.

That new technologies do indeed have powerful implications for the societies which incorporate them, is discussed at length by Marilyn Strathern in her account of the new reproductive technologies. These pose interesting questions for the way people act on what they know. Technological intervention to assist conception, for instance, is also intervention in the modernist representation of kinship as the social or cultural construction of natural facts. What new knowledge does it embody?

Strathern sees two rather different consequences. First, these technologies are understood to supplement and thus *stand in* for other processes, exemplified by surrogacy arrangements which preserve some of the naturalism of unassisted birth while drawing on implantation techniques. Traditional relationships are thus held in place in the way both the technology (helping nature) and the surrogacy (divisions of maternal roles) are interpreted. The second point is that such novel technologies effect a radical displacement, substituting certain kinds of understanding for others. Most significant is technology's own rationale: it works in the way money buys, or genes express themselves.

She suggests that both modernist and postmodernist politics operate in parallel. The former appeals to certain relationships, such as that between nature and culture and derives justification from the claim to be strengthening the foundations (of for example the family); whereas the latter justifies itself through effectiveness, an effectiveness of image and technique upon the consumer–customer. The 'real worlds' of commercial transaction and of genetic identity are contiguous with a cultural postmodernism that presupposes that everything is accessible. While surrogate motherhood generates profound debate, the issue of genetic identity is presented as self-evident. However, Strathern concludes, there is a sense in which no interpretation is required to make evident the meaning genes have for personal identity and no relationships between persons seem necessary to their effectiveness. Genes come 'already interpreted'.

Central to these discussions on technology and the emerging world of postmodern patterning in which human agents must engage, has been the issue of ethical procedures and the attainment of the good, as Martins and Strathern both emphasise. Roy Boyne's chapter attempts to place the character of ethics in a postmodernist framework. Drawing initially on Lyotard, especially *Le Différend*, Boyne seeks to present the problem of the presentation of the unpresentable, the sublime as a window through which the possibility of postmodernist ethics might be glimpsed. That is, for Boyne the siting of

Lyotard's groundless subjectivity may be found through the work of art and its construction. After an excursus into Kant, Boyne concludes by suggesting a reformulation of the categorical imperative within a postmodern frame.

9 Technology, modernity, politics

Herminio Martins

In an extraordinarily influential article the historian of medieval science and technology Lynn White (1967) attributed to Christianity, specifically Latin Western Christianity, the basic legitimation for the technological drive of the West towards the 'domination of nature'. The very considerable scholarly literature triggered by this article has shown that White's provocative blanket indictment of the alleged biblical sanctions for the technological domination of outer nature was too sweeping. Within Western Christianity various strong theological traditions warrant a wide variety of attitudes towards the exploitation of natural resources and the limits of anthropocentric considerations in the appropriation of non-human forms of life. Even whilst using the idiom of 'domination of nature', traditions of stewardship and co-operation with nature have been quite persistent and sustained by good theological authorities. Christian teachings have been and continue to be many-stranded in their theological prescriptions on nature, technology, animals, biomedical ethics, etc.[1]

By contrast, references to the 'domination of nature' in sociological literature have generally been rather undifferentiated and the underlying attitudes are widely called, quite interchangeably, Promethean *or* Faustian (the influence of the Frankfurt School has been quite significant in bringing about this conflation). This chapter argues that invocations of the 'domination', 'mastery' or 'conquest' of nature in nineteenth- and twentieth-century social thought have by no means carried invariably the same implications. It attempts to bring out the sharp differences between two ideal-typical traditions, the Promethean (particularly marked in the wake of the French Revolution) and the Faustian (culminating in the work of the single most influential contemporary philosopher of technology, Heidegger). Both traditions of thought on the domination of nature display internal variants which can only be dealt with rather cursorily in a short paper. Briefly, the Promethean tradition links the technological domination of nature to human purposes and above all to human welfare, to the emancipation of the entire

150

species and particularly of the 'most numerous and poorest classes' (in the Saint-Simonian formulation). The Faustian tradition seeks to unmask Promethean claims and either embraces or seeks to overcome (with no clear and unequivocal solution) technological nihilism, the condition whereby technology serves no human purpose beyond its own expression.

The French Positivists, leading exponents of a Promethean view of technology, depart from Rousseau's theodicy.[2] The most radical teaching of Rousseau, according to Cassirer (1963 [1954]), was the doctrine that human ills arise in and from society: this theodicy ignores natural evil (as shown by Rousseau's response to the great Lisbon earthquake) and concentrates on evil which can and must be rectified by social and indeed political action. This over-socialised theodicy was regarded by many thinkers in the wake of the French Revolution as having provided a powerful stimulus to revolutionary and totalistic politics and is perhaps at the root of the 'longing for total revolution' which pervades post-Kantian German Idealism (Yack, 1992 [1986]). Saint-Simon and his followers acknowledged the force of Rousseau's moral teaching yet wanted to obviate the strife and violence of insurrectionary and revolutionary politics. Technology was, in their view, the great instrument for the rapid and comprehensive amelioration of the human condition, particularly of the 'most numerous and poorest class'. A scientific-industrial society would enable the structures of human oppression diagnosed in Rousseau's theodicy to be overcome and to yield to a domination-free condition of society and history ('from the government of persons to the administration of things', a Saint-Simonian formula endorsed by many non-Positivist thinkers, socialist and non-socialist). It cannot be too strongly emphasised that for Saint-Simon and the much-maligned French Positivist tradition 'the only useful kind of human action exerted by humans is that exerted over things. The action of human beings on other human beings is always, in itself, harmful to the species, owing to the double destruction which it entails; it only becomes useful in so far as it is secondary and it helps bring about a greater action over nature' (Saint-Simon, cited in Jouvenel, 1976: 179).

Technical civilisation as post-history

Curiously enough, the fullest and most sophisticated theorisation of the end of politics (in any strong sense of the term) with and through the prevalence of the administration of things is not to be found in the nineteenth-century socialist and anarchist treatises and tracts that advocated, celebrated and prophesied such an outcome for societal evolution. Such a theorisation, albeit in scattered texts, emerges in the work on the critical and substantive philosophy of history by Antoine-Augustin Cournot (1801–77). The recent notoriety of the semi-Hegelian theme of the end of history (Fukuyama, 1992) revived in the wake of the collapse of state socialism has drawn attention once again in the English-speaking world to his social and historical thought (Anderson, 1992). The locutions 'post-history' and 'post-historic' were actually coined independently by French commentators on his work early this century (Bouglé, 1905) and by American (Seidenberg, 1950) scholars in the last four decades mostly in connection with an invocation of his theory of history and especially of its bearing on the future of advanced industrial societies. In a debate on the theme of industrialisation and technocracy in 1949, Georges Friedmann claimed for Cournot the title of *the* or at least *a* prophet of technical civilisation (Friedmann, 1966). At any rate, Cournot was the most systematic of the nineteenth-century thinkers who argued for the likelihood or even the inevitability of what were later to be called the end of ideology, the end of utopia, the end of politics or the end of history, where 'end' does not necessarily mean extinction or termination but can be variously construed as exhaustion, completion, fulfilment or consummation, as in Hegel.[3]

Cournot's general philosophical account of human history and society may be seen as partly governed by a cluster of binary oppositions: chance and necessity central to his natural philosophy as a whole and to his account of scientific induction and probability by which he is best known to philosophical readers, reason and instinct, the passions and the interests. His concept of objective chance was doubtless his single most influential contribution to French philosophy and represented a major instance of the great series of attempts throughout the history of nineteenth-century French thought to limit and circumscribe the scope and stringency of scientific and metaphysical determinism. In this endeavour positive theorisations – whether in the philosophy of nature, the philosophy of organic life or the philosophy of mind – of contingency, chance, probability, indeterminacy, natural spontaneity and creativity and of course libertarian free will or minimally a compatibilist stance with soft determinism emerged within the mainstream rationalist outlook shared by Cournot as well, less surprisingly, in the strictures of its critics. This persistent anti-Laplacean and indeed to some extent anti-Cartesian theme in French philosophy runs through the philosophical concerns of a number of socialist thinkers, most notably Renouvier who argued more vigorously than most that ethical socialism of which he was perhaps the leading exponent in France is incompatible with the historical determinism found in Saint-Simon and in scientific socialism as well as with every other form of necessitarianism. This anti-Laplacean strain can be detected even in strictly scientific work not least in the pioneering contributions on deterministic chaos in mathematical physics by Poincaré, which opened up an area of inquiry (nonlinear dynamics) which has enjoyed a tremendous vogue of late.

By 'chance' Cournot means the unforeseeable occurrences which come about as the result of the intersection or coincidence of two or more previously independent causal series; unforeseeability even in principle, although important for us in setting limits for human knowledge and control, is not of the essence of the matter for Cournot argues that even for a superior intelligence such occurrences would remain fortuitous: chance thus is not the product of our ignorance. Such fortuitous occurrences could be unique historical events, whether in cosmogony or human affairs, but statistical regularities can emerge under some descriptions (which capture the non-unique features of otherwise unique events) and social constancies in behavioural rates can be fairly reliable. Causal necessity – or rather the intersection of severally necessary, heretofore independent causal series – generates chance and conversely chance under certain circumstances of fungibility generates statistical regularities or macro-phenomena, although chance can also, of course, beget chance.

Anticipating the linguistic turn in twentieth-century analytical philosophy of history Cournot sees the three great time-phases of human collective existence – triadic stadial schemes were irresistible then as now – as calling for different kinds of discourse. The first or what he calls the 'ethnological' phase is characterised in substantive terms by the preponderance of instinct over reason, of the unreflective over the deliberate and planful: this might be called the socio-biological phase by contrast to the post-historic which might be called socio-mechanical. In the main, massive routines of instinct, habit and custom obtain, punctuated by natural or human calamities. The most fitting form of discourse to record collective experience in this phase would be annals or chronicles.

The second phase or history proper involves a growth of rationality in thought and action, an admixture of passions and interests among the spring of action with sufficient scope and opportunities for 'event-making' (Hook, 1955 [1943]) historical figures, world-historical deeds and master-works, 'colossal' (Cournot's own term) events of which the French Revolution and its aftermath represented for him and perhaps for most of his coevals, almost the paradigm case. Hence the most tempting genre for historiography is narrative, for deeds and works may be seen as strings of historical accidents necessarily datable and essentially bound to proper names. However, Cournot does not, like some contemporary analytical or hermeneutic philosophers of history, advocate pure narrative as the sole or privileged mode of historiographic discourse (for all epochs and cultures, as the question of differential genres for different modes of historicality is infrequently raised) although he repeatedly evokes the 'great dramas' of the *historic* phase. Certainly for Cournot the second or historic phase of human societies is the 'narratable' phase *par excellence*. However, precisely because the historic phase entails a mix of chance and necessity, of scientific law and accident even great figures and great deeds are neither self-intelligible nor wholly beyond rational explanation but have to be situated in terms of underlying impersonal forces and longer-run processes. Accordingly, pure narrative is not adequate for a satisfactory historiographic account whilst a nomological, covering law type of explanation subsuming historic events or other *explananda* under the laws of the theoretical social sciences (chiefly economics) would run up against the epistemological obstacle of historical accidents without which indeed there would be no history proper, human or otherwise. Cournot might well have concurred with Gallie's thesis: no story, no history (Gallie, 1964). Only a mix of narrative and analysis can do justice to the dual character of the 'historic' mode of existence since system and accident, chance and necessity, the nomological and the aleatory belong together in this sphere. What he called 'historical etiology' searches for deeper causes than the discrete datable events, sheer accidents and proper names of narrative, and may bring out the 'solidary' character of superficially independent causal series, revealing the hidden necessity of apparently chance events. Chance *per se*, however, is ineliminable, not because of the limitations of our knowledge of initial and boundary conditions which could be overcome by us or at least by a Laplacean Demon but owing rather to the nature of things.

The third, terminal phase of this historico-philosophical scheme later to be called the 'post-historic' is, strictly speaking, for Cournot a condition or ideal limit which may be approached ever more closely without actually reaching it at any time. In this phase the great collective passions (religious, political, national) conducive to memorable, narratable deeds but also to ferocious zero-sum and negative-sum games yield more and more to the peaceable play of economic interest and *le doux commerce*: the contrast between the passions and the interests is set forth very much in an eighteenth-century way (Hirschman, 1977) but Cournot specifically refers to *political* passions and what he called 'political faiths' in the wake of the French Revolution as liable to mitigation and erosion in an increasingly commercial society. A historical society in which religious or political passions thrive is likely to be one marked by the resort to violence by religious denominations, parties and social movements and in which the drive to international war may well be salient: contemporaries of Cournot theorised Absolute War (Clausewitz) and the Absolute Terror (Hegel and others). The radically agonistic character of such societies and the uncertainties of battles and wars fought by passionate contenders afford much of the dramatic interest of traditional narrative historiography and of the historic mode of existence. It should be added that for Cournot the post-historic phase presents itself in the typical form of gazettes and statistical bulletins, the end of history being also the 'end' of historical narrative and 'narratability'.

A post-historic society is one geared to the conquest of nature through the strenuous pursuit of scientific discovery, technical invention and innovation, and economic growth. Like the Saint-Simonians and Comte, Cournot envisaged future technical advance as substantially dependent on prior scientific progress and Cournot's quite elaborate classification of the sciences precedes and grounds his classification of the technologies. Cournot appears to subscribe beforehand to something like the twentieth-century theses of the routinisation of economic innovation (Schumpeter, 1943) and of the invention of the method(s) of scientific-technical invention (Whitehead, 1925) without betraying any significant concern over possible intrinsic limits of scientific progress, which might bar further fundamental technological advance. More accurately, he *does* recognise and indeed insists on one quite fundamental epistemic barrier or *ignorabimus* of considerable relevance for the history of technological Prometheanism: organic life will never be understood in as fundamental a way – at least as far as scientific cognition is concerned – as the physical or the human worlds, both of which are susceptible to indefinite mechanisation in a way that organic life would never be.[4] The striking refutation of this limitative thesis by the recent advances of genetics and molecular biology and the flood of ever more widely applied and ever more potent biotechnologies implementing them conjures up a spectre of universal planetary mechanisation which he never entertained. For in his scheme of thought whilst the physical and the human worlds may be mechanisable (and the principle of the mechanisability of the human world underlies his construct of the post-historic civilisation) the world of living nature would remain, by and large, gloriously recalcitrant to mechanisation, though not, of course, immune to human depredations such as deforestation. Despite this allegedly intractable limitation on our knowledge and power he believed that our growing knowledge of inanimate nature and of such features of organic nature as may be scientifically accessible to us sufficed for *indefinite* but not infinite technical perfectibility and material progress.

Technological Prometheans such as Cournot whose outlook was formed in the first half of the nineteenth century, were thus not necessarily committed as widespread current stereotypes would have led us to believe either to the ideal of total scientific knowledge, as in the Laplacean vision or to a project of the universal technological domination of Nature. These self-restrictions may have stemmed in part simply from failures of scientific or utopian imagination but were also in any case deduced from explicit grand axioms of strict epistemic and hence technological limitation: such presuppositions concerning the limits of what can be known, of what can be done and what can be made have surely to be taken into account in order to properly appreciate the import of what the technological Prometheans meant by the 'conquest of nature'.

In his last book Cournot labelled his metaphysical outlook 'trans-rationalism': whilst maintaining his faith in reason and science he affirmed that a number of fundamental questions in natural philosophy (especially regarding the 'mysteries', as he called them, of the origin of life and biological evolution) were beyond the reach of scientific rationality and that our options in such matters should be guided by the 'instincts of the soul' (Cournot, 1875). This prophet of technical civilisation cannot be charged with scientific hubris (and the Positivist Littré concurred with 'trans-rationalism'). Such a civilisation, according to the theorist of post-history, would require religious faith and wise political elites. He was a 'trans-rationalist' also with regard to the possibility of providing a justification of sovereign political authority that could withstand rational criticism. In this context he maintained: 'it is the lot of human reason to betray its insufficiency precisely in dealing with the issues which most concern human destiny' (Cournot, 1861: 465).

Finite and infinite versions of the Promethean project

Exponents of the contemporary ecological consciousness, with their deep, even eschatological, sense of the imminent or already-transgressed natural or social limits to sustainable economic growth or even to a sustainable 'steady state' economy, typically assert or imply the wholesale bankruptcy of the Promethean project. However, not every significant historic version of the Promethean project at least from Bacon onwards was necessarily committed to an unqualified vision of limitless material progress, staking everything on an infinitely munificent, cornucopian technology, ignoring all pertinent limiting boundary conditions, side-constraints or collateral assumptions about human demography, energy regimes, the moral status of other animals, environmental quality or aesthetics, the nature and scale of anthropogenic change in the natural world and the fitting attitudes towards our planetary abode.

Among these collateral assumptions not the least important were those concerning the future size or growth rates of the human population that would not defeat the hope for progress and the optimal demographic regime for industrial societies. Issues about the 'mode of reproduction', about the problematical and fateful interactions between *homo faber* and *homo parens*, greatly exercised in one way or another most Prometheans, at any rate after Malthus – however critical they were of his specific formulations and overtones (their attempted solutions were usually tortured but they recognised this problem-complex as an especially daunting one). The great exceptions were, notoriously, Marx and Engels, who instead castigated such preoccupations as reactionary obscurantism and worse. This virulent anti-Malthusianism led them to rule out Malthus-type explanations even in animal population biology and thereby to underestimate the import of Darwinian evolutionary theory and the 'Darwinian world-view' as a whole. Even though Engels particularly could be quite sombre about the scale of long-lasting, possibly irreversible environmental degradation brought about by unwitting as well as deliberate human action, so much so that he has been enlisted by some admirers as an ecological prophet, he completely failed to forecast the full import of the demographic factors in the Great Climacteric. The strong prejudices in general Russian thought against Malthusian population theory and its implications were inherited by Russian Marxism which in the main manifested a strong pro-natalist bias, certainly into the 1950s, and an aversion to regarding demographic constraints as limitative, in local or global terms, in any but a provisional sense thereby contributing further to the exorbitation of the role of technology and by implication to the estimation of received natural ecosystems as expendable (Todes, 1989).

The 'infinitisation' of Technological Prometheanism which occurred in Russian Marxism becomes more understandable when seen against the background of the apocalyptic and chiliastic atmosphere in Russia in the first two decades of the century. It was in Russia also that one of the most radical versions of Christian Technological Prometheanism arose and can be seen in the writings of the Orthodox lay theologian or religious philosopher, Nicholas Fedorov (1828–1903). It is no exaggeration to say that his doctrine of the Common Task of humanity involves the 'most grand and the most radical utopia which is known in the history of human thought' (Berdyaev, 1947: 155). Like the Russian Marxists, Fedorov advocated the 'unity of theory and practice', the involvement of all in scientific and technical activity and the unity of humankind in a titanic techno-scientific mobilisation. The goals of this planetary mobilisation and 'consciousness-raising' ('the planet becomes conscious of self') are not simply the abolition of misery, disease, ignorance, war, oppression, exploitation but the restoration of life – the resurrection of all human dead. For, he argues, what is the point of changing life if you can't change death? This Common Task would involve eventually the humanising or spiritualising not just of the earth but of the cosmos. Thus science and technology become part-vehicles for the salvific history of the species and the cosmos. It should be noted, however, that Fedorov was also concerned about the despoliation of the environment through the misuse of technology and science and if he envisaged the engineering of other planets to receive human life (what is now called 'terra formation') it was not out of disregard for the potential environmental degradation brought about by industrialism. Whilst Fedorovian inspiration has been claimed for the great undertakings in geographical engineering in the USSR, disregard for environmental impacts was not a precept of the utopian.[5]

In fact 'finite' versions of the Promethean project were not rare or minor ones as can be demonstrated by considering, for example, Auguste Comte, the putative founder of 'technocratic positivism', as claimed by not unsympathetic commentators (Geiger, 1973). This is particularly significant because this outlook has been targeted by many contemporary critics of modernity as virtually the hegemonic ideology, or operational code of an environmentally reckless industrial society. Comte's famous formula 'savoir pour prévoir, prévoir pour pouvoir' ('to know in order to predict, to predict in order to be able to act') is still widely quoted as encapsulating this whole outlook. The Heideggerians' claim that 'technocractic positivism' is but one vehicle of what they call 'the Enframing' (now the most common translation of what the master called *Gestell*), a technologically enframed world being one in which everything becomes raw material, resources or standing reserves (e.g. Heim, 1987). Yet Comte and other French theorists of scientific civilisation of the same period did not naively extrapolate the recently magnified world-transforming powers of technology and of the market economy as conjointly sustainable at the same or enhanced pace over the long run, in an exponential or even merely linear fashion. If anything, the implicit overall model of technological macro-history in

Comte entails something like what we could anachronistically call a 'technological transition' by analogy with the twentieth-century concept of 'demographic transition': a very long period of slow technical advance is followed by the prodigious surge of technical inventions and innovations of the early scientific-industrial society which in turn should abate in a third and final phase with the consolidation of this social formation. For Comte envisages a 'positive' post-industrial world in which the promotion of techno-economic interests or the 'conquest of nature' would yield to the higher and nobler concerns of the self-transformation of the moral agents involving moral, *not* industrial perfectibility, action upon the self and not upon the outer world.

In any case, Comte did not expect continual technical revolutions in future. Such technical revolutions would, in his view, be doubly precluded. On the one hand, even with the future growth of scientific knowledge, technical advances would not necessarily follow, for developments in basic science could not generate technical advances without concomitant growth in descriptive and concrete sciences which was unlikely to take place (Ducassé, 1958 [1956]). On the other hand, Comte, as is well known, ruled out in principle continued breakthroughs in the sciences of the microscopic world, and indeed throughout the natural sciences. Curiously enough though he did venture the technological conjecture (Arbousse-Bastide, 1957) that tidal energy might provide a major source of power for industry, although as an early formulation of a 'soft energy path' for industrial civilisation this has, so far, turned out to be a bad technical guess within the spectrum of the environmentally benign, renewable energy paths. But Comte did not believe in the feasibility or desirability of the unlimited expansion of human material wants. His concern for novel complementary or alternative energy sources reflects the sense that the currently tapped sources of energy might not suffice to meet even a modest level of economic aspiration in the not too distant future (and, like Fourier, he did assume or at least hope for moderate population growth and alimentation largely consisting of liquids and gases!).

Comte, of course, did not entertain a modern concept of energy which emerges with the development of thermodynamics. The Second Law of Thermodynamics (or Entropy Law) provided not only cosmological frissons but also much concern over the prospects of technological civilisation.[6] The Energy Question already in the late nineteenth century defines a problem-complex mediating between the Social Question and the emerging 'Natural Question' (Moscovici, 1974) and instigated much rethinking of the nature and prospects of a socialist economy. 'Energy catastrophism' has been a recurrent position with energy as the key limiting factor in economic growth. Two positive utopian positions have polarised the field of energy speculation – tektopian utopianism and ecological utopianism. The term 'tektopian' was coined by a British thermodynamicist to designate an energy regime with a very high ratio of inanimate energy slaves to the human population, to which technical progress brings us ever closer (Ubbelohde, 1963 [1954]). Here we propose to radicalise the definition to match the grandeur of the techno-dreams involved. A tektopia in this modified sense is a utopian vision of an ideal energy regime with effectively infinite, cheap, reliable, safe energy sources which lack intractable, unwanted and unforeseen environmental side-effects, proximal or distal in space or over time; and which are fairly easily manageable in technical, administrative and political terms. The British radiochemist Frederick Soddy already in the early 1900s, had argued strenuously that the world was poised between tektopia (infinite energy supplies could be tapped from nuclear fission) and catastrophe (running out of fossil fuel resources to sustain, let alone develop, industrial civilisation in the not too distant future). The dichotomy cornucopia/catastrophe is endemic in this kind of speculation, as if the alternatives were mutually exclusive and exhaustive.[7]

A recrudescence of the tektopian imagination occurred, curiously enough, with Alexandre Kojève, whose celebrated lectures in the 1930s on Hegel's *Phenomenology of Spirit* with their emphasis on the theme of the 'end of history' are partly responsible (through intermediaries) for this current vogue (Fukuyama, 1992). Kojève, a senior civil servant of the European Community and political adviser to President de Gaulle, claimed in a paper published in 1964 that the industrial utilisation of nuclear power – which was still in its early days at the time – ushered in the 'end of history' (Kojève, 1964). The latest version of tektopianism is the notorious techno-dream of 'cold fusion', which has been pursued to the tune of billions of dollars. The counter-utopia to tektopianism, ecological utopianism, often dismissed as 'primitive', also belongs to the story of Promethean humanism and not simply to that of the wholesale rejection of scientific rationality and technological purposiveness (Martinez-Alier, 1990 [1987]). Comte's own conception of the positive-industrial society, certainly, is not at all a tektopian one.

It should be apparent that no precise match obtains between these three phases of technological macro-history which we have reconstructed from Comte's teaching and those of his kernel Law of the Three States which governs the master succession of systems of generalised cognitive orientations through human history (though in the sociological system of Positivism various kinds of social institutions were correlated with this law). This incongruence is perhaps not surprising in a perspective where cognitive systems rather than material practices co-determine long-run social dynamics. However, even in classical Marxian historical materialism where technological advance appears to enjoy the overall status of a prime mover, no precise match obtains, oddly enough, between the pivotal junctures of technological history and the key world-historical transitions from mode of production to mode of production nor with any specificity in the *prospective* breakthrough from capitalism to socialism. In classical Marxism and through Leninism a completely open technological horizon of illimitable growth of the productive forces supposedly capable of overcoming every natural obstacle and scarcity and also by implication the ravages and secondary scarcities wrought inadvertently or otherwise by their own workings, furnished perhaps the central message, the kerygma of its variant of Western redemptive activism. What was unique in the Marxist synthesis was the conjoining of the 'technological sublime', the exaltation of mighty technical deeds and works and the apotheosis of inevitable technical progress, and of the 'political sublime', the exaltation of the terrible beauty of total revolution. A critical ambiguity of Marxism stems from its emphasis on the relentlessness of global technical advance and the very long-term thrust of 'technological orthogenesis' (Meyer, 1950) coupled with the categorical rejection of any notion of the autonomy of technology (though Adorno did argue for the increasing importance of 'technological fetishism' as against 'commodity fetishism' in advanced industrial capitalism). It cannot be too strongly emphasised that for other Prometheans technological progress provided the *alternative* to the totalistic revolutionary politics legitimated through Rousseau's oversocialised theodicy, though they might all subscribe to the Saint-Simonian directional formula 'from the government of persons to the administration of things' and regarded industrial society as essentially peaceable.

Turning to the utopian socialists we find in the major work of the most active disciple of Fourier, Victor Considérant (a military engineer by training like many of the followers of Saint-Simon or Comte) a *visionary* model of civilisations as following a two-phase rhythm in which the first phase, of technological ascent, is normally followed – if the life-course of the civilisation is not arrested – by one predominantly characterised by a burgeoning of 'social inventions' (an expression he used with deliberateness) and the arts of association (phalansteries and the like!) (Considérant, 1835). This could be seen as an early version of what the French philosopher of technology Louis Weber later called a 'law of two states', involving a recurrent alternation and not a unique linear sequence unlike the famous Law of the Three States, in which an epoch of sustained technological progress is followed by one in which the perfecting of the arts of living (on the basis of the technical achievements of the previous epoch) takes over as the leading priority.[8] Considérant believed that the epochal shift to co-operative, humane, aesthetic and other supra-technological concerns of the second phase of our civilisation was imminent.[9]

It is very misleading to assert or to imply that either generic Prometheanism or 'technocratic positivism' entails a utilitarian ethic (in the sense of universalistic ethical *hedonism*). Let us consider first the alleged 'technocratic positivists'. The provision of ever-higher standards of material want satisfaction for ever larger numbers, flowing from an ever-dynamic, expansive, planetary techno-economy, whilst integral to the normative images of the future entertained by Saint-Simon and those Saint-Simonians who were closest to a utilitarian moral philosophy and to the political economy of liberal capitalism, is not at all a desideratum for the Comtean scenario for the next and last stage or 'definitive equilibrium' of scientific-industrial society. In any case the expansion of material welfare is not construed by Comte as self-justifying but rather almost solely prized as a precondition, a support and an agency for the fostering of what is of the utmost importance in the positive-industrial type of society, altruistic love or love of Humanity as a whole: 'love as its principle, order for its basis, and progress for its end' (rather misleadingly reduced to just 'order and progress' in most citations). Far from advocating the 'colonisation of the life-world' in scientific-industrial society Comte wanted to put an end to the 'long insurrection of the mind against the heart'. He anticipated recent advocacy of the 'disestablishment of science' (Bronowski, 1971), the extrication of scientific pursuits from the circuits of power and wealth. Whilst he was increasingly distrustful of professional engineers and scientists, he discerned an elective affinity between Positivism and the urban proletariat as well as women, both largely neglected by the educational and scientific establishments. As we have noted he did not expect either scientific or technical revolutions to go on indefinitely. For all these reasons, he may be seen as the founder of *anti-technocratic* Positivism, startling as this claim may seem in the light of current clichés. But it is certainly the case that neither branch of classical Positivism, whether technocratic or anti-technocratic, valued political or intellectual liberty highly or discerned the importance that parliamentary government was assuming and would continue to enjoy as a political paradigm for Western and westernising societies. With the advantage of writing in

1875, Cournot could assert that the 'reign of industry is the reign of democracy'.

Other Prometheans like Proudhon and Renouvier prized above all justice *and* freedom: it would be difficult to find two thinkers as intoxicated with these values as they and as committed to their autonomy. Renouvier, especially, asserted what would now be called the 'lexical' priority of liberty with the utmost emphasis (he had learned from the disasters of 1848), and elaborated a rational ethic whose regulative ideal is the Kantian Republic of Ends, the realm of the maximal compossible flourishing of persons, to which goal the provision of material welfare through technical progress and distributive measures of justice-seeking and solidarity-affirming social policy affords only necessary aids (or the 'hindering of hindrances' to such flourishing). Proudhon, who regarded machines as 'emissions of the spirit', believed that industrial society, whether capitalist or run by labour-managed enterprises, would generate ever more and ever better machines. Yet he also affirmed that an ever-more mechanised economy would not bring about continuously rising levels of material well-being as a result of the perverse effect which he called the 'law of poverty'. One of the examples he gave of the operation of the 'law of poverty' is still apposite as a parable of everyday life in the technological society: he forecast that increasing speeds in the means of transport would fail to shorten the median time taken by the journey to work in great cities (Proudhon 1867 [1861]: vol. I, t.II, 126–44). Similarly, he believed that work would go on becoming more intense and demanding in an increasingly mechanised world. None of these Prometheans, except some of the Saint-Simonians, endorsed a cornucopian technology scenario and even less a chrematistic economy geared to the unremitting commercialisation or commodification of all life.[10]

The Faustian image of technology

The first comprehensive articulation of a Faustian view of technology and science, at any rate within an account of world history, was that of Spengler in the two volumes of his major work, *The Decline of the West*, the first volume of which appeared late in 1918 to coincide (unintentionally) with the sudden and totally unexpected military and industrial collapse of Germany. It had an immediate and extraordinary impact and whilst it attracted a good deal of controversy – it was attacked by such diverse and significant figures as Max Weber (who engaged in a public debate with Spengler) and Otto Neurath – some commentators have discovered a 'capitulation to Spenglerism' even within the scientific community (Forman, 1971). The book was evaluated in the English-speaking world largely as one of the most bizarre exhibits in the intellectual chamber of horrors called the speculative or metaphysical philosophy of history. Yet its influence in its country of origin was not so much due to its academic pretensions in 'totalising' world-history as in its reading of the signs of the times, in purporting to decipher the riddle of the future, in providing (in the analogy with clinical medicine offered in it) both a diagnosis of the times and a prognosis for the West and the world at a juncture of grave crisis. What is of principal interest here is that the work sets forth an image of technology and science which became, in one version or another, virtually hegemonic in Germany during the Weimar Republic and in the Third Reich.

Other visionaries of technology, such as Ernst Jünger, who claimed to speak for the 'front generation' as one of the most decorated soldiers in the German army in World War One, had a significant impact not least on Heidegger who came to present, like some other thinkers, a more philosophically sophisticated variant of the Faustian image of technology.[11] The variants put forward by academic philosophers still bear a family resemblance to Spengler's, and while often free of his overtly racist discourse continue to share his cultural relativism and militant nationalism.

One of the most general claims of the Faustian image concerns the conceptual or ontological dependence of science on technology. Science, or rather modern natural science, may appear detached from pragmatic involvements or technically barren for long periods of time. While in logical empiricism or critical rationalism the tests of scientificity overlap with the requirements of technical relevance, the Faustian claim is that science always subserves a 'technological *a priori*', as the Left Heideggerian Marcuse put it. Consider the thesis of the logical symmetry of scientific explanation and prediction: although argued for on strictly epistemological grounds it also vindicates the technological import of science. The emphasis on predictive success as against retrodictive substantiation vindicates technological import if only as a by-product of methodological requirements. The Faustian theorists, however, *start* from the hidden technological agenda of science and do not regard the technological fertility of science as a by-product of prior, independently characterisable epistemological virtues or methodological merits. Whilst the Faustian theorists did not work out detailed accounts of the epistemic roles of instrumentation and experimentation in natural science their strong emphasis on the material embodiment of scientific methods and procedures ('the violent examination of nature in order to dominate it') contrasts sharply with the neglect of such issues in specialist work in the epistemology and methodology of science during that period. Rather, the Faustians would claim that the mode of apperception of modern science is such as to view natural entities and processes solely and exclusively from the standpoint of their accessibility to experimental manipulation and practical control. Thus, scientific procedures and schemes presuppose a technical orientation even when they do not lead to actual physical experiments or to successful practical applications for long periods of historical time.

The technological character of science has also been very sharply asserted by some scholars in the logical empiricist movement. Thus Philipp Frank, a physicist and philosopher of science, a one-time collaborator and biographer of Einstein, wrote in 1954:

in modern science, a theory is regarded as an instrument that serves toward some definite purpose. It has to be helpful in predicting future observable facts on the basis of facts that have been observed in the past and the present. It should also be helpful in the construction of machines and devices that can save us time and labor. A scientific theory is, in a sense, a tool that produces other tools according to a practical scheme . . . the building of a scientific theory is not essentially different from the building of an airplane. (Frank, 1961 [1954]: 22–3)[12]

Closely related to the claim about the priority of technology in relation to science – *ontological* if not always historical (Ihde, 1983) – is the epistemological thesis that scientific procedures do not aim at truth (verisimilitude) or at a grasp of the inner nature (causal powers) of things but solely at the fullest comprehension of phenomena strictly for the purposes of prediction and control of the phenomenal world. The Faustians differ from the Positivist Prometheans inasmuch as they do not rule out, as a matter of principle, other kinds of claims to knowledge of the inner nature of reality; indeed they often insist on the legitimacy, autonomy and even the superiority of other forms of knowledge and understanding of human, supersensory or absolute reality. It is to the non-scientific, even non-rational, modes of knowledge, relations to being, or forms of ontological disclosure that Faustian theorists appealed to overcome the predicaments of technological modernity – though often they embraced, rather than attempted to transcend, technological nihilism.

This approach implies that modern technology and modern science are not just the latest and finest chapters in the global cognitive history of the species and the overall progress of the human mind, as the French Positivists and many exponents of the idea of progress vehemently affirmed. Rather for the Faustian theorists modern technology and modern exact science do not simply build on earlier achievements but involve a radical break with earlier science and technics. In some ways this claim anticipates recent fashionable theses concerning the incommensurability of successive cognitive paradigms or categorial frameworks and radical meaning-variance in the key terms in the history of the natural sciences. Spengler's historicisation of mathematics[13] exemplifies this stress on conceptual, intuitional and categorial discontinuities even in the area of thought where Platonism has commanded most support in our own time.

Recent analyses of the supposed radical discontinuities or 'paradigm-shifts' within the history of the exact sciences argue that the incommensurability of successive paradigms (and hence the impossibility of scientific progress through the accumulation of knowledge) does not preclude – though it certainly does not ensure – their comparability. Similarly, Spengler argued that the incommensurability of cultures did not preclude their comparability and in his 'Wagnerian prose-poem' (as his masterwork was described by some critics) some procedures of cross-cultural comparison were advanced (analogy, homology, parallelism, synchronicity, etc. are among the formal categories of his 'cultural morphology'). It should be added that Spengler saw deep differences between *nations* within the same culture and endorsed, indeed radicalised, Duhem's sharp contrast between the national styles of French and 'English' physics (though the 'English' physicists most attacked were Scots like Clerk Maxwell). It should be added parenthetically that Duhem's book on physical theory had a better reception in the German-speaking world than in France and even Max Weber commented favourably on the thesis of the existence of national styles in the exact sciences advanced therein. Spengler generalised and radicalised the idea of national styles in physical theory (actually, in Duhem's view different epistemological and methodological inclinations). This notion had flourished in the higher propaganda of World War One with attacks, for example, by French and German physicists and chemists on the other country's national style of scientific work (indeed Duhem published a vitriolic attack on 'German science' during the war). Spengler's epistemological relativism was certainly multifaceted.

For Spengler, the relevant historical individual is Western or Faustian Culture, which emerges around AD 900 and involves a major breach of continuity with earlier phases of systematic thought, mathematics, metaphysics, technics (including drastic changes in the intuitions of time, space, number, etc.). The import of this thesis can only be appreciated if we realise that this 'morphology of culture' was one of the expressions of the major asymmetrical dichotomy between 'culture' and 'civilisation' which pervaded German thought for several decades and which set the terms of reference for the major discussions in the philosophy of technology during the Weimar period (Herf, 1984).[14] This set of terms constituted not so much a pair of contrasting analytical categories as polar expressive symbols: 'culture' stood for ultimate values or attitudes constitutive of a national, ethnic or other particularist identity whilst 'civilisation' stood for those instrumental values which can be shared across cultural boundaries which therefore seemed to belong to a lower order of being and meaning.[15] The Faustians tied modern technology, which seemed to most of the German academic mandarins (Ringer, 1969) or '*Weltanschauung* professors' to belong exclusively to the realm of civilisation, to *cultural* presuppositions which did not grow out of earlier technics or other cultures but involved a sharp reorientation whereby modern technical culture was endowed with a new and distinctive spirit. Similarly Scheler (1970 [1915]) asked: Why is it that the classical Greeks did not develop even the germ of a systematic, rational technology given their superlative mathematical achievements and intellectual genius? The most common answers to this once often asked question were that they lacked some vital cultural resource or alternatively that structural socio-economic obstacles (the institution of slavery being the one most often invoked) prevented them from pursuing the path of technical advance. Crudely, Scheler's answer was that the Greeks did not do so because they were not interested in doing so. He models this answer quite explicitly on the theory of art history of Alois Riegl and its key concept of the 'artistic intention', 'artistic will' or 'will to form' (*Kunstwollen*) which Riegl deploys to account for the sharply contrasted figurative styles of the Egyptians and classical Greeks: it was not that Egyptian artists lacked skills and artistic maturity, or operated at a lower level of cognitive development, quite simply they had different goals. There is in this approach an aestheticisa-tion of technology: technical cultures or styles differ not primarily in terms of their devices, skills and capacities (and other varieties of 'tacit knowledge') but in terms of their underlying overall root-intention or the technological counterpart of the *Kunstwollen*. Riegl in fact had wanted both to stress the discontinuity of artistic intentions across cultures and periods *and* also to preserve some sense of linear develop-ment in art history without managing to combine the two in a coherent or even particularly impressive conceptual scheme or historiographic practice; it was the striking emphasis on shifts in root-intentions that was the most fertile stimulus outside his own field.

A corollary of this view on which Spengler placed much more emphasis than any of the other exponents of the Faustian image of technology is that modern Western technical culture was essentially

non-transferable and whereas gadgets, machines and weapons, factories
and laboratories could be adopted or even produced by non-Western
cultures, the technological drive to world mastery of modern Western
culture would inevitably be relinquished. Spengler made an important
advance in preparing the legitimation of technology and science-as-
technology which was amplified by the engineer-philosophers of Weimar
Germany, who sought to emphasise the cultural (non-instrumental,
ethnonational) in contradistinction to the civilisational (instrumental,
calculative, transferable, universalistic) facets of technology (Herf,
1984). In this perspective technology does not stem primarily from a
prior cognitive rationality ('sovereign reason') but can be seen as
manifesting the basic values ('sovereign will') of a culture (this may be
called an *expressivist* theory of technology).[16] By attributing to modern
technology a distinctive spirit or ethos wholly alien to that of all other
technical cultures – the drive towards world mastery, the appropriation
of all nature, or planetary domination – the Faustian theorists also
rejected standard utilitarian accounts and justifications. Nothing is more
striking than the animus evinced by the Faustian theorists against the
'vulgar' belief that the purpose or at any rate the major function of
technology is to relieve the wretched material lot of the greatest number.
Such a conception was anathema to them for it trivialised and obfus-
cated the inner meaning and drive of modern Western technology.
Heidegger, in a famous passage, characterised Americanism and Bol-
shevism as 'metaphysically identical' because they professed both to
develop technology to the full and to make it into a vehicle for the
satisfaction of the wants of the many. In particular, he never appears at
any time in his long career to have regarded the condition or cultures of
non-Western peoples as worthy of any significant philosophical interest
– except perhaps Japan – and as to the Western masses their vocation
was 'followership'.

Many Faustian writers claimed that mass production, under both
American democratic capitalism and Soviet state socialism, typically
produced goods lacking in aesthetic value whilst 'true' industrial technology had much in common with traditional handicrafts, and this claim
was often reiterated by the engineer philosophers seeking to legitimate
industrial technology in the Weimar period. As a result of the late
accelerated industrialisation of Germany, artisanal production was more
rapidly overtaken by large-scale technically advanced industry than in
any other major country. Both in Germany and elsewhere there were
also Left variants of the ideal of an industrial aesthetic: some argued that
modern industry made possible the mass production of aesthetically
satisfying goods instead of the craft production of luxury goods for the

few. Others envisaged the labour process and the means of production, i.e. machines and factories, becoming more aesthetically significant (Sorel, 1901).[17]

The Faustian image of modern technology was always and necessarily an 'infinist' one. For according to this image what is at the root of modern technology is will, the 'will to power' which in the last analysis is nothing but the 'will to will'. So in sharp contrast to Promethean theories of technology there can be no question of a principle of 'sufficiency', an inner or built-in resistance to its dynamism, for no definite state of affairs can count as final satisfaction for the will to power. The climate of opinion at the time of Germany's defeat in World War One favoured Faustian analyses: in 1919 the Austrian economist and social theorist Schumpeter argued that imperialism in the strict sense should not be equated with mere territorial expansion or appetite for booty but rather with the objectless drive for mastery without end (Schumpeter, 1950). However, this strong concept of imperialism was construed by him as non-capitalist and pre-modern, and in its contemporary manifestations, atavistic, whilst for the Faustian theorists, modern technology is Faustian in sharp contrast to non-modern technical cultures. For example, in Scheler there is an elective affinity between Faustian technology – the drive towards unlimited appropriation of nature – and capitalism – the drive towards unlimited capital accumulation.

In one way or another, Faustian theories of technology regard technology as destiny. In place of the Promethean vision of the rationality of science, technology and material progress inherited by classical Marxism with its faith in the rationality of history, the Faustians affirm not so much a necessitarian as, so to speak, a destinarian view of technology and history. In their rhetoric of 'fate' and 'destiny' they stand in sharp opposition not only to any belief in the intelligibility of history as a law-governed process or as a vehicle of dialectical logic but also to any libertarian view of the neutrality or the purely instrumental character of technology. Certainly, it was the theorisation of technology that was most affected by this widely shared destinarian discourse. However, according to the 'Forman thesis', Heisenberg's 1927 Uncertainty Principle reflected this general climate of thought in which claims of natural necessity were uncongenial and the vindication of physical *science* best effected through the vocabulary of acausality (Forman, 1971). A weak version of this thesis would be more credible, viz. that in the general intellectual climate of Weimar Germany the public image of hard science benefited from the presentation of the radical indeterminism of quantum mechanics which arose through its internal dynamics as a cognitive enterprise.[18] That a key principle in the most advanced sector of physical science appeared to be in sympathy with the anti-causal prepossessions of the intellectual environment was certainly a bonus for a beleaguered scientific community.

One feature worth noting in the light of the recent wave of sweeping attacks on the Enlightenment as the *fons et origo* of the catastrophic onslaught on the Aristotelian–Thomist moral–civic outlook and ensuing ruination of our moral world, is that despite their deep loathing of the Enlightenment most Faustians took a much broader retrospective time-horizon in their putative historico-philosophical genealogy of our current technological predicaments. For Spengler, as already noted, the Faustian culture in which we are fated to dwell until its inexorable death goes back to the tenth century AD. In Heidegger's 'history of being', modern technology is grounded in a long-lived 'Western metaphysics' which insofar as we can speak of a *terminus a quo* may be traced to Plato and Aristotle. Western metaphysics has been from its inception a 'productionist metaphysics' in which root metaphors of making and producing saturate ontic discourse – thus the Platonic *eidos*, the super-empirical pattern, projects craft production on to the relation between being and entities (Zimmerman, 1990). For Heidegger, and quite a number of thinkers who however much they dissent from major features of his thought endorse this characterisation, Western productionist metaphysics has endured into our times and in a sense today's all-conquering technology is the consummation or completion of this metaphysics: 'the essence of technology is nothing technological'.

The Faustian theorists of technology were mostly deeply antipathetic to liberal and democratic values and institutions either in general terms or in their German manifestations (Scheler is again a partial exception). But, more importantly, their conception of technology implied that the true vocation of modern technology could only be fulfilled in societies that rejected Western liberal, democratic, universalistic, egalitarian values. The image of technology-as-culture so strenuously propagated by the engineer-philosophers anxious to legitimate technology with the politico-cultural Right implied an elective affinity between modern technology and authoritarian rule, as well as between modern technology and a social order organised round the principles of hierarchy, authority and discipline. For technology to fulfil its destiny it must fulfil 'authentic' national concerns – of the German community which stood for, as well as against, the West. Heidegger, notoriously, could never make sense of the technological success of the democratic West in and after World War Two.

In the 1940s with their increasing historical and cultural pessimism,

Adorno and Horkheimer moved towards something like a left-wing version of the Faustian view of technology. They traced the 'dialectic of the Enlightenment' beyond the Enlightenment to the ancient Greeks, if not to classical Greek metaphysics, rather than to the historically specific features of the modern world. Whilst their ethical stance is wholly at variance with that of the standard Weimar Faustians they conflated the Promethean image of technology which they inherited from classical Marxism with the Faustian image of technology which they received from Heidegger and other kindred thinkers. For them 'the domination of Nature' was now uniquely identified with the will to will, the drive towards unlimited appropriation of outer and inner nature. Accordingly they equated generic 'positivism' with its crudest technocratic variant – not only a disputable exegesis but a lamentable failure to render justice to the more temperate versions of the Promethean tradition. Whilst their specific analyses of the implications of modern technology especially in the area of the 'culture industry' could be illuminating, their overall view of technology as a project of illimitable domination of nature simply echoed Faustian accounts and lacked a fundamental critical re-working of the Faustian tradition. Despite a critique of the 'jargon of authenticity' they did not scrutinise the Faustian theories of technology with the same intellectual energy they devoted to castigating 'positivism'. In Horkheimer's writings, the drive for the domination of nature appears to lack any definite psycho-cultural let alone historical institutional anchorage:

The true critique of reason will necessarily uncover the deepest layers of civilisation and explore its earliest history. From the time when reason became the instrument of human domination of human and extra-human nature by man – that is to say, from its very beginnings – it has been frustrated in its own intention of discovering the truth. This is due to the fact that it made nature a mere object, and that it failed to discover the trace of itself in such objectivisation, in the concepts of matter and things not less than in those of gods and spirit. (Horkheimer, 1974 [1947]: 176)

Adorno and Horkheimer identified scientific and technical rationality as pure instrumental rationality, which they saw as wholly alien to the dialectical rationality (or negative dialectics) which alone can carry through the project of human emancipation. Scheler, on the other hand, had earlier worked out a tripartite scheme of orientations to the world, in which, in addition to the technical-scientific mode of cognition he posited a religious mode aiming at salvific knowledge and a metaphysical orientation to the world aiming at apodictic knowledge of essences, values or material *a prioris*. Insofar as Scheler had a positive solution to offer to the predicaments of technological humanity it was to recommend that it accept the guidance of an elite of metaphysicians with their privileged access to the axiological and eidetic realm and their unrivalled capacity to form a truly integrated world-view which could play the role in 'self-cultivation' (*Bildung*) that post-Kantian German idealism and Humboldtian neo-humanism had aimed at. In fact the conception of *Bildung* was appropriated by the radical Right for their own nihilism (Mosse, 1985).

Another tripartite scheme of basic modes of cognition in which natural science is identified solely with technically relevant knowledge was put forward by the philosophical sociologist Hans Freyer in 1930. For Freyer the three basic epistemic attitudes are those of 'under-standing', the 'self-recognition of existential reality' and that of 'natural science'. 'Understanding' underlies the humanities or hermeneutical sciences. The 'self-recognition of existential reality' underlies sociology which for this author (like philosophy for Hegel), is construed in an activist and decisional sense. Sociology is impossible or unintelligible apart from the will to change social reality in one direction or another and especially in the light of the 'privileged moments' or windows of historical opportunity which it diagnoses. It is, in its way, as voluntaristic as natural science but also 'decisional' in the stream of historical events. Freyer characterised the epistemic attitude of natural science as follows:

[Man] wants to live on the earth, he wants to cultivate it, i.e. to include it among human creations. The epistemic attitude of the natural sciences is unimaginable without this quite primary fact of the will – the technological will, taken in the broadest sense. What elements constitute the complex processes of nature, which laws govern them, and which types of material systems exist whose inclusion in the natural process will create a particular situation B from a given situation A – these questions represent the hidden rudder of discovery in the natural sciences and give rise to all of the concepts they develop. This epistemic attitude does not imply the intervention of heterogeneous motives of utility, but lies within the object of knowledge itself and in the living relation between a person and the object. Modern Western science has certainly implemented in a particularly radical and unscrupulous way this ethos of violent or treacherous examination of nature in order to dominate it step by step. But, on the other hand, this historical form of thought in the natural sciences, which is familiar to us and which we of course take for granted, is based on a generally valid epistemic attitude that is required by the matter itself. (quoted in Wiggerhaus, 1994)

This scheme may have provided in part the inspiration of the typology of basic knowledge-interests formulated by Habermas: the key point here is that he construes the knowledge-interests of the scientific enterprise of the empirical-analytical sciences as exclusively those of prediction and control, whilst communicative rationality, the only basis for hope in the emancipatory project of modernity, lies completely outside the instrumental rationality of science and technology. Although Habermas has emerged in the last decade or so as one of the foremost philosophical figures in the defence of the project of modernity in the ongoing Quarrel of the Moderns and the Postmoderns it is not clear how far he has substantially modified the quasi-Faustian conception of science and technology which he inherited from the Frankfurt School. So, paradoxically, even in the case of one of the most important defenders of the Enlightenment project there is no longer the confidence in the elective affinity of the values and norms of modern science and the modern secular humanistic project which largely pervaded Promethean traditions. Yet even under the regime of contemporary industrialised techno-science it can be argued that discursive practices in setting validity claims within the scientific community warrant the attribution of communicative rationality in that terrain (Radder, 1988).[19]

Concluding remarks

Hannah Arendt wrote in her classic study of totalitarianism that what was most striking in such regimes was not so much their drive for total power as their ambitions for the transformation of human nature. In the present conjuncture within democratic capitalist societies such an ambition could probably not be voiced in political ideological terms by any major contender in normal politics.

At least until recently biopolitical ventures culminating in the compulsory euthanasia programme introduced by the Nazis right from the start of their rule appeared to have been totally discredited. Yet the rapid advances in biological techno-science building on the molecular genetics breakthrough of the 1950s suggest that the biotechnological possibilities of the transformation of human beings over the next twenty-five years or more raise fundamental ethical and political issues. It is no longer a matter of centralised state biocracy but rather the consequences of myriad piecemeal decisions about the application of biotechnologies, such as the new reproductive technologies, somatic and germline genetic engineering incessantly coming on stream. Where moral theology had to develop casuistic procedures to manage social and cultural changes which were eroding religious hegemony, today by contrast, bioethical and biojurisprudential casuistry rationalises, mitigates but in the main ratifies the overall advance of biotechnologies.

Faith in the comprehensive rational direction of society appears to have finally evaporated with the breakdown of state socialism yet biotechnologists in their projects for the biological engineering of human beings demonstrate a new version of the hubris which recently collapsed in political terms. But moral imagination and civic courage of a high order will be needed to resist the tyranny of technological possibilities.

NOTES

1 White's essay has been anthologised in a number of collections on environ-mental studies (most recently in Pojman, 1994), the philosophy and the sociology of technology. It has been addressed by a considerable critical literature over two decades. The Stewardship tradition enjoins restraint in the utilisation of natural resources for the sake of future generations. The Co-operation with Nature tradition favours eliciting natural powers rather than the reshaping of the natural world according to alien designs. Relevant discussions of these traditions within Latin Western Christianity may be found in Passmore (1974) and Attfield (1983). It may be noted that Heidegger, at least in statements of the 1930s, also impugned Christianity in a wholesale fashion as conducive to environmental recklessness.

2 We use the term 'Positivism' to designate the historic movement of 'Positive Philosophy' in order to obviate the negative and misplaced associations which the term 'positivism', now one of the most widespread dyslogisms in the social and human sciences, is likely to carry with most readers. What Collingwood meant by 'positivist metaphysics', Parsons by the 'positivist theory of action', the Frankfurt School by its indiscriminate use of the rubric or ethnomethodology in thus labelling the theory and practice of mainstream social science need not bear on 'Positivism'. Halfpenny has distinguished twelve senses of the term, with Comte's work partaking of four of these; doubtless even more senses could be adduced (Halfpenny, 1982). It should be noted that Durkheim in his lectures on socialism treated Saint-Simon as the founder of Positive Philosophy, which he regarded as the most important philosophical movement in France since Descartes (Durkheim, 1962). The core of 'Positivism' was the Law of the Three States, which had a double role as the central thesis of 'social dynamics' and as the key theorem of the historical epistemology of the sciences (or its 'encyclopaedic law' as Comte called it).

3 The fullest account of Cournot's theory of history is still Ruyer (1930). The literature in English on Cournot (except as a mathematical economist) is sparse indeed but see the excellent chapter by Anderson (1992).

4 In this confidence that the realm of organic life would remain fundamentally inaccessible to mathematical-experimental science unlike the physical and the human worlds, Cournot anticipates Bergson who argued for this view in terms of a new metaphysic. But in any case this faith in the unmechanisa-bility of the organic world was widely shared in nineteenth- and early twentieth-century philosophy of technology and whatever the pertinent thinkers say about the 'conquest of nature' must be understood in the context of this faith (Martins, 1993). Like Comte, Cournot endorsed an over-socialised theory of mind but particularly stressed that a great deal of

human mental life was subject to instrumentalisation and rationalisation. It is only insofar as our mental life is grounded in the organic that it is recalcitrant to economic, social and cultural rationalisation or mechanisation.

5 There has been a revival of interest in the West in Fedorov's thought, signalled by the publication of an English translation of a collection of his writing (1990). The obsession with longevity and immortality in Russian culture had its impact amongst some Russian Marxists and may have had a bearing on the embalming of Lenin. It is interesting to note that in the period 1890–1914 at least three non-religious thinkers with a positive attitude towards modern technology expressed confidence in the imminence of the conquest of death in human beings: F. C. S. Schiller, Henri Bergson and Octave Hamelin. The latter argued that a civilisation dedicated to both rational technology and the 'cult of the human person' should secure the redemption of all human beings, including the resurrection of the dead. Hamelin was a staunch republican, democrat and socialist. The way in which faith in *apocastasis* unites Fedorov, Hamelin and the mystical materialist Walter Benjamin shows how far Western redemptive activism can reach (their respective religious backgrounds being Orthodox, Protestant and Jewish).

6 The Entropy Law was called by Bergson the most metaphysical of all scientific laws because of its depth of philosophical implications for cosmogony and the nature of Time. It was called by Georgescu-Roegen the most 'economic' of natural-scientific laws because of its implications for the nature of real-life economic processes and the bearing it has on a radical reconstruction of economic science (Georgescu-Roegen, 1971). For the same reasons, and others – e.g. the relationship between 'entropy' and 'information', a key category of our technological society – it could also be called the most technological of the laws of nature.

7 Soddy was a more complex figure than these remarks may suggest. He became greatly concerned about the monetary system of the world economy and a severe critic of academic economics which he dismissed as a totally barren enterprise. A self-proclaimed disciple of Ruskin he distinguished between 'chrematistics' as a theory of (illusory) wealth from the science of the real economy which has to incorporate physical energy balances in economic transactions and other interfaces between economy and nature (Martinez-Alier, 1990; Trenn, 1979). 'Chrematistics', almost always a pejorative term, is of course a flag word for critics of the untrammelled market economy and of orthodox academic economics (whether neoclassical, Austrian, Keynesian or even *Marxisant*): neo-Thomists, disciples of Karl Polanyi, Left Aristotelians, ecological economists, etc.

8 Though this author is careful to point out that the distinction is more analytical than chronological, more a matter of relative emphases than of complete breaks, so that in fact there can be an overlap between the two phases (Weber, 1911).

9 Considérant envisaged the possibility that anthropogenic environmental change could arrest the growth of civilisation. Like many other scholars in the first half of the nineteenth century he warned against the possible

catastrophic effects of deforestation on local and regional climates. In the light of current world-wide concern about deforestation in the Amazonian region it is interesting to note that he was especially worried about the chances of an environmental disaster of planetary import in the Americas.

10 Comte assumed that a basic function of modern technology would be not only to abridge human toil but also that of animals, through reduced dependence on animal power. Comte, Cournot, Proudhon, Renouvier all emphatically rejected the Cartesian view of animals as automata and indeed any conception of animals as essentially machines of some kind. They not only ascribed sentience to animals but regarded them as endowed with a mental life which brought at least the higher mammals close to human beings. Indeed for Comte the basic stratum of the religious life, fetishism, is shared by the higher animals and early human civilisation: it should be recalled that he viewed the Religion of Humanity as a kind of neo-fetishism! Renouvier's major treatise on moral philosophy contained an important discussion on the ethics of the treatment of animals which has gone largely unnoticed (Renouvier, 1869). In it he argued that a rational ethic requires us to minimise the suffering we inflict on animals and even enjoins a positive 'duty of kindness' to them. More generally, he posited a general obligation of 'respect for nature', an expression which has only recently enjoyed a wide currency and become the watchword of a biocentric outlook in environmental philosophy (Taylor, 1986). Note that Renouvier defined himself as a thinker in the Enlightenment tradition.

11 Jünger's emphasis on industrialised 'total war', 'total mobilisation', the human typus of the worker-soldier as the mark of our epoch and on the metaphysical role of pain found a very receptive audience in Weimar Germany. Jünger's writings had a profound impact on Heidegger as has been shown in detail, very cogently by Zimmerman (1990). The claims made by Jünger concerning the inevitability and positive value of war and especially on how war is not a distortion but a fulfilment of the vocation of technology were shared by most Faustian theorists. The Promethean Positivists naively believed that scientific-industrial society was inherently peaceable and had no misgivings about the advent of perpetual peace.

Heidegger read Spengler quite early (1919) with a 'mixture of admiration and rejection', annotated his copy quite extensively and discussed its themes in university lecture courses and other academic occasions over a number of years. A certain number of the most resonant terms of *The Decline of the West* also appear in Heideggerese, e.g. 'concern' (*Sorge*) which Spengler defines as the 'primal feeling' (*Urgefühl*), 'existence' (*Dasein*) and others. Whilst Heidegger does not appear to have been particularly struck by Spengler's views on technology in that book, they both agree that the essence of technology is nothing technological, that technology is grounded in the elementary structures of life, that technology is destiny, etc. For a most informative account of Heidegger's reception of Spengler see Volpi (1991).

12 It should be added, however, that the point of the aeroplane parable for this founder-member of the Vienna Circle was to elucidate the role of extra-scientific factors in certain phases of scientific thought. For, he argued, just as in selecting the type of aeroplane to be built criteria of morally and

politically guided appraisal constrain the choice of the mix of safety and speed, 'fun and endurance', similar considerations may apply in scientific theory choice. The lexicographic 'preferences' for logical consistency and empirical validation together with the presumptions favouring simplicity, elegance and mathematical beauty do not suffice to uniquely and completely determine theory-choice at least in the domain of 'theories of high generality'. Hence moral, religious, ideological preferences may well come into play in guiding choice amongst otherwise underdetermined rival theoretical proposals. These extra-scientific considerations belong to the 'pragmatics' (as distinct from semantics and syntactics) of scientific inquiry and Frank's rather forlorn hope was that the social sciences could incorporate 'pragmatics' (the study of 'human engineering') into a unified science of science. (Frank, 1961 [1954] and 1957). Theories of high generality included conceptions of the nature and modality of determinism and indeterminism in the physical world such as the ones advanced in quantum mechanics which are addressed sociologically by the 'Forman Thesis' discussed in the text below. Frank had been of course a keen participant in the discussions in the philosophy of physical causality in the 1930s.

13 Spengler's general orientation to the history of mathematical knowledge has been evoked as 'foundational' by contributors to the 'materialist sociology of mathematics' (Restivo, 1983). But they have to mitigate the strong form of cultural-historical relativism crucial to Spengler's approach. Spengler, indeed, did not merely reject but despised philosophical materialism. His own 'explanation' of the variability of number-worlds was in terms of 'culture souls' (though since he rejected causal explanation a better term would be 'hermeneutic', or even better, 'physiognomic' account).

14 The wide use of the asymmetrical dichotomy culture/civilisation by the politico-cultural Right in Wilhelmine and Weimar Germany is surely a phenomenon of intellectual pathology. Perhaps the only notable German sociologist to make analytical use of this pair of terms was Alfred Weber in his typology of social, cultural and civilisational processes. Norbert Elias, who had been a pupil of the younger Weber, discussed the historical semantics of the German usage of these terms in his magnum opus (Elias, 1978 [1939]). Braudel also paid some attention to the topic but the most comprehensive survey of the use of these terms is to be found in the book by Béréton (1975).

15 For Spengler 'civilisation' was the late, decadent phase of the history of a 'Culture'; however, the majority of those who made much of the dichotomy in German thought did not follow him in this respect, though Spengler's usage also relegates 'civilisation' to the sphere of inferior values.

16 An expressivist theory of technology may seem oxymoronic as technology is normally understood as purely instrumental but it flows naturally from the extraordinary emphasis on 'expression' in all branches of the human sciences in German thought of the period. 'Expressivism' is usually treated in the context of Hegelian communitarian political philosophy but it also profoundly affected the philosophy of language and the philosophy of culture, and it pervades 'the philosophy of life' (*Lebensphilosophie*). Spengler's 'cultural morphology' construes science and mathematics as expressive and

the master quality for the student of human culture, life and personality is defined as 'physiognomic tact'. The expressivism of Klages not least in his work on graphology had a great impact on Benjamin. (Roberts is very informative on Klages and his reception by Benjamin: see Roberts, 1982). For Spengler the scope of 'expression' is virtually ontological so that one could almost say 'to be is to be expressed'. On Spengler's expressivism see Gurisatti (1991).

The Romantic conception of language as the spirit of a people which as an organic whole becomes a kind of living being was racialised by the Nazis and one may argue that 'the failure of Nazism was, in a sense, the failure of a philosophy of language' (Gusdorf, 1953, 31). Similar remarks might be made about the Nazi version of the expressionist philosophy of technology.

17 Sorel, who wrote a number of thoughtful papers in the philosophy of science and technology, had argued as early as 1905 that the scientific laboratory and the automatic factory were becoming increasingly alike. Modern science for him had no longer anything to do with natural philosophy and everything to do with 'experimental practice'. Scientific determinism appertains only to the 'artificial nature' of laboratory experimentation (Sorel, 1905). He thus anticipates Bachelard's 'rational materialism' and its conception of *phénom-énotechnique* which some sociologists of science regard as the classical formulation of the concept of techno-science (Bachelard, 1953). For Sorel continual technical, material progress is a necessary condition of moral progress, and in this sense he counts as a Promethean in the present scheme.

18 Even if one rejects Forman's strong thesis as yet another example of externalist excesses in the historical sociology of scientific knowledge, his richly textured monograph is well worth reading in conjunction with the works of Herf and Zimmerman on the German philosophy of technology in the same period. Curiously enough, neither work does in fact refer to Forman (Herf, 1984; Zimmerman, 1990).

19 The revival of interest in the American Pragmatist movement has led to a reconsideration of the public philosophy of Dewey, for whom – as also for Mead – modern science and democracy were like, consonant, mutually reinforcing enterprises (Hickman, 1990). But it is not at all clear how such a public philosophy could be restated under the regime of contemporary industrialised techno-science.

BIBLIOGRAPHY

Anderson, P. (1992) *A Zone of Engagement*. London: Verso Books.
Arbousse-Bastide, P. (1957) *La doctrine de l'éducation universelle dans la philosophie d'Auguste Comte*. Paris: Presses Universitaires de France (2 vols.).
Attfield, R. (1983) *The Ethics of Environmental Concern*. Oxford: Blackwell.
Bachelard, G. (1953) *Le matérialisme rationnel*. Paris: Presses Universitaires de France.
Berdyaev, N. (1947) *The Russian Idea*. London: Geoffrey Bles.
Béréton, P. (1975) *Histoire des mots: culture et civilisation*. Paris: Presses de la Fondation Nationale des Sciences Politiques.

Bouglé, C. (1905) 'Les rapports de l'histoire et de la science sociale d'après Cournot', *Revue de métaphysique et de morale*, 13: 349–76.

Bronowski, J. (1971) 'The Disestablishment of Science', in W. Fuller, (ed.), *The Social Impact of Modern Biology*. London: Routledge and Kegan Paul, 233–43.

Cassirer, E. (1963 [1954]) *The Question of Jean-Jacques Rousseau*. New York: Columbia University Press.

Considérant, V. (1835) *Destinée sociale*. Vol. I. Paris.

Cournot, A.-A. (1861) *Traité de l'enchaînement des idées fondamentales dans les sciences et dans l'histoire*. Paris: Hachette.

(1875), *Matérialisme, vitalisme, rationalisme*. Paris: Hachette.

Ducassé, P. (1958 [1956]) 'Auguste Comte et la philosophie des techniques', *Actes du Congrès International d'histoire des sciences*, 3: 1151–4.

Duhem, P. (1991 [1906]) *La théorie physique – son objet – sa structure*. Paris: Vrin.

Durkheim, E. (1962) *Socialism*. New York: Collier Books.

Elias, N. (1978 [1939]) *The Civilizing Process*. Oxford: Blackwell.

Fedorov, N. (1990) *What Was Man Created For? The Philosophy of the Common Task*. s.l. Honeyglen Publishing.

Forman, P. (1971) 'Weimar Culture, Causality and Quantum Theory, 1918–1927: adaptation by German Physicists and Mathematicians to a Hostile Intellectual Environment', *Historical Studies in the Physical Sciences*, 3: 1–115.

Frank, P. (1957) *Philosophy of Science – the Link between Science and Philosophy*. Englewood Cliffs, NJ: Prentice Hall.

(1961 [1954]) 'The Variety of Reasons for the Acceptance of Scientific Theories', in P. Frank (ed.), *The Validation of Scientific Theories*. New York: Collier Books, 13–26.

Friedmann, G. (1966) *Sept études sur la technique*. Paris: Gonthier.

Fukuyama, F. (1992) *The End of History and the Last Man*. Harmondsworth: Penguin Books.

Gallie, W. B. (1964) *Philosophy and the Historical Understanding*. London: Chatto & Windus.

Geiger, T. (1973) *The Fortunes of the West*. Madison, WI: University of Wisconsin Press.

Georgescu-Roegen, N. (1971) *The Entropy Law and the Economic Process*. Cambridge, MA: Harvard University Press.

Gurisatti, G. (1991) 'Il tramonto dell' expressione. Spengler e la fisiognomica', in S. Zecchi (ed.), *Sul destino – Estetica 1991*. Bologna: Il Mulino.

Gusdorf, G. (1953) *La parole*. Paris: Presses Universitaires de France.

Halfpenny, P. (1982) *Positivism and Sociology: Explaining Social Life*. London: George Allen & Unwin.

Heim, M. (1987) *Electric Language – a Philosophical Study of Word Processing*. New Haven, CT: Yale University Press.

Herf, J. (1984) *Reactionary Modernism: Technology, Culture and Politics in Weimar and the Third Reich*. Cambridge: Cambridge University Press.

Hickman, L. (1990) *John Dewey's Pragmatic Technology*. Bloomington: Indiana University Press.

Hirschman, A. O. (1977) *The Passions and the Interests: Political Arguments for Capitalism Before its Triumph*. Princeton: Princeton University Press.

Hook, S. (1955 [1943]) *The Hero in History: A Study in Limitation and Possibility*. Boston: Beacon Press.

Horkheimer, M. (1974 [1947]) *The Eclipse of Reason*. New York: Seabury Press.

Ihde, D. (1983) *Existential Technics*. Albany, NY: State University of New York Press.

Jouvenel, B. de (1976) *Les débuts de l'État moderne – une histoire des idées politiques au XIXᵉ siècle*. Paris: Fayard.

Kojève, A. (1964) 'L'origine chrétienne de la science moderne', in I. B. Cohen and R. Taton (eds.), *L'aventure de la science – Mélanges Alexandre Koyré*. Paris: Hermann, Vol. II, 295–306.

Martinez-Alier, J. (1990 [1987]) *Ecological Economics – Energy, Environment and Society*. Oxford: Blackwell.

Martins, H. (1993), 'Hegel, Texas: Issues in the Philosophy and Sociology of Technology', in H. Martins (ed.), *Knowledge and Passion: Essays in Honour of John Rex*. London: I. B. Tauris: 226–49.

Meyer, F. (1950) *La problématique de l'évolution*. Paris: Presses Universitaires de France.

Moscovici, S. (1974) 'Le Marxisme et la question naturelle', in *Hommes domestiques et hommes sauvages*. Paris: Union générale d'éditions.

Mosse, G. (1985) *German Jews Beyond Judaism*, Bloomington, Indiana: Indiana University Press.

Passmore. J. (1974) *Man's Responsibility for Nature*. London: Duckworth.

Pojman, L. J. (1994) *Environmental Ethics*. Boston: Bartlett and Jones.

Proudhon, P.-J. (1867 [1861]) *La guerre et la paix*. Bruxelles.

Radder, H. (1988) *The Material Realisation of Science*. Assen: Van Gorcum.

Renouvier, C. (1869) *La science de la morale*. Paris: Ladrange (2 vols.).

Restivo, S. (1983) *The Social Relations of Physics, Mysticism and Mathematics*. Dordrecht: Reidel.

Ringer, F. (1969) *The Decline of the German Mandarins: the German Academic Community, 1890–1933*. Cambridge, MA: Harvard University Press.

Roberts, J. (1982) *Walter Benjamin*. London: Macmillan.

Ruyer, R. (1930) *L'humanité de l'avenir d'après Cournot*. Paris: Alcan.

Scheler, M. (1970 [1915]) *L'homme du ressentiment*. Paris: Gallimard.

Schumpeter, J. (1943) *Capitalism, Socialism and Democracy*. London: Allen & Unwin.

(1950), *Imperialism and Social Classes*. New York: Oxford University Press.

Seidenberg, R. (1950) *Post-historic Man*. Chapel Hill, NC: University of North Carolina Press.

Sorel, G. (1901) 'La valeur sociale de l'art', *Revue de métaphysique et de morale*, 9: 252–78.

(1905) 'Les préoccupations métaphysiques des physiciens modernes', *Revue de métaphysique et de morale* 13: 859–89.

Taylor, P. (1986) *Respect for Nature: A Theory of Environmental Ethics*. Princeton, NJ: Princeton University Press.

Todes, D. P. (1989) *Darwin Without Malthus: The Struggle for Existence in Russian Revolutionary Thought*. New York: Oxford University Press.

Trenn, T. J. (1979) 'The Central Role of Energy in Soddy's Holistic and Critical Approach to Nuclear Science, Economics and Social Responsibility', *British Journal for the Philosophy of Science*, 12: 261–76.

Ubbelohde, A. (1963 [1954]) *Man and Energy*. Harmondsworth: Penguin.

Volpi, F. (1991) 'Heidegger lettore edito e inedito di Spengler', in S. Zecchi, *Sul destino – Estetica 1991*. Bologna: Il Mulino, 209–49.

Weber, L. (1911) 'La loi des trois états et la loi des deux états', *Revue de métaphysique et de morale*, 19: 597–603.

White, L. (1967) 'The Historical Roots of our Ecologic Crisis', *Science*, 155 (10 March 1967), no. 3767: 1203–7.

Whitehead, A. N. (1925) *Science and the Modern World*. New York: Macmillan.

Wiggerhaus, R. (1994) *The Frankfurt School: Its History, Theories and Political Significance*. Cambridge: Polity Press.

Yack, B. (1992 [1986]) *The Longing for Total Revolution*. Berkeley, CA: University of California Press.

Zimmerman, M. (1990) *Heidegger's Confrontation with Modernity: Technology, Politics, Art*. Bloomington, Indiana: Indiana University Press.

10 Surrogates and substitutes: new practices for old?

Marilyn Strathern

In commenting on the way surrogacy has appeared at the eye of the storm surrounding assisted conception, Derek Morgan records a complaint. It is not his; it comes from those who would wish to defend even in these circumstances what he presumes most would also wish to defend in general: the legal understanding that takes the mother of a child to be she who gives birth to it. The complaint is that parenthood has instead become defined as 'genetic and intrafamilial'. In this view, 'genetic niceties' should not stand in the way of recognising the authenticity of gestational mother: the person 'who takes and rears the child rather than she who gives birth is properly the surrogate. The woman giving birth is *the* mother' (paraphrased by Morgan, 1989: 56, his emphasis). Nelson and Nelson (1989: 86) point out that the current *OED* definitions of 'mother' (woman who has given birth) and 'surrogate' (one who acts in the place of another) would suggest that the surrogate is the woman to whom the child is surrendered. Yet popular usage seems determined to have it the other way round.[1] The term surrogate appears irrevocably and stubbornly tied to the woman who in these circumstances bears the child. There are, I shall suggest, some interesting reasons for that stubbornness.

Morgan, whose field is health-care law in Britain, stresses the familial as well as genetic presumptions here. He regards surrogacy itself 'as a by-product of the industry which has created the nuclear family' (1989: 55; and see Haimes, 1990). Drawing on British examples known in the courts or to the press, he documents the still recent demand for surrogacy in the context of changing attitudes to fertility and the possibility of couples realising some form of genetic parenthood even when the woman cannot bear the child herself.[2] The possibility has been opened up through new techniques to assist conception. Most dramatically, procedures such as in-vitro fertilisation and embryo transfer have made it possible to separate the procreation of an embryo from its gestation. At the nub of surrogacy agreements is the intention of a woman gestating an embryo/foetus to hand the child when it is born

182

over to other persons (typically a couple) who can often (it does not necessarily follow) claim some kind of procreative tie to it. He argues that it is the contemporary emphasis placed on the nuclear family, 'energised' by a parallel emphasis on individual self-fulfilment, which encourages couples otherwise unable to have children to complete themselves/their family through such agreements.[3]

A similar argument is offered from the United States by Janet Dolgin, lawyer and anthropologist. Considering various cases of contested parenthood brought to American courts, she concludes that decisions handed down in judgement are only intelligible when seen as protecting a certain vision of the nuclear family (1992; see also 1990a, 1990b).[4] In surrogacy agreements where the commissioning parents are those with whom egg or sperm originated, judgements in their favour are often justified by reference to 'genetic' parentage as natural parentage. She notes that when all that is at issue is the donation of ova the claim does not arise, and the gestational mother is taken to be the natural mother of the child she bears. Thus a woman who does no more than receive eggs by ovum donation is not called a 'surrogate', any more than the egg donor is. The definition of natural parentage is contextual, and again, the context seems shaped by ideas about the family. Examining the reasoning behind specific cases, Dolgin shows the way in which outcomes invariably find in favour of those persons whose parental aspirations[5] fit most closely a nuclear enactment of family life.

To these British and American commentaries, I wish to add a further dimension. My concern is less with the family than with the genetic niceties themselves. The dimension is the politics of modernity, and in the late twentieth century I take that politics as contextualised by the condition of knowledge called postmodern. In the eye of these storms is a question about the representational practices on which ideas about parenthood turn.

Surrogate and substitute

There is, I believe, a very good reason why the term surrogate will go on being used for the woman who carries a child on behalf of another. It draws attention to the role of interpretation in understandings of human life. In so doing the term makes explicit a mode of understanding the world indigenous to twentieth-century Euro-American cultures.[6]

Everything we may call modernism renders this mode simultaneously constructionist and foundationalist. I say nothing new here, but let me synthesise it briefly for a new context. Interpreting the world is regarded as inherent to human consciousness as social life is to human practice.

Society is regarded in turn as built both on and after the facts of nature, nature in the twentieth century axiomatically including biology. The natural thus appears as an order of reality to which people must attend/ interpret, though they are understood both as taking this order to be the foundation of their efforts (it encompasses them) and as constructing other orders of reality for themselves (representation is in turn all-encompassing). Seeking out knowledge about the foundations on which to construct the world (in the double sense of interpretation/building a social order) is based on the same premise of doubt that drives scientific enquiry: a working uncertainty about the adequacy of representation.

Social life is thus a self-evident exemplar of human constructions. It exploits, moulds and imitates nature all at once, the crucial point being that all and any of these are embraced in the perception of a relationship between orders of reality. Susan Oyama (1985) would trace pre-modern antecedents in the relationship between 'matter' and 'form'. What gives a modernist cast to the contemporary perception of such a relationship is the substantive place accorded to human ingenuity in the double process of constructing and interpreting. As a result, reality may appear in now the foundation, now the edifice.

The modernity that bases social institutions on natural foundations also endorses a modernism that seeks the context and reasons for those institutions. It has an investment in 'making explicit' the conditions of existence, whether these are in the realm of 'natural' or 'social' affairs. If Euro-Americans thus presuppose that human activity includes efforts to interpret and hence represent the world, then language, symbolism, the way people 'express' themselves all create orders of reality built on and after other orders of reality. Indeed signification is held to afford infinite possibilities in the very relationship it creates between what is seen to be given and what is seen to be the outcome of human ingenuity itself. In terms of the world's cultures, this constitutes a set of specific representational practices. Euro-Americans create meaning by dividing phenomena into those whose meaning is self-evident and those whose meaning has to be made explicit, and the practices we can identify as modernism consist in the further (foundationalist, constructionist) activity of making this explicit as a set of relationships. The conditions under which such relationships become of no concern we might then identify as postmodern.

The 'surrogate mother' makes explicit the relationship between gestation and other factors in childbirth. The meaning of surrogacy is thus established *by reference* to those other factors and to those circumstances where gestation is part of a self-evident maternity. Gestation may be interpreted as 'more' or 'less' biological and as 'more' or 'less' indicative of authentic maternity or motherhood, depending on the context. It itself is not diagnostic of surrogacy. The diagnostic issue is that one woman is perceived to be carrying a child *for another* woman – and this is a specific representational strategy. In acting on behalf of another woman, she represents a facet of motherhood but is not herself the real mother. She is a stand-in, metonymically occupying the place of the mother for a while, discharging an important function, but always in reference to another person who by implication is the real[7] parent. Indeed, it is precisely because she stands in for that element that otherwise defines motherhood that she is the surrogate. As modernists Euro-Americans are, it seems to me, very clear on this. Contest only arises when *the relationship* between the surrogate and the woman on whose behalf she is bearing the child breaks down. The relationship in question is at once social, between persons, and conceptual, between the significance of what the persons are doing. When gestation is claimed to be definitive of her own motherhood, the surrogate is no longer simply a surrogate.

This might sound self-evident, but it carries an intriguing corollary. In terms of the popular categorisations of these issues in late twentieth-century Euro-American cultures, the surrogate role is quite straightforward: one person stands in for another. *The enigmatic role becomes that of the 'real' parent.* It is how to determine what is real that becomes a source of doubt.

The enigma is already there in the complaint to which I have alluded. Surrogacy does not seem to lead to agonising scrutiny of what makes a woman intend to act on another's behalf; the question of who might be the real mother may well do so. The definition of surrogacy belongs to the social world of agreements and contracts between persons (cf. Dolgin, 1990b). The real mother, by contrast, is established by an appeal to some natural characteristic, in turn likely to be established as biological in character, whether it is no more than the wish (the 'biological drive') to be a parent. The dispute noted by Morgan arises, I suggest, not from ambiguity surrounding the definition of surrogate, but from ambiguity in respect of the real or natural mother. A stand-in is always a surrogate, and that is all there is to it. Problems arise when persons claim they are not after all a stand-in but the real thing. In these modernist constructions, the real thing is made to appear and is thus represented by other things that stand for it. Here orders of reality are relativised: a surrogate is never the real thing, by definition. But one order of reality can also *substitute* for another. We might say for instance that the real world created by the possibilities of new reproductive technology inevitably substitutes for a real world whose possibilities were tied to other means.[8] In the same way new knowledge substitutes for old: it constitutes an order of reality in its own right. However, new techniques and new knowledge are often championed not as substitutes for the old but as continuous with and part of it. They may even pass themselves off as mere surrogates.

I treat people's explorations of new parenting possibilities as an indigenous hermeneutics. Before making it yield what might be modernist and what might be postmodern in the politics that is also here, let me explain the difference I have introduced between surrogate and substitute. Each constructs reality in a distinctive way.

The surrogate: assisting nature

In the field of reproduction, new technologies are regarded as facilitating biological process. This includes 'assisting' conception. We may consider that birth itself has long been so assisted (cf. Martin, 1987), although at present (beyond monitoring procedures) what are generally called the new reproductive technologies do not 'assist' gestation or nurture or those after-birth body processes once regarded as fundamentally biological in nature.[9] Insofar as the technologies focus on conception, they focus on the fertile union of male and female gametes and on the viability of the embryo. In this, artificial insemination, in-vitro fertilisation or other practices such as GIFT (gamete intra-fallopian transfer) simply stand in, so the justification goes, for natural body processes.[10] Not themselves natural, they make up for natural impairment in the same way as the woman who acts on behalf of another's motherhood is a surrogate mother. We could consider them surrogate processes.

What makes a surrogate mother 'like' a mother yet not the real mother is the fact that she assists the real mother to overcome a particular impairment. While her gestation of the child is a complete substitute for the commissioning mother's role in gestation, by itself it is an incomplete act that only makes (interpretive) sense when seen as part of the total process by which the real mother is created. (If there were no 'real' mother to receive the child, her act by itself would be meaningless.) In the same way, technology is 'like' the natural processes it assists yet is not the natural process itself. Again, technological intervention attends to some particular bit of the whole developmental sequence that creates a child; each act of assistance as such is only given meaning, however, by a successful outcome that is simultaneously a natural one – an egg is fertilised, a child is born. (If there were no encompassing 'natural process', the interventions would have no outcome.)

Appropriately in the case of the mother and by extrapolation, I have suggested, in the case of technology, these are indeed surrogate acts. The contrast with procedures of ovum donation mentioned by Dolgin renders this evident in the case of the mother. In making a gift the donor alienates her rights to the eggs; the eggs may still carry her identity, but she cannot dispose of them further, and in popular parlance they make neither the donor nor the recipient a surrogate. Rather, donated eggs substitute for the commissioning mother's eggs – in Euro-American cultures a 'gift' is a complete act that requires no further interpretation. In the case of these medical technologies, however, 'technology' is also perceived to be more than surrogate insofar as its efficacy is complete in itself, for efficacy requires no further interpretation beyond the evidence that it works. I return to this observation later.

For the moment I note that the surrogate who keeps her agreement is an uncontested surrogate. The act was shown to have been literally altruistic. So, too, technology. As long as technology is simply 'giving nature a helping hand' (cf. Hirsch, 1993: 77), then it appears akin to natural resources which can be put to the benefit of society. As one speaker in the debates surrounding the passage of the British Human Fertilisation and Embryology Bill spoke of the development of technology itself: 'research and experimentation are a natural part of the development of the human condition' (quoted in Franklin, 1993: 113).

The substitute: assisting commerce

A nuance that in other circumstances might carry little weight will serve here as heuristic. I have wished to make something of the difference between two constructions: 'standing in' the place of another and 'taking' the place of another. It is the difference between what is seen to require interpretation by reference to another person or order of reality (surrogacy), and the supplanting of one by the other (substitution). When we talk of one person acting on the behalf of or in the stead of another, the act itself will not tell us whether this is surrogacy or substitution. We have to know whether the original, supplemented and assisted as it may be, remains the reference point, or whether the original is displaced. The difference is no more nor less than the visibility of the relationship between them. The 'surrogate mother' shows this clearly. She is a surrogate as long as her relationship with the 'other' mother is intact; should she claim the child to be hers, however, she then seemingly takes the place of that other woman. She now substitutes for her. But her very willingness to act as a surrogate may already carry a substitutive possibility of a kind. In the place of what would otherwise be considered a desire to help there may instead be a desire for money. It is interesting that the substitution of a maternal impulse by a commercial one is also frequently regarded as problematic.

There is nothing surrogate about commerce. Profit is thought to contain its own rationale; there is no end to the reasons for which it is sought, but that is not the point – the point is that acting for profit in and of itself requires no explanation or interpretation. Money is money. In late twentieth-century Euro-American cultures, the market is in itself an end as well as a means, for it is a kind of political regulator in its own right. I suspect that the equivocations surrounding the commercial possibilities of surrogacy arrangements turn in part on the substitutive and thus displacement effect that money introduces.[11]

The present British government holds before it a model of American enterprise. Especially in matters to do with the relationship between private and state funding, institution after institution has either been set free from or else made financially accountable to the state, in order to follow what is perceived as the spirit of American commercial success. For example, advocating the extension of higher education through the diversification of funding in 1989, the then Secretary of State for Education and Science was quite clear about the model Britain had to follow. 'In a market-led and multi-funded setting', he said, 'the structures of higher education will be much more diversified, as they are in the United States' (reported in the *Times Higher Education Supplement*, 13 January 1989). The market is associated with the production of variety, so that such an education system will be 'better able to meet the needs of different types'. At the same time, diversity of needs is not an axiomatic rationale for the market. It is also assumed that the British would not want their institutions to be American in every respect, and the very quality that is so openly admired or, more accurately, that gives the British one of their stereotypes about American culture, is also what in other situations holds people back. There are certain areas of enterprise that British practices protect from commerce and where, despite the diversity of needs, market forces are not regarded as appropriate. On the contrary it is feared commerce would displace other cherished values.

Also in 1989, the government's Human Fertilisation and Embryology Bill (1990) was being debated in the British Parliament. The Bill was intended to set up a licensing authority for certain treatments of infertility and associated embryo research. While the government's position was that both treatment and research should be encouraged with multiple benefits in view, it drew back from allowing the market to intervene as a mechanism for regulating supply and demand. An explicit provision in the Act debars the donors of gametes from being able to profit from the donation (S12(e)), and persons who wish to seek an order to be treated as parents of a child from donated gametes or a surrogacy arrangement cannot do so if money has changed hands (S30(7)). The commercialisation of surrogacy by third parties already involved a criminal offence.[12] Whatever the range of types of needs, market-led and multi-funded possibilities were rejected in favour of only permitting surrogacy arrangements to proceed if they were in effect conducted on a private basis. In the background was the idea that only such a context would sustain the value of altruism that made the agreement acceptable. During the debate, acknowledgement had been made of the fact that in the United States a greater emphasis on commerce in all types of relationships put money into a different moral category from its place in Britain.

According to Wolfram (1989: 188; and see Cannell, 1990), there was a direct connection between the British provision and what were perceived as American practices. The government's initial Committee of Enquiry into the issues that became the focus of the Act had been published in July 1984 as the Warnock Report. It already contained a recommendation that surrogacy agencies should be outlawed. Within a few months, as Wolfram says, surrogacy hit the British headlines with the case of 'Baby Cotton': an American agency set up in Britain had arranged for Mrs Cotton to be paid some $10,000 to gestate a baby she had conceived through artificial insemination. A Bill was rushed through Parliament, and within a year the Surrogacy Arrangements Act (1985) had ruled that anyone involved in surrogacy arrangements for money was acting criminally. It was conceded that the United States 'was a much more commercial society' (Wolfram, 1989: 192). The opening paragraph of Wolfram's commentary sums up the British attitude towards their American counterparts:

In the parliamentary debates which led to the banning of commercial surrogacy in the United Kingdom in 1985 it was admitted that 'commercial surrogacy has been successful in the United States' and that 'we all admire many parts of the United States ethos' (Hansard, 1985 [6th series], vol. 77, column 37): '[America] is a great innovator' (Hansard, 1985, vol. 77, column 42). But it was also added 'that we do not always try to emulate [the United States]' (Hansard, 1985, vol. 77, column 37), 'surrogate motherhood is one type of experiment that need never have arrived on our shores' (Hansard, 1985, vol. 77, column 42–43). (Wolfram, 1989: 187, footnote omitted)

Here is an example of substitution: the fear is that an American ethos might displace a British one. And what is supposed to characterise this particular ethos is that it in turn makes explicit the displacement effect of money itself. In fact money has been of comparable concern in the United States, at least as reported in some of the cases considered by Dolgin. While a major disquiet voiced by the American courts with respect to gestational surrogacy has been the potential disembodiment of motherhood, in surrogacy disputes where the surrogate mother also supplies the egg, this disquiet is overruled by another: 'hardly a judge has issued an opinion in a surrogacy case without lamenting the risk of . . . commodification' (n.d.: 21). The reference here is to what money can buy or sell. Money also signifies contract. But there were judges who, when faced with the claims of a surrogate to be the real mother, could not bring themselves to endorse the morality of contract above the morality of motherhood (n.d.: 31). The surrogate who sets aside an agreement in favour of her own maternal impulses in effect substitutes an instinctive maternity for instinctive commerce. Neither the maternal impulse nor commerce have, in this context, to be explained further.

A potential politics lies in adjudications over what does and does not require explanation. It is blatantly modernist insofar as it rests in the relationship between what is seen to require interpretation by reference to other things and what is seen to be intelligible in its own right. Thus do moderns 'construct' their worlds out of what they make explicit and what they take for granted. The other side of constructionism is foundationalism, and to this I turn.

New practices for old?

In these views and values, it would seem that the altruism (if only minimally the altruism sealed in a contract) that otherwise justifies surrogacy can be displaced by other orders of phenomena which then appear as 'the real thing'. For the woman it may be either motherhood or commerce. Money, as an end in itself, typifies that possibility; so does the presumed maternal impulse.

Yet I suggested that when they are so paired it is not the surrogate but the 'real' mother who appears the more enigmatic of the two. Why should this be the case when the impulse to motherhood appears to require no interpretation? On the contrary, 'real' motherhood has its foundations both in biology and the social recognition of biology, so the 'real' mother always has either nature or society on her side; by the same token, when a 'surrogate' acts on behalf of a 'real' mother it is because the real mother's claims are already there.[13] Thus a commissioning mother can be considered a real mother, whether by Nature (some commissioning parties can also claim a genetic tie; all can claim the natural desire to be a parent), or Society (the commissioning parties may be seeking legal support for their claims, or can demonstrate they can provide the child with everything that defines good parenting). Where is the enigma? The enigma rests in the very necessity to conserve the foundations on which the real thing is established. Competing foundations take away one another's axiomatic (and thus foundational) status.

I touch briefly on two conserving strategies, the first to do with the regulating role of society and the second with the evidence that nature produces of itself. Regulation is foundational here: modernist Euro-Americans take society's capacity to organise and regulate the social world as its own self-evident foundation in the same way as nature is known by its internal design.[14]

Old practices: keeping the ethics

Moderns look to make explicit the relationship between different orders of reality. In the field of new reproductive technologies, the relationship between technology and biology is like the two components of maternity that have now entered popular parlance, the social and the biological; this in turn is like the two components of biological motherhood made explicit in surrogacy, genetic (of which more anon) and gestational.[15] The relationship may or may not be symmetrical. When surrogacy cases are debated in terms of a contrast between the genetic and the gestational tie, an asymmetry is assumed: one or the other must take precedence. Indeed, surrogacy always implies such an asymmetry (it points to 'the real thing' elsewhere). This is also true in the relationship between technology and biology where technology simply assists biological process. At the same time technology is regarded as in a relationship of sorts with society. Technology is seen to be built on and derived from the same materials that 'nature' uses but with the further input of human ingenuity and human intentions for it, which are geared to social purposes. Its foundational rationale thus belongs to society.

For as long as social ends remain stable, technological innovation does not, in this modernist view, have to mean social innovation. On the contrary, as in the promotion of the nuclear family new procedures may fulfil old goals: the use of technology is taken to have a foundation in social values it leaves unchallenged. This no doubt facilitates what in Britain Wolfram (1989: 190) mischievously notes as one of the commonest 'political platforms' in debates concerning legislative change: either that no change is at issue or else that what arises is a consequence of a change already made; conversely, she notes, the political platform against change may well be that it is change. In a society that values individual well-being, it is considered morally proper for technology to be turned to the ends of medical among other forms of welfare. This is largely the basis on which developments in gene therapy are justified. However, if surrogacy is at the eye of the storm as far as reproductive medicine is concerned, then gene therapy is the storm that surrounds the continuing development of genetic knowledge. I quote from *Science and Public Affairs*, a joint publication of the British Association for the Advancement of Science (BAAS) and the Royal Society.

The 1991 magazine published a discussion between several distinguished workers in the field from a panel convened by the Royal Society under the title 'Embryos and Ethics'. Its intention was to allay anxiety by clearing away confused thinking. The opening paper pointed out that it was difficult to predict long-term outcomes; in the short term, however, the position seems clear:

> Our new-found ability to manipulate our genes is giving rise to a certain amount of public concern. In fact the application of human recombinant DNA technology *does not raise any fundamentally new ethical issues*, at least not yet.
>
> Genetic screening and prenatal diagnosis have been accepted procedures for many years; our new technology will simply increase the number of diseases that can be avoided in this way . . . Organ transplantation is quite acceptable; replacing defective genes is, in essence, no different to replacing whole organs. (Weatherall, 1991: 28, my emphasis)

New technology, then, but old ethics.[16] New possibilities for human health but no new ethical issues because the kinds of decision individuals have to face have already been encountered in medical practice. The new field simply highlights existing issues. Another contributor complains that much confusion is caused by considering ethics in the abstract and running different issues together: one should instead consider each individual issue as it arises with respect to the specific persons whom it concerns (Baird, 1991: 35).[17]

The Royal Society meeting was attended by members from the Committee on the Ethics of Gene Therapy which presented its report to the British Parliament the following year (Clothier, 1992). The report is a landmark: it is also a fascinating document, though I draw from it both more and less than was no doubt intended.

The report was requested because, among other things, it was acknowledged that gene therapy may 'introduce new and possibly far-reaching ethical issues which have not previously had to be considered' (1.11). The presumption of the report is that before gene therapy is introduced into medical practice it must be ethically acceptable;[18] for instance, such therapy must stand the tests of 'safety and effectiveness in relation to other treatments' (1.12). However, its general finding is that the basis for an ethical position already exists: it offers the 'tentative view that gene therapy should initially be regarded as research involving human subjects' (8.3). Somatic cell therapy is directed to the specific individual with a disorder, and the conditions for such an application of genetic knowledge are met by already established guidelines for research with medical patients (such as preserving the subject's rights and liberties and ensuring that procedures are carried out with respect to the well-being of the subject). 'Somatic cell gene therapy will be a new kind of treatment, but it does not represent a major departure from established medical practice, nor does it, in our view, pose new ethical challenges' (8.8).

Ethics is defined, and is done so in terms of its foundations. 'We begin from the basis that ethics are . . . moral convictions' and these convictions 'are in general derived from a compound of natural philosophy and religion' (3.1). As statements of principle these convictions are intuitive – 'the rules and duties derived from them are wrought by moral reasoning'. Other rules and duties, it adds, are derived from utilitarian principles concerning assessments of benefit and harm 'to individuals and to society'. There seems to be an equivocation here. The moral convictions are those of 'thoughtful, conscientious and informed people, to be rejected only when they are in conflict with other convictions which better stand the test of reflection', that is, of individuals in interaction with others, in short one may say of individuals in society. At the same time 'individuals' and 'society' are also the object of moral reasoning. So what is based on what?

In the view of the report, human effort is clearly required to transform intuitive principles into rights and duties that will guide people's actions. Current medical ethics presumably provides a foundation for ethics in the area of gene therapy because they already enshrine the outcome of hard moral reasoning. So the finding of 'no new ethical issues' is based on already established practice. Yet what appears to be an unequivocal foundation can also be open to doubt. It is the processes of regulation that are also in need of regulation. Thus it is acknowledged (3.8) that different codes of practice and means of regulation have evolved to cover different areas that treatment may in fact bring together. We may ask in any case of the part generally attributed to human effort. Like gene manipulation, such regulation is presumably always subject to further human ingenuity.

The phrase 'human ingenuity' appears in the opening statement of the report (1.1): now 'human ingenuity makes it possible to manipulate [genetic] messages deliberately' that could before 'be altered only by accident or chance'. The whole purpose of the Committee's enquiry derived from the fact that such manipulations might yield harm as well as benefit. This is because the potential of genetic processes is unknown. That genes have potential is, however, self-evident. Indeed the reality of genetic potential need have no other foundation than itself (genetic potential). The Report opens with this statement: 'Genes are the essence of life: they carry the coded messages that are stored in every living cell, telling it how to function and multiply and when to do so (1.1).' Here there seems no equivocation about what regulates what: genes regulate cells. And that asymmetrical relationship would appear to offer a partial analogy between the creative gene and human ingenuity itself. Genes tell living cells how to function, while it is the ability to manipulate genes that will (albeit in a more limited sense) affect functioning of individuals and society. We might say that ingenuity is thus placed at the basis of human activity in the world, including its own self-regulation. But by the same token it is also the force that fuels the way human beings act on (try to regulate) a world apprehended as being beyond themselves and thus apply themselves to what is already given in their circumstances. Here what I have read as an analogy gives way to a familiar symmetry: human ingenuity is also no more than a part of the functioning of individuals and society that is ultimately rendered contingent on biological possibilities for life as such. The incontrovertible reality here is that 'genes are the essence of life'.

It is human ingenuity that gives rise to the ethical problems in the first place. But in the (modernist) formulation of the kind we are given in the report, the *idea* of human ingenuity is, as I have suggested for the idea of surrogacy, quite straightforward. I would instead look for an enigma in the foundation on which human ingenuity itself is held to rest and to which it is applied: the reality of which genes are the essence.

New practices: keeping the biology

The view of genes as regulating life through ensuring the functioning of living cells neatly upstages one modernist view of society. Modern society is known through its organisational structures, above all in its regulation of human nature, the social order it imposes on what is otherwise imagined as chaotic and intractable. That is how it gives evidence of itself (where else do Euro-Americans find society but in the 'rules' by which it regulates individual behaviour?).[19] Genes introduce a further order of reality: they are (in this view) the ultimate rules.

As a reference to the distinction between living things (organisms) and inorganic matter, the opening statement about life in the Clothier report is unremarkable. But the statement can also be seen in the light of a process of cultural transformation that has produced certain specific late twentieth-century Euro-American understandings. I refer in particular to the sequence that has turned 'nature' into 'biology' and biology into 'genetics'. It is found, for instance, in changing definitions of the procreative basis of parenthood in Euro-American kinship, and is found as a sequence of enigmas.[20] What is enigmatic is what is to be taken as the real thing. Certainly in ideas about procreation, the real thing is ever open to new interpretation. Thus those disputes over surrogate motherhood show the point at which 'biology' ceases to be an axiomatic foundation for motherhood. I do not mean simply the way in which 'social' motherhood may be opposed to 'biological' motherhood, but in the way in which *what is biological about biological motherhood* has to be made explicit. This is what makes the claims of the real mother enigmatic. How will the real thing show itself? On what will it be founded? Is it still biology, and if so in what way do we see the unmistakable signs of biological process?

If new medical technologies have brought the biological component of procreation into greater rather than lesser prominence, it is, so to speak, technology's kind of biology that is thus brought into prominence. In assisting conception, such technologies also substitute one kind of understanding about the significance of biology in human relations for another. The focus is on the pairing of gametes, and gametes are held to be important for the genes they contain. What comes to be seen as the foundation for biogenetic kinship is the genetic tie. As a consequence, when dispute turns on the kinds of claims that parties can make in relation to one another, the appeal to biology may be understood as an appeal to genetic connection.

I cite some renditions from recent press reports, and return to the hermeneutic context of surrogacy arrangements. Other contexts can be expected to yield different interpretations of 'the biological', including the fact that outside technological intervention the carrying mother is still referred to in general as the natural or biological mother, a usage that (as we have seen) may include mothers who bear children from donated gametes. Nonetheless, as in popular interpretations of surrogacy as an 'interpretation' or construction of motherhood, the foundation of all life in genes seems to need no interpretation. Indeed (as we shall see) if popular usage is stubborn on the issue of who is the surrogate, it is also stubborn on the significance of genes.

Some months after the Royal Society meeting, the London *Daily Telegraph* (8 August 1991) published a news item from New York headlined 'American woman to have daughter's twins'. The woman, pictured tending a hanging plant, clearly pregnant, was reported as carrying a foetus created by her daughter's and daughter's husband's gametes but 'implanted' in her because her daughter had no uterus. The *New York Times* (5 August 1991) had run the same story and picture the day before, its headline being 'When grandmother is the mother, until birth'. The British version commented that it was the question of the surrogate mother's relationship to the twins that was perplexing American commentators. There was no problem about the legality of the pregnancy. Both reports also went out of their way to state that no money was involved, and gave the mother's statement that she would have been horrified at the thought of being paid: she did it altruistically as an act of love. ('Very kind, generous . . . [and therefore] ethically admirable', was the opinion of one 'ethicist'.) What the reports take for granted is the significance of the gametes.

The daughter is cited as saying that there is no question in her mind but that the twins will be 'hers'. The *New York Times* article quotes two other cases, one of a sister being the gestational surrogate, and one of a Californian woman who received payment. In the former case, the commissioning couple was reported as becoming 'the parents of triplets, *their own biological children* borne by Mrs R's sister'; while in the Californian law suit, 'the court awarded custody to the couple who . . . [were] the *biological parents* of the child' (my emphasis in both cases). The biological parents are, in these citations, those who supplied the gametes; the significance of supplying the gametes lies in the assumption that this makes them 'the' genetic parents. Indeed being the source of the eggs and sperm and having a genetic connection are generally taken as synonymous. Thus genetic connection conserves the priority given to biology.

The British version of the article summarised the American outcome as follows: 'The courts have established precedents that in a dispute, the resulting child goes to the biological . . . parents, rather than the woman who gave birth.' The statement is followed by one from a home correspondent who draws an explicit parallel with the British situation. Since no money was involved, the issue of commercialisation did not arise, though the article cannot refrain from referring to the banning of commercial surrogacy in Britain. It repeats the point about the biological identity of the mother, ending with a reference to the Human Fertilisation and Embryology Act which will 'enable the courts to declare the biological mother the legal mother'. The reference is to the provision in the HFE Act that allows parental orders to be made in favour of a couple one or both of whose gametes were used to bring about the creation of an embryo (S30). The day after the British report, the *International Herald Tribune* published a syndicated précis of the *New*

York Times article. It repeats the case of the Californian woman who had to relinquish the child she was carrying and hand it over to the 'biological parents'. It was emphatic:

And recently a California woman in whose uterus an embryo had been implanted was ordered by the court to relinquish a baby *to which she had no biological ties whatever* (7 August 1991; my emphasis).

What lies in common between these pieces of reportage, then, is what is indeed taken for granted: the biological tie is demonstrated in the origin of the gametes, and the gametes are the source of genetic connection.[21]

Even here, however, the human ingenuity by which the genetic link is thus conserved as the basis of biology introduces its own order of reality. I cannot resist drawing the parallel with the place of commerce in surrogacy. There, it will be recalled, money worked to substitutive effect. Here, foundationally, it further validates the genetic claim. My renditions of the *Daily Telegraph* summary left a couple of words out. The full sentence reads (my emphasis): 'The [American] courts have established [that] the resulting child goes to the biological *or purchasing* parents, rather than the woman who gave birth.' In the words of the original *New York Times* piece, 'The court awarded custody to the couple *who paid her*, the biological parents of the child.' Of course we can understand the 'purchasing parents' as the 'commissioning parents', those with the capacity and intent to be parents.[22] And in British practice there can be no public 'purchase'. Yet this further validation raises a query against the foundational status of the genetic tie.

Do we glimpse a dimension that makes the genetic tie enigmatic – that there are reasons for emphasising it? Insofar as the genetic tie takes precedence only by having been actively sought out, it has in a sense thus been 'chosen'. Now while in the short term there may be nothing new; in the long term, Weatherall observed, future developments in molecular biology may indeed raise fundamental new ethical issues. One such set of ethical problems can be seen on the horizon: 'as we become more efficient at predicting the genetic make-up of individuals, how far will we be justified in offering parental choice?' (Weatherall, 1991: 29). What kind of choice, he asks, should a parent have to bring a defective child into the world? That choice is of course subsumed in the prior choice by which parenthood is in the first place claimed on a genetic basis.

Yet equally, in these views I have collected together, genes will go on having their effects whether or not people choose to make them the basis of kinship. Indeed rather than thinking of genes as the foundation of a life biologically conceived, it would seem sufficient to take genes themselves, in the words of the Clothier report, as the essence of life. In considering this sufficiency, I also want to suggest how 'the genes' attract not only a modernist but a postmodern 'hermeneutics'.

New–old politics

My account began with a complaint about popular understandings of processes that stubbornly seem to flow in the face of other evidence. Morgan was of course recording someone else's complaint, with the intention of demonstrating how diverse interpretations of maternity implicate one another. He draws out the paradoxes between the different positions people take in order to clarify the reasons for particular choices in the matter, thus exposing how enigmatic claims about the real thing are. In this he is party to an interpretive strategy that seeks the contexts and reasons for positions. There are layers to people's understandings and interests, as there are layers to people's constructions of events or the foundations on which things appear to rest. Indeed in the various sets of data that he brings to the discussion of the problem, Morgan deliberately moves between different types of evidence. In making the relationship between them explicit, he demonstrates the social conditions under which people make particular kinds of claims. The very practice of sifting through such claims also mobilises a sense of social responsibility. This, as he says at the end of his chapter, is the responsibility of determining who is affected by the reproductive revolution, what the implications for individuals are, what we do in making – as in debating surrogacy – surrogate-born children publicly visible.

I take Morgan's concern with ethical issues as endorsed in some of the representational practices of modernism. Thus he makes explicit the interaction between the development of new technologies and the values of the society that sustains/regulates them. Whether we think of it as the desire to find inner truth behind surface appearances or as the type of reflexivity characteristic of modernity (Giddens, 1991: 14),[23] such explicitness makes room for a modernist politics. Modernist politics adjudicates between different social interests precisely because of the way in which it brings different orders of reality, and thus the different bases for people's claims, into relationship.

But just as human ingenuity is, culturally speaking, the substantive mechanism which makes modernist reflexivity possible, there is substantive weight to be placed on those moments where enquiry concerns 'the genes'. In the surrogacy debates genes enter as an uncontested reality; in debates concerning gene therapy their reality has to be made explicit.

But in either case ideas about genes are already determined by the regulatory functions read into them. Yet where a modernist might be interested in these regulatory functions because they work like rules, a postmodernist might be content with the efficacy of the mechanism. The former would require an interpretation in terms of relationships; the latter would subsume relationships under an interest in outcome. Here I turn to a second complaint. It is a complaint about stubbornness not in popular but in scientific understandings. However, I believe it resonates with popular and equally stubborn understandings about genes as the ultimate rules. The complaint is pertinent for its appeal to politics.

Writing of the way Euro-Americans interpret their understandings of organic development, Oyama says:

An attempt to explain development by such means is unintelligible at best and theoretically, *politically* and morally *dangerous* at worst because it encourages us to predict limits in situations whose critical parameters may be unknown to us (Oyama, 1985: 63, my emphasis).

The means in question are those metaphors of 'rule' and 'instruction' which endow the gene with its self-fulfilling 'plan', its future potential, and lend rhetorical weight to the image of genes carrying 'coded messages' that enable them to 'tell' cells what to do. Among the dangers of such metaphors, in her view, is precisely the way they encourage people to think in terms of a relationship between different orders of reality. After all, I may add in this context, they can encourage complacency about change – new technology creates no new ethical problems because the social justifications are the same. But her account goes far further than this.

Describing genes as containing messages that 'control' the functioning of a cell suggests that it is the message that gives 'form' to 'matter', making the code an independent and prior order of reality,[24] albeit in the case of genes in 'interaction' with the environment. Oyama's complaint concerns the fate of this last proviso. Interactionism seems both universally adopted, in scientific writings, and yet consistently marginalised (Oyama, 1985: 7). This seems no more so than when an interactionist paradigm simply repeats the original dualism of form and matter. Her interest is in the fact that alternative descriptions are possible. Thus Oyama prefers to use 'interaction' to refer not to the relationship between genes and the conditions under which genes are manifest (their environment) but to the whole process of organic development as such. Genes are in this view an *outcome* of developmental processes. Indeed she suggests that in the difference between inherited and acquired characteristics, what is inherited is developmental means, including an organism's pertinent environment, while what is acquired by construction is the nature of the organism (Oyama, 1985: 125). Like Morgan she talks of interactions, then, but in a context I shall suggest that gives them a quite different effect.

One would have to conclude from her account that at least as far as relationships between whole organisms are concerned, *there is no such thing as 'a' genetic tie*. Or rather, that 'the genes' do not create it. Instead, we have to understand genes as created by the same developmental processes that have as their outcome both the potentials and the characteristics of the organism.[25] This is true from the start of individual 'life'. Speaking of the human potential of a fertilised egg, Birke, Himmelweit and Vines (1990: 73, emphasis removed) point out that such a potential 'exists only in the interaction between the changing, developing embryo and its human environment – a woman'. Yet, they add, somehow the concern with potential has focused on the genes to the exclusion of much else.

The politics to which Oyama draws attention rests in representational practice: in making explicit not only the language of description but the context in which it is read and what gets excluded (the politics of the 'text' reveals the politics of the critic). It invites one to read the Clothier report and the paper I quoted from *Science and Public Affairs* with quite new eyes. Alongside the description of genes as encoding messages, they also in fact both present an interactionist view. Thus the Clothier report (4: 17) observes that 'the quality of humanness' which characterises each individual [person] comes from 'the interaction of . . . genes and external influences throughout life'. Weatherall judiciously refers to those disorders which:

result from complex interactions of environmental factors with our genetic constitution which render us either more or less likely to develop these conditions after similar environmental exposure. (Weatherall, 1991: 25)

He suggests that even more important than understanding the molecular basis of disorders that are 'primarily genetic in origin' is the challenge of starting 'to dissect the complex interactions between our environment and our genetic make-up' (Weatherall, 1991: 25). The invitation to further dualism ('dissect') aside, there is nothing here that suggests a priority of one over the other. And if one divests the description of the shadow image of a freestanding individual ('our genetic make-up') and the world 'in' which it stands ('our environment'), then there is nothing to prevent one reading environment as the means of the developmental process itself, of which an individual's genetic make-up would be an outcome. And now that popular under-standings have seized on the significance of 'biology', there is nothing here that would prevent lay persons thinking of biology as that whole set of 'complex interactions'. It thus appears as a blatant example of what Wolfram would call a political platform to declare that someone could be 'the genetic, biological and natural' parent of a child *to the exclusion* of the gestational parent.

This particular declaration is contained in an American judgement handed down in a disputed surrogacy case (Dolgin, n.d.: 33). It shows the problem that comes when descriptions that derive their rhetorical power from social life (the gene, like an individual, is imagined as existing 'in' an environment) are put back into it (if the genes are 'in' the person or 'in' the gamete then what surrounds them is simply environ-ment). Thus the same judge stated that biological facts had different implications depending on the parties involved, in effect different kinds of efficacy depending on the person of the mother. In this case, the gestational mother was like a foster mother who simply provided care and nurture to the child for the period that the natural (genetic) mother could not. She was its (temporary) environment. The gestational mother – without whom, as some biologists would assert, the child would have no genetic make-up – he then categorised as an 'hereditary stranger' to the child.

Thus do we see the reduction of biology to genetics, and *the reduction of genetics* to 'the genes' 'in' the gametes. Armed with Oyama's alter-native model of interaction one can see this as the (unintended) politics of representational practice. It is characteristically modernist. It attends ('chooses') some types of knowledge to the exclusion of others, layered in terms of what is to be made explicit (genetics is proof of biology) and what is taken for granted (genes come with the gametes). And this is similar to the kind of layering that Oyama carefully undoes in taking apart the metaphor of 'rules'. Rules, she suggests, are what Euro-Americans imagine they will need in order to make things that will work.

Rules and instructions, in other words, are what we formulate on the basis of observation of the universe *to be simulated*. They are what we must use to produce results that resemble the operation of a system that runs without 'rules' as we know them, but rather, produces orderly outcomes by virtue of its evolving nature and its interactions. (Oyama, 1985: 62)

But in taking apart the metaphor of rules she also problematises how we might think of relationship at all.

In her critique of the (false) place that the idea of rules holds in descriptions of natural process, Oyama explicitly avoids reproducing the modernist model of the world that, presuming different orders of reality, must therefore search constantly for the relationships between them. Instead she offers a view of an emergent world. There can be no blueprint or plan of it for any blueprint or plan that truly reflected ontogenesis (coming into being) could only be a description of the phenomenon itself (Oyama, 1985: 63).[26] There are in that sense no relationships to be uncovered, only phenomena to be described. It follows that there is no enigma attached to phenomena for there is no ulterior reality to which reference has to be made, and no proof of that reality needed. Will interpretative practice become the sequencing of things as they are laid out to view, to use a postmodern metaphor, the journey between points that can never become positions? It is not just that there is no difference between interpretation and the real thing but that the only possible interpretations must be the real thing.

The enigma of the real contained a politics of a kind. What was modernist was the way in which the real was held to be a matter of interpretation or human construction upon an already given world; what is postmodern is the way in which such representational practices are superseded by the simple possibility of making things – including interpretations – work. One judges by effect and by capacity. Thus might one think of the mother as self-referentially defined, where self-reference need not rest on any prior claim to reality. The mother is simply she who has been made effective, by technology, by legislation, by a court order. But then she may have to sustain that judgement by continuing to give evidence of the capacity to parent.

How do we interpret, then, the merging of interpretation and the real thing that is given in those models that work best of all: the 'technology' that plays back an understanding of the world in terms of its own effectiveness? 'By reinforcing technology, one "reinforces" reality' (Lyotard, 1984: 47; and cf. Latour, 1991). What has been largely true in the application of science, that one can make things work without understanding why they work, has become culturally visible in what late moderns and postmoderns alike hypostatise as 'high technology', an epithet that has certainly been used of the medical procedures that assist conception. Indeed what people take to be 'technology' is the know-how that requires no interpretation and no justification beyond itself: it simply demonstrates that the ideas that built it work. In short, it validates itself in its effects.[27]

Finding the rules in the genes has long been open to criticism. Tim Ingold (1990: 217) refers to the 'trick' of imagining that if substantive traits can be identified gene by gene then an organism appears con-stituted by the sum of its genes. Genes become vested with exclusive 'responsibility' for organisation, despite the fact that organisation can only be a property of the organism as a whole. The transparency of this trick is not new. In a culture that is self-consciously 'technological', however, a new trick can be pulled with the genes themselves: gene therapy can make certain interpretations of them work.

Here is a political issue. How will new understandings of 'the genes' be translated back into social practice? I cheer when I read Oyama saying that as long as 'coming into being is understood as the instantiation of preexisting form, the fundamental aspects, and therefore the fundamental contradictions, of our ways of construing life will reconstruct themselves into new versions of the [modernist] homunculoid gene' (1985: 141). I can translate that into a politics that recognises positions while taking no particular position as given. As she remarks a few pages later, developmental pathways are not set in any substantive way by either genome or environment. But I am chilled when I read the sentence above this remark: 'influences and constraints on responsiveness are a function of both the presenting stimuli and of the results of past selections, response and integrations, [such] that organisms organize their surroundings as much as they are organized by them' (1985: 150). This may be a perfectly adequate (indeed the only possible) picture of organic development, and is suitably unlayered for post-modernist taste. Yet the political truth is we live in a mixed world. There never will be a pure postmodern moment[28] and there cannot therefore be an uncontaminated audience for such views.

On the contrary there are modernists out there who will seize on descriptions of the natural world precisely because they think it is an order of reality that will justify social practice. They will not realise that such language is about the *in*admissibility of inferring from the mutual being of organism and surroundings a justification for other things. Read it with old eyes, and that passage could be a mandate for disregarding ethics altogether in the interests of binding persons more closely to the realisation of themselves in what they can get access to. Indeed it could almost be taken as a mandate for consumerist politics, postmodern only in veneer, where everyone should be set free to create their own environments – as in the wonderful merging of purchasing power and biological identity that came together in popular renditions of surrogacy cases.

NOTES

This chapter derives from interests developed during research undertaken in the context of an ESRC-funded project R000 23 2537; the support of the ESRC is gratefully acknowledged, as is the expertise of other members of the project:

Jeanette Edwards, Sarah Franklin, Eric Hirsch and Frances Price (Edwards et al. 1993). Sarah Franklin is to be thanked for her further comments on this chapter, and both her and Debbora Battaglia for several conversations, as is Pnina Werbner for the stimulus of her paper on Salman Rushdie. I am grateful to the participants at Durham for their comments on the 1992 talk from which this also derives and to colleagues at the University of Wisconsin for comments on a sister version.

1 This 'popular' view corresponds to the definition adopted in the 1985 Surrogacy Arrangements Act which banned commercial surrogacy (' "Surrogate mother" means a woman who carries a child in pursuance with an arrangement' (S 1)). See note 12.

2 To be understood in part in the context of a decline of babies available for adoption. At the same time the publicity given to gestational surrogacy (see below) seems to have heightened the possibility that it will be persons who otherwise have a genetic claim to the child who seek out surrogacy. That claim does not of course necessarily follow.

    The term 'surrogate' used alone refers (1) generally to all forms of maternal surrogacy and (2) specifically to a woman who has been inseminated (artificially or otherwise) by one of the parties with whom she has the agreement but whose child is born from her ovum as well as uterus. 'Gestational surrogate' distinguishes the woman whose child is formed wholly from gametes (sperm and egg) derived from other persons. She is presumed to have no genetic connection to the child. (I return to this point below.) The number of relational permutations that can be derived from gestatory and genetic parentage is laid out in Haimes (1992: 120–2).

3 He makes this argument against the complaint that surrogacy cuts into fundamental values and disturbs the integrity of family life. In his view, the desire to enter into such agreements also responds to the integrity of family life.

4 I am grateful to Janet Dolgin for her comments.

5 Procreative intent is a significant part of popular (and legal) understandings of the kind of parentage claimed by a commissioning couple (Morgan, 1989: 59; for an anthropological comment, see Strathern, 1995). But invariably such intent is only interpreted as authentic if realisable in a 'family' context. This apparently guarantees what seemed most important of all to a number of the decisions Dolgin records: the likelihood of a woman being able to provide 'proper' maternal care once the child is born.

6 I try to give something of an interweaving between British and American observations. But while my examples are only British and American, I use the hybrid Euro-American for a community of discourse both larger and smaller than simple identification by country would indicate. I pluralise it in referring to Euro-American cultures only to indicate the way it is promulgated in diverse contexts. Note for instance that the Glover report to the European Commission cites American experience in its discussion of surrogacy arrangements (Glover, 1989: 68f.). I should add that cultural analysis of the kind offered here has its limitations; for a relevant critique, from a sociology of knowledge perspective and one that draws on material from the field of neo-natal care, see Anspach, 1989a.

7 The relationship between different orders of reality is rendered in this case as one between the real and a surrogate for it. The surrogate offers 'real' gestation but not 'real' maternity.

8 Elsewhere (Strathern, 1994) I have explicated the difference in terms of displacements. What I here call 'surrogate' corresponds to the way analogies routinely displace one state of affairs by another but where the original sequence can always be restored. What I here call 'substitute' follows usage also in that paper, namely the radical displacement that comes from making the implicit explicit, for example, uncovering assumptions in such a way as to pre-empt their return to an axiomatic status.

9 Though intensive neo-natal care is a focus of technological developments of its own (see the several contributions to Whiteford and Poland, 1989, especially Anspach, 1989b).

10 As many feminist writers have pointed out, the yardstick of natural process is, in this view, fertility and productivity, so that the condition of the infertile body is thought to be abnormal. Morgan (1989: 72–3) dwells on the 'construction' of fertility.

11 The 'taint of commerce' can be attached to both the surrogate and the commissioning parties. 'They see children as a market. Just another commodity to be bought and sold' (quoted in Hirsch, 1993: 88).

12 The Surrogacy Arrangements Act 1985 was the one piece of legislation stemming from the initial Warnock report (1985) that appeared before the much-delayed Human Fertilisation and Embryology Bill was finally brought to Parliament. The HFE Act 1990 reinforced the 1985 Act with the further provision that no contract for surrogacy could be held binding on the parties (S36(1)).

13 This is a symbolic construction. There is nothing in a surrogacy agreement that means that the claims of the commissioning parents have to be grounded in such biological (or social) justification. It is when the agreement fails that the foundations of motherhood are contested.

14 The point is made at length in Strathern, 1992. The following argument about regulation owes much to Franklin's (1993) analysis of another debate.

15 Oyama's (1985) essay expands the succession of metaphors through which this relationship is reproduced.

16 However, he does go on to detail a number of moral issues already on the horizon. Despite the confidence of the claim just quoted, the whole tone of the discussion is measured and cautious, and advocates public debate. 'There are ethical issues that, although not new, are being highlighted by this new field. It is important therefore that in our haste to reap the extraordinary benefits that may arise from human DNA manipulation, we do not ignore them and that we debate them in their new context' (Weatherall, 1991: 28).

17 Baird's comment is apropos the variability of ethics 'from society to society; and within society from individual to individual' (1991: 35). This in turn confuses levels of analysis. One might wish to endorse the first and query the second. Indeed the second observation is likely to justify a tendency that Lee and Morgan (1989: 6) deplore in the case of law, a refusal to see the scene- (of technological innovation) as-a-whole. Far from it being a 'confusion', we

delude ourselves by separating out problems as though they could be picked off one by one. (Any one is already a version of, implicates and derives from others.)

18 The first of the Committee's terms of reference was to draw up guidance for the medical profession on the treatment of genetic disorders by genetic modifications of human body cells in contradistinction to germ line cells, though the report has a brief chapter on Germ Line Gene Therapy, concluding that insufficient knowledge exists to evaluate the risks to future generations and recommending that no modification of the germ line should be attempted.

19 On the general point see Ingold (1989: 500). On the language of rules applied to understandings of the genome, see Oyama (1985: 50–63); on the language of rules applied to understandings of law in society, see in general Fitzpatrick, 1992.

20 I refer to a sequence in the sense of a devolution of concepts. All these terms and their 'old' and 'new' meanings may of course be in cultural circulation at the same time.

21 For an 'earlier' view, see the Glover report, which is careful to suggest that biological links may be formed by more than one way: a couple's claim to parenthood may be 'backed up by at least one biological link, whether semen, eggs *or* pregnancy and childbirth' (Glover, 1989: 57; my emphasis).

22 The juxtaposition of commercial and biological idiom is explicit in other contexts. Consider the following: 'there are good indications that mimicking biological processes to help make complex decisions can increase business yields. Now finance companies are investigating whether it is possible to evolve the best solution – starting from a set of random solutions. Genetic algorithms are computer processes which treat a problem as an environment, and solutions as life-forms struggling to survive. The algorithms try to find the "fittest" solutions by forcing the life-forms to adapt and change over generations. The researchers say that the pattern recognition techniques evolved by the automated systems apply to the actual stock market, and that genetic algorithms could generate real market trading profits.' (*The Guardian*, report on Proceedings of the Neural Networks and Genetic Algorithms Seminar, Santa Fe, 1991.)

23 For Giddens, the particular reflexivity of modernity lies in the extent to which descriptions of social life organise and alter those aspects of life they describe. It is to be distinguished from reflexive monitoring common to all human activity by its effect: 'the susceptibility of most aspects of social activity to chronic revision in the light of new information or knowledge' (1991: 20). If, as he says, science is based on the methodological principle of doubt, then the modernism that gives rhetorical value to science is based on exploration and the search for new information that will deepen layers of reality. Exactly the same could be said of modernist aesthetics, as it could of attempts to ground ethics in an intrinsic or essential human nature (cf. Shusterman, 1988: 339).

24 One might have thought that insofar as 'genes' are seen to work on 'living cells' then it would be the latter and not the former that is taken as a foundational reality. This is not how the Clothier report is likely to be read.

In fact the reality conferred by the genes themselves may create a category of person where on other grounds none could be presumed to exist. The *Sunday Mirror* (10 January 1993), reporting the possibility that foetal cells could be used to produce ovaries in infertile women, quotes a researcher as saying that the woman giving birth 'would not be the baby's real mother'. 'The doctor explains: "The baby's genetic mother is the dead foetus."' (My thanks to Steven Sharples for drawing my attention to this.)

25 See the discussion in Ingold, 1990. Ingold (1991: 368) puts this understanding with great clarity: 'I have no intention of denying the existence of the gene, or of its importance as a regulator of physiological and developmental processes. I would point out, however, that it is the structure of evolutionary theory, not the molecular structure of the genome, that dictates the latter's role as a carrier of encoded information. The theory requires a vehicle that would import form into the organism and DNA seemed to fit the bill. Yet in reality, genes exist nowhere except inside organisms, and the reactions that they set in train depend entirely on that organismic context. Only within the particular contexts of their activities, therefore, can genes be said to specify, or to be programmatically "for", anything at all. In other words, far from serving as vehicles for injecting meaning into the organic world, genes take their meanings from the relational properties of that world itself. More generally, organic form is not revealed or expressed but rather originates within processes of development, and every developmental system is constituted as a nexus of relations between manifold reactants both within the organism (including the genome) and beyond it, in relevant aspects of its environmen' (Oyama, 1986: 34).

26 The concept of 'description' introduces its own dualism – only the phenomenon itself is an adequate description of itself (and hence no description). But the reduction or miniaturisation of 'descriptions' is probably essential to the capacity for criticism, much along the lines of Ingold's (1989: 502) argument concerning the development of language as in the first place a modelling and monitoring device rather than a substitute for non-verbal communication.

27 This does not mean to say it does not create uncertainties (see Price, 1990). But the uncertainties lie in how results are to be interpreted, not in whether there will be results. Thus technology may be assumed efficacious but give rise to uncertain interpretations of the outcome (as in ambiguous readings of ultrasonography), or else the efficacy of the result for the patient/client may be seen to depend on a multitude of other factors (as in in-vitro fertilisation).

28 I find Liz Stanley's observations helpful. No new social order ('postmodernity') is required to justify postmodernism as a critique of modernist (she would say 'modern') modes of self-representation; postmodernity's claim 'to be the condition of contemporary society [consists] only in invocations of it' (1992: 15). It is of course thoroughly appropriate that postmodernist commentary does not have to appear as a manifestation of any particular social order. Rather, postmodernist theory colonises anti-foundational features of modernism to work its criticism (and cf. Lyotard, 1984: 79).

BIBLIOGRAPHY

Anspach, R. R. (1989a) 'Life-and-death decisions and the sociology of knowledge: the case of neo-natal intensive care', in *New Approaches to Human Reproduction*, ed. L. M. Whiteford and M. L. Poland, Boulder: Westview Press.

(1989b) 'From principles to practice: life-and-death decisions in the intensive-care nursery', in *New Approaches to Human Reproduction*, ed. L. M. Whiteford and M. L. Poland. Boulder: Westview Press.

Baird, D. (1991) 'Committees and Individuals', *Science and Public Affairs*, The Royal Society, BAAS: 33–5.

Birke, L., Himmelweit, S. and Vines, G. (1990) *Tomorrow's Child: Reproductive Technologies in the 90s*. London: Virago.

Cannell, F. (1990) 'Concepts of parenthood: the Warnock Report, the Gillick debate, and modern myths', *American Ethnologist*, 17: 667–86.

Clothier, C. M. (1992) *Report of the Committee on the Ethics of Gene Therapy*. London: HMSO.

Dolgin, J. L. (1990a) 'Status and contract in feminist legal theory of the family: a reply to Bartlett, *Women's Rights Law Reporter*, 12: 103–13.

(1990b) 'Status and contract in surrogate motherhood: an illumination of the surrogacy debate', *Buffalo Law Review*, 38: 515–50.

(1992) 'Family law and the facts of family', in S. Yanagisako and C. Delaney (eds.), *Naturalizing Power*. New York: Routledge.

Edwards, J. *et al.* (1993) *Technologies of Procreation: Kinship in the Age of Assisted Conception*. Manchester: Manchester University Press.

Fitzpatrick, P. (1992) *The Mythology of Modern Law*. London: Routledge.

Franklin, S. (1993) 'Making representations: the parliamentary debate on the Human Fertilisation and Embryology Act', in J. Edwards et al., *Technologies of Procreation: Kinship in the Age of Assisted Conception*. Manchester: Manchester University Press.

Giddens, A. (1991) *Modernity and Self-Identity: Self and Society in the Late Modern Age*. Oxford: Polity Press.

Glover, J. et al. (1989) *Fertility and the Family*. The Glover Report on Reproductive Technologies to the European Commission. London: Fourth Estate.

Haimes, E. (1990) 'Recreating the family? Policy considerations relating to the "new" reproductive technologies', in M. McNeil *et al.* (eds.), *The New Reproductive Technologies*. London: Macmillan.

(1992) 'Gamete donation and the social management of genetic origins', in M. Stacey (ed.), *Changing Human Reproduction: Social Science Perspectives*. London: Sage.

Hirsch, E. (1993) 'Negotiated limits: interviews in south-east England', in J. Edwards et al., *Technologies of Procreation: Kinship in the Age of Assisted Conception*. Manchester: Manchester University Press.

Ingold, T. (1989) 'The social and environmental relations of human beings and other animals', in *Comparative Socioecology: the behavioural ecology of humans and other mammals*, ed. V. Standen and R. A. Foley. Oxford: Blackwell Scientific Publications.

(1990) 'An anthropologist looks at biology', *Man*, 25: 208–29.

(1991) 'Becoming persons: consciousness and sociality in human evolution', *Cultural Dynamics*, 4: 355–78.

Latour, B. (1991) 'Materials of power: technology is society made durable', in J. Law (ed.), *A Sociology of Monsters: Essays on Power, Technology and Domination*. London: Routledge.

Lee, R. and Morgan, D. (1989) 'Is birth important?', in R. Lee and D. Morgan (eds.), *Birthrights: Law and Ethics at the Beginning of Life*. London: Routledge.

Lyotard, J.-F. (1984 [1979]) *The Postmodern Condition: A Report on Knowledge*. Trans. G. Bennington and B. Massumi. Manchester: Manchester University Press.

Martin, E. (1987) *The Woman in the Body. A Cultural Analysis of Reproduction*. Boston: Beacon Press.

Morgan, D. (1989) 'Surrogacy: an introductory essay', in R. Lee and D. Morgan (eds.), *Birthrights: Law and Ethics at the Beginnings of Life*. London: Routledge.

Nelson, H. L. and Nelson, J. L. (1989) 'Cutting motherhood in two: Some suspicions concerning surrogacy', *Hypatia*, 4: 85–94.

Oyama, S. (1985) *The Ontogeny of Information: Developmental Systems and Evolution*. Cambridge: Cambridge University Press.

Price, F. V. (1990) 'The management of uncertainty in obstetric practice: Ultrasonography, *in vitro* fertilisation and embryo transfer', in M. McNeil et al. (eds.), *The New Reproductive Technologies*. London: Macmillan.

Shusterman, R. (1988) 'Postmodernist aestheticism: a new moral philosophy?' *Theory, Culture and Society*, 5: 337–55.

Stanley, L. (1992) *The auto-biographical I: The Theory and Practice of Feminist Auto/biography*. Manchester: Manchester University Press.

Strathern, M. (1992) *After Nature: English Kinship in the Late Twentieth Century*. Cambridge: Cambridge University Press.

(1994) 'Displacing knowledge: technology and the consequences for kinship', in *Life and Death under High Technology Medicine*, ed. I. Robinson. Manchester: Fulbright Papers, No. 15.

(1995) 'Disembodied choice', in *Other Intentions: Cultural Contexts and the Attribution of Inner States*, ed. L. Rosen. Santa Fe: School of American Research Press.

Warnock, M. (1985) *A Question of Life: The Warnock Report on Human Fertilisation and Embryology*, Oxford: Basil Blackwell.

Weatherall, D. (1991) 'Manipulating human nature', *Science and Public Affairs*, The Royal Society, BAAS: 25–31.

Whiteford, L. M. and Poland, M. L. eds. (1989) *New Approaches to Human Reproduction: Social and Ethical Dimensions*. Boulder: Westview Press.

Wolfram, S. (1989) 'Surrogacy in the United Kingdom', in *New Approaches to Human Reproduction: Social and Ethical Dimensions*, ed. L. M. Whiteford and M. L. Poland. Boulder: Westview Press.

11   Postmodernism, the sublime and ethics

Roy Boyne

It has been suggested that the postmodern task is the presentation of the unpresentable, that the postmodern condition is crystallised most positively in the avant-garde's resistance to metalinguistic dictatorship.[1] It may seem unlikely that the mere forward exploration towards extension of stylistic reach and expansion of discursive articulation is the principal challenge of our era. Surely Lyotard's construction of the postmodern task as the realisation of the sublime is aimed at more than the artistic and poetic encounter with difference? It is difficult to be so certain.

If postmodernity is only about a garrulous, splattering confrontation with the difference that is the sublime, then its key style will be that of the sprawling intersection: leading perhaps to complex compromise and plural reconciliation as an essentially fuzzy mode which is nevertheless beyond conflict and confrontation. This is a tempting view. It may even be part of the story. It certainly seems the case that the main lines of Western political culture seem to have been moving towards negotiation as the principal junction rather than towards the crossed wire of obdurate opposition. However, there is something more. There is an aspiration. What can be found in the work of theorists like Michel Foucault and Jean-François Lyotard, in the work of novelists like Umberto Eco, and in the work of many artists is the strong feeling that there is a hidden dimension of present culture that is inexpressible but crucially important. This dimension cannot be named. By definition it is beyond our intellectual grasp. The artistic and theoretical task of the present day may, leading from this, be defined as one of focusing, of bringing what is just out of reach into focus.

While this may seem a modest task, make no mistake that what lies just out of reach is anticipated as a switch which will take us into a new epoch, and there is, of course, no royal road to its discovery. So, it is hardly surprising that plural and sceptical methodologies have been employed in all sorts of fields as ways of probing forwards, sideways and backwards. Have these probings produced anything yet? If we were to attempt to understand postmodernism from within a modernist frame

210

(setting aside the too obvious paradoxes which arise from posing such a question), we would ask whether any progress was being made. Procedurally, and within the modernist spirit, an attempt to jettison what will not take us further and to hold on to possibilities that do exist is perfectly defensible, and even invaluable. Nevertheless, it will be the case that attempts to prune and graft will, at this point in the formation of future culture, appear to be structured by a will to power, and to be located within the modality of pure assertion. This is inevitable. The principles are not established, the axiomata are far from clear, the process of casting-off which precedes 'mature' scientific investigation is inappropriate. There can be no settling of accounts for postmodernism for a good time yet.

Bearing that in mind, I will advance the proposition that the next phase of postmodern cultural theory will bear on the development of limit-subjectivity. This emergent understanding of conditioned subjectivity will not judge the status of the subject by reference to an outmoded ideal of a free-floating subject which exists in a mythical state of absolute primacy and inviolable essence. Limit-subjectivity will come to be understood as grounded in history, politics, culture and inter-subjectivity, and will come to be defined in terms of its reflexive appreciation of those grounds, and of their consequences for the exercise of the subject's agency. Limit-subjects are powerful subjects. However, their powers are necessarily circumscribed, and their energy sources are contingently renewable rather than infinite. The unconditioned subject was always a theological conceit, but the structuralist's abandonment of the subject was surely an over-reaction. The postmodern theory of limit-subjectivity will emerge in some fashion out of the intersection of sociology, aesthetics and ethics. It will focus in on what we intuitively grasp but cannot quite express.

Lyotard and the différend

The Postmodern Condition is an attack on certain ruling ideas, those of scientific imperialism, progress toward utopia, and the accessibility of every aspect of the natural and social world to the demystifying and rationalising operations of the knowledge-machine. Lyotard's book never really examined the issue of subjectivity, but it is clear that these ideas which he criticised rest upon a philosophy of objectivism and an ethics of decisionism. Who observes? Who decides? Neither question can be answered satisfactorily within the terms of the ruling ideas of scientific modernism. For finally the place from which the observations and decisions are made cannot be accounted for. One crucial implication of this is that the discourse of rationality is fractured. Rationalisation as both process and ideology aspires to completeness. But the total coverage sought is unavailable. This unavailability is serious. A key consequence is that there can be no rational legislation of the political. The 'Here' in 'Here I stand' is outside the paradigm. This is especially disturbing when we contemplate the structural–technological–cultural momentum of the West, because then, not only do we seem to be faced with a phenomenon which all but exceeds our imaginations and any personal political will that we might have, we also, at least within the modernist frame of reference, seem to lack the possibility of any language which might even provide the simplest description of our condition as subjects (the competition between psychoanalysis, behaviourism, cognitivism and the various schools of ethics is extraordinarily underdeveloped, so that we are offered just a collection of parochial systems of thought which are all, more or less, established in self-referential terms).

This placing of the subject *en abîme* allows us to understand some of the dynamics that coax Lyotard into telling us that there is terror at the heart of this postmodern world. This terror arises because the postmodern world is one without guidelines, yet it is a world which will develop with the subject rather than in opposition to its ultimate mystery: God is dead, anything is possible.

Can we respond beyond the apprehension that the challenge of grounded and therefore limited subjectivity may inspire? There are, it is said, no metanarratives that can guide us, no great syntheses to provide us with visions of a desirable future: science has spawned ecological nightmares, Marxist fantasies of an equal society have brought about the Gulag, advances in medicine have led us to the edge of a market in bodies. If knowledge cannot be reduced to the singularity of science, and if the inevitable syntheses of different forms of knowledge are bound to fail (since success would reduce plurality to singularity, and thereby re-establish what we now feel to be impossible – the genuine hegemony of science), does this mean that temporary alliances and regional harmonies are all that can be expected? It may be that such a limiting of horizons is desirable. It does, however, seem rather daunting to imagine new forms of subjectivity based on notions which are all conditioned by the idea of the limit. The symbol of God, as archetype of unconstrained subjectivity is one that we have all become comfortable with, and to be atheistic is one thing, but to give up what in us is redolent of theistic symbolics is quite another. Think also that if Nietzsche was one of postmodernism's precursors, then to move towards conceptions of limit-subjectivity is hardly within the dauntless, difference-embracing spirit of the *Übermensch*. Furthermore, our concerns may not all be selfish, and based on apprehensions of space- and time-limited forms of subjectivity. There is another negative side, a lurking concern that if we forsake all totalising and metanarrativistic concepts and aspirations, there will still be metanarratives that remain, and that they will be unchallenged since we would no longer accept the possibility of their existence. This is a serious concern. We may be beyond belief in the possibility of genuine metanarrative, but this does not mean that we can renounce the fight against the appalling false metanarratives that linger on. If postmodernity inspires hope, it is because of its promise for the subject's self-invention and self-responsi-bility; if it inspires concern, it is because its implicit advocacy of weak but grounded subjectivity is not accompanied by a political under-standing of metanarrative renunciation.

Lyotard's reflections on language pragmatics and justice provide a partial response to some of these concerns. The positive side relates to the impetus to redefine the state of things as but a local constellation whose seemingly permanent boundary lines are due to entrenched ways of thinking, ruling, administering and so on, in short, to the ways of performing that we cannot or will not see beyond. What is positive here is the implication that we need not define the bits of the whole in the way that we do. We can, as Lyotard explains, make new moves. Deconstruction may have been one such move. To take an example: to speak of positive and negative is to speak of a dualism that reduces to oneness. If we take the example of truth and falsehood, we can see that the everyday conceptual idiom treats that dualism as an expression of the oneness of truth. Truth is the defining term, and falsehood is secondary. Truth, like justice or beauty, is a concept which tends to totalise. Now, Lyotard seems to imply that deconstructing such usages is not enough. He seems to suggest that we may be on the edge of a world which is beyond privilege, so that to speak, *à la* Derrida, of privileging the other, is not really to face the irreducible pluralism of the post-modern. Now, as an example, that is fine as far as it goes, and the implied critique of early Derrida may be acceptable, but where is Lyotard's new move? We may be convinced of the need, but we are still short of the innovation. Lyotard would see us connect, only connect. It will be the world that will provide the move, rather than Lyotard. This is obviously disappointing, since it makes of his position something of a modernist refuge, as he himself, as a self, is not fully involved in (and thereby limited by) the new moves which will come to define the future. The negative side of Lyotard's language pragmatics is, then, its appar-ently extraordinarily weak politics, its seeming lack of concern about possible consequences, its far from Pascalian wager that the current basis of calculating the odds will be entirely overturned by the very act of placing the stake, and its apparent lack of self-investment.

Excursus: living postmodern pluralism

What if Lyotard's gamble is made? What if he is not premature in his thought, and we are at the very outermost, beginning-most limit of a world which cannot be totalised. If we are heading into that world, of what lies further within we can have, I suggest, no conception. If we truly have to face pluralism as the essence of a world which is never to be totalised, and if facing this irreducible pluralism is beginning to happen now, then we have only just started to feel our way. It will not be so easy to go beyond good and evil, and fear would be an understandable response to what lies ahead. Such an advent of ontological plurality would certainly signal once and for all the failure of the rational project and thereby excise the arrogance and terror which lay at its core. But lack of guarantees brings its own unease. How would we prepare the way? Educational strategies might be adopted that would seek to smash the false fixity of our various routines. But which of us will bring up our children thus? And there exists the formidable technical problem of parental socialisation into limited subjectivity (which may appear to be based on meaninglessness and profound negativity). How is this to be done in such a way as to preserve a certain energy for the postmodern child (or will we have transcended genetic imperatives at this point)? An aesthetic effect might make clear what is involved. Imagine living the infinite extension of an irrational number, in a vain quest for some purpose, some end, for finality, one digit succeeds another: green numbers to infinity on the black background of an IBM screen. As each new figure appears on the screen, a pattern may be created or an earlier one destroyed, and that is all there is. Would it not be tempting to stop at some point, and make more of a particular sequence than it deserved? And why not, when the alternative is a list whose only meaning would seem to be that it would be always longer than the number you first thought of? What do we say about this temptation to halt the process, to make the best of the numbers that have already appeared, or perhaps to ignore the last few in favour of an earlier pattern? Who will demand that the numbers are faced ever anew, and deny the satisfaction of respite? Who can truly pluralise?

But perhaps the vision of pluralism implicit in the above is too extreme, and the social-psychological consequence of metanarrative decline is not the human being as accident or contingency. Might it not be the case that the postmodernist hyperbole with which we have been contending arises mostly in virtue of the imperative to reject old-style thought? If we focus not on the rejection of the past but rather on embracing what is to come, then we may find more of a balanced view. Let us see.

The notion that we should acknowledge the presence of worlds not yet experienceable is clearly not straightforward. But this transgression of 'common sense' is hardly without precedent (consider the case of 'anti-matter', for example), and it is of considerable moment for the aesthetics of modern art, a field in which Lyotard at one time had placed a degree of hope for the future. Artists have often seen themselves as seeking to escape the boundaries of mundane perception, and they have frequently affirmed how hard this is to do. But is their effort genuinely directed towards the future? In other words, is postmodern art (whether it calls itself that or not) a truly valuable way of facing the apprehension which attends knowing the world as ineffably unstable and endlessly defined by doomed particularity? Or is it mere consolation? A bold view of contemporary art might base itself on a denial of essential difference between, shall we say, a painting by Kiefer and the devastation of Dresden at the end of the Second World War: the world, all of it, would be seen as performance, its value residing only in the fact that performance passes time. Now it is certainly possible that the consolations of the aesthetic are not consolations at all, but rather the effect of a pure realism finally reached, a realisation that there is no depth, only the sensational experience of the play of surfaces and the working through of performances. But there is reason to think that art is not so ontologically uncompromising.

Is the fear of a knife through your skin, of a total rejection of you by your friends and colleagues, or of cancer cells proliferating in your body, just an aspect of surface happenstance? Could such fears be otherwise in just two days' time? Conceivably so, but such surfaces are strong. They will endure for a time yet. And fear is an aspect of them. The machinery of consolation, reassurance, forgetfulness, the technology of doubt as we might call it (described in Kierkegaard's account of Abraham on Mount Moriah[2]), still leads us to believe – even though we may be at the very dawn of the postmodern – that our fears are abnormal, that they will disappear on our arrival at some ultimate saving realm of comfort and redemption. One has to be strong to remain in fear, to embrace, for example, civil war as egological liberation. Does art serve such strength? Or is it, perhaps like religion, a form of consolation? Wasn't Michel Butor right to speak of Mark Rothko's work as 'a kind of prayer to an unknown god'?[3] Do we not live lives dedicated to the appeasement of the future? Might it even be that there is no art that is not complicit with that dedication, that does not console us with the sensation of the present?

Every word that I write, every meal that I eat, every painting that I see, or piece of music that I listen to, everything that I do is stigmatised by a'withdrawal from the pagan and polyvalent future of which Lyotard's earlier work seemed to speak. There are, I suggest, millions like me. Distraction is our mode of being. Distraction is at the heart of it. Was this not always the case? Wasn't the story teller always the one who would make you glad to live from second to second in the endless succession of self-cancelling nows? Imagine the scene when we convince ourselves that the next digits of our irrational number will be just one of two rather than any of ten, and that this patterning will go on for some little time yet. One can almost feel nerves relax as the opium smoke pervades the laboratory – we can trust in the future, even if just for a little while!! The plea from the masses is, please can we take our eyes off the future? We have had enough of wondering if the crop will go bad leaving us to die in the winter's chill. If this really is postcapitalism can we please forgo the bourgeois habits of deferred gratification, of living the macroeconomist's equation that saving equals investment, of dissipating the pleasure of the text as we write in accordance with the strict rules of argumentation, relevance and the need to impress?

The hard fact is, of course, that Lyotard is right to say that reality is a question of the future. But he was somewhat naive to suggest that we can open ourselves to all of its possibilities. He saw the contradictions even at the time of writing *Economie libidinale*, asserting that he was not one of the 'liberators of desire'. He was well aware that we still live in a capitalist world in which we have to look to exercise a modicum of control over what is ahead. Self-discipline remains the recommended model, and if this is just too hard, then perhaps a little support is needed. Consider this statement from Lyotard on the sublime:

Here then is a breakdown of the sublime sensation: a very big, very powerful object threatens . . . and stuns the soul (at lower intensities, the soul is at this point seized with admiration, veneration, respect). The soul is dumb, immobilised, as good as dead. Art, by distancing this menace, procures a measure of relief, of delight.[4]

The implication seems to be that there is a 'collusion' between art (as a 'for instance' in this case) and the present, rather than a real connection to the future. In this formulation, the sublime functions to sustain the present order (and this is not to mention its capacity to symbolise the 'greatness and grandeur' of wealth and power). It may be correct to say that the artistic attempt to intimate that which is beyond presentation will 'undo spiritual assumptions regarding time', but this opening of temporality is only likely to promote the intensification of the present, as the art consumer is swallowed up by the work, and is thus allowed some respite from the burdens of constrained existence. What more, beyond this temporary relief, is there here other than a certain self-satisfaction arising out of a largely unmomentous recognition of having faced something beyond discourse, beyond figure? With the energy of the sublime strategically harnessed to cultural consumption, the politics of avant-garde art are the politics of consolation and distraction.

What can we retrieve following this critique? Lyotard's *Le Différend* acknowledges the detranscendentalising of the sublime. It does this by using Wittgenstein's formulations about language games, and it assumes that these formulations can also be applied to the notion of 'form of life', although this is not made explicit. Now, then, it is a question of the autonomy of language games, of, for example, art as language game. The hermetic nature of language games establishes a place for the sublime. This place is the outside which cannot be thought from inside: 'whereof we cannot speak, thereof we must be silent' – the soul is again struck dumb. Lyotard's quest, in *Le Différend*, will be to force our lips to open, so that we speak where before there was only a silence imposed by a seemingly inexorable logic. The sublime will be brought back into time, as the politics of a world which will explode into all kinds of voice, and which will frown upon the traditional silences of exit and loyalty. It is at this point that the previous criticism, of Lyotard as purveyor of weak politics, is answered.

Le Différend searches for the possibility of new forms of connection between the political and the juridical. Consider the following:

When the group Red Army Faction makes an incursion and destroys the American computer in Heidelberg, that is war, the group considers itself at war, it is waging war and it is actually destroying a part of the forces of the adversary . . . that is part of the rather exact game that is a two-sided war. But when the same group kidnaps Schleyer and blackmails a third party with Schleyer's death as the stake, then we are in an altogether different violence which has no relation to the previous one.[5]

This appears not to be a good example of incommensurability. They are two strategies, and we might think that they are easily containable within the same game. Some may know this now. But are there not those for whom these two strategies cannot be conceivable in those terms? For whom they are really incommensurable?

While Lyotard's particular example might not be particularly sharp, the general point which he makes is quite clear. It is that there are many instances of incommensurable games, and the grinding edge between these games may be of enormous social significance (consider the edge between terrorism and democratic politics). The choice between such incommensurable games cannot even be posed, without the choice already having been made. It cannot be guided by any *logic*. Incommensurability can be dealt with by force: the destruction of the other game. But can there be a judgement between two incommensurable games? Would such a judgement, if it were possible, become a third game which in swallowing the other two games becomes the only game? These questions are, in Lyotard's view, the very stuff of the sublime, no longer transcendental but social, no longer assigned to a stabilising function but now precisely destabilising and restabilising at the same time. They are the starting point of *Le Différend*, which sees language lagging behind the event, which asks therefore that the effort be made to talk and write ourselves into the present, which, so to speak, is the future. It is a question of linking incommensurable discourses, of doing this apparently impossible thing rather than seeking a rule which will prescribe how it is to be done, or which will explain why it cannot be done. That there is no such rule is the first principle of *Le Différend*, and, for Lyotard is the root of politics. We are now, of course, returned to our opening trial definition of postmodernism as extension of reach and expansion of articulation.

We have seen, however, that what counts as an incommensurability from one perspective, may count as a potential compatibility from another. This is ultimately the main problem in Lyotard's reformulation of the postmodern task in terms of the concept of the *différend*. Lyotard takes incommensurability as a given about the world; whereas, the incommensurabilities which concern him are more properly redescribed as incommensurabilities between differently constituted (and therefore limited rather than universal) subjectivities. Lyotard's unexamined reliance upon a modernist form of universal subjectivity holds back his development as a practical theorist of emerging postmodernity.

Let us summarise. The movement of postmodern being, which begins with a conception of the future as utter opportunity, is initially undertaken by Lyotard only through the allusive monuments of modern art. Such a confrontation with the openness before us is, in truth, no confrontation at all, but rather a determined avoidance, self-concealment in a sensual present. It made sense, then, for Lyotard to turn to a new understanding of sociality as a heterogeneous collection of forms of phrasing, and to engage theoretically in what we might think of as a form of social Heideggerianism: the unconcealing of the social, through the specification of what at first seems unspecifiable, the links between differences. This is to be done without a guide, the rules of our proceeding being established as we proceed. We simultaneously penetrate and displace the sublime as we say what formerly could not be said, and link what formerly could not be linked, seeing what we have done only after we have done it. Therefore, Lyotard's detranscendentalised social sublime is a given of the world, an unexamined presupposition turned into realised potential.

With the shift from aesthetics to language pragmatics, Lyotard's version of postmodern subjectivity continues to be truly hard, requiring an abasement before or leap into a given but unknown world. In the end the subject is based on will, and is still an incarnation of the Nietzschean gesture. While postmodernity may be defined as a waiting game, a hesitation at the end of modernity as we await what is to come, in Lyotard's conception the waiting is active not passive. One waits for the event to come by doing all that it is possible to do to bring it into being. Lyotard's future awaits us as a stream of events which are, to a significant extent, willed from hiding into appearance.

In the ultimate, what we can now see is that Lyotard's version of postmodernity continues with the modernist theme of groundless subjectivity. What is more, it continues with this even though the tasks and certainties which are seen to lie ahead are more daunting than ever before. This constitutes the weakest point of postmodern theory, and explains the general concern with theorising forms of subjectivity which have recently come to the fore, largely in the guise of theorising the body. Lyotard's inclination towards an implicit understanding of subjectivity based on will to power is, however, capable of being (as he himself did with the sublime) detranscendentalised. The limits that are found following this are both physical and social. The issue of physical limits leads us into theorisations of the body within a tradition perhaps inaugurated by Merleau-Ponty. The concern with the social limits of postmodern subjectivity takes us into the realm of ethics, within a tradition begun by Kant. The second part of this essay constitutes merely an opening engagement with that latter tradition.

Re-claiming Kant on morality

There is no doubt a willed blindness in the present situation, which is the necessary accompaniment to any search for clarity. But, unavoidably susceptible to the ruses of metaphor though this may sound, it is surely possible that limit-subjectivity cannot float free, that it needs an anchor point, a first hold in the rock, a point from which to make the next move. A subject of limited scope and power whose ground is to be found only in the particularities of experience: does this not sound like an empiricist dream? But we already asked, 'Who dreams?', and know that the true subject of the empiricist world-view is far from restricted. Kant offers the only, even part-developed path. *The Critique of Pure Reason* like the *Groundwork of the Metaphysics of Morals* begins with limited subjectivity.

Kant believed that the principle of morality is an a priori principle. That is to say, he believed that the idea of morality is not deducible from experience, but is somehow independent of experience and prior to it. As an a priori principle, morality grounds and limits subjectivity. Is it possible to incorporate such a principle into the postmodern problematic? Would such a move (and I am mindful here of Lyotard's injunction that new moves are of the essence) place us back within the modernist metanarrative frame? Or, is a postmodern moral law a real possibility?

To begin with, we have to ask about the nature of a priori judgements. We can draw an analogy with logic. One of the basic laws of logic is that a thing cannot be both itself and something else at the same time; for example, a table is a table, and if it is such, then it is not, for example, a bottle of wine. In propositional logic, the law of identity, as this law is called, is expressed very simply by writing: $a = a$. Now, in Kant's thinking, we do not derive this law of logic from experience. Rather, it an a priori law, a formal precondition which must hold for any subject's experience of any physical world. Is such a language of formal preconditions, the formulation of conditions of existence, neutral with regard to the modernity–postmodernity divide? This is a difficult question, but if we follow Kant's argument in *The Critique of Pure Reason* the answer would seem to be that postmodernity and the a priori need not be foreign to each other. Obviously this requires some demonstration.

As far as Kant is concerned, there are just two kinds of judgements. They are either analytic or synthetic. For the purposes of this inquiry, let us assume the adequacy of this position and leave aside the criticism of Kantian thought that it is disabled since it only focuses on subject-predicate relations (which, for my purposes is no disability, but rather an advantage, since it is precisely those relations within postmodernity which are of current concern). If the predicate is entailed by the subject (as in the phrase 'a morally constituted subject is behaviourally limited'), the judgement is analytic. If the predicate is not contained by the subject (as in the phrase 'a postmodern subject is morally constituted'), the judgement is synthetic. It has been said on many occasions that analytic judgements explain, while synthetic judgements inform. Kant argued that these judgements take two forms – a priori and a posteriori. He defined a priori judgements as those which are true for all subjects no matter what their experience, while a posteriori judgements are derived from particular experience. Judgements as judgements may be true or false. That is clearly so in the case of a posteriori judgements, and it is important to recognise that it is also the case with a priori judgements. Kant's classification, then, allows for four general forms of judgement: synthetic and analytic a priori and synthetic and analytic a posteriori, and for each of these four forms we have, just like the insurance investigator, to contend with false claims. For Kant, morality/freedom as precondition of subjectivity was not the only example of a synthetic a priori. These judgements, whose predicates are not determined by their subjects, and which are also invariable within the particular experiential world, include – at least, this is how Kant saw it – the basic laws of mathematics, the rule of causation in natural science, as well as (the focus of our discussion) the basic law of precedence of moral duty over desire. It is crucial to note that for all these a priori judgements, what is at issue is here the constitution of subjectivity.

Before we can draw a conclusion about the potential fit or misfit between the a priori and postmodernity, we need to clarify the nature of the synthetic a priori. Probably the single most fundamental objection to the whole of Kant's critical philosophy, which he himself saw as an extended argument for the possibility and indeed necessity of the synthetic a priori, is that that no judgement can be both synthetic and a priori. A synthetic judgement informs about what is the case, while an a priori judgement is by definition necessary and logically independent of the variations within experience. How can the two be put together? The answer to this criticism is that synthetic necessity is not like analytic necessity. Analytic judgements are necessary in the sense that their denial results in contradiction. But synthetic necessity is not like that. To say that every quadratic equation can be resolved is to make a judgement which, if not true universally, would invalidate the laws of algebra. If, on the other hand, we argue that there need be no morality for postmodernity, we will only be saying that postmodernity will not have a moral law as one of its conditions of existence. In other words, synthetic necessity refers to the specific preconditions of experience of a particular world, rather than to the universal preconditions of any world at all, and if we are to talk about the specific preconditions of one world rather than another, it surely follows that elements of the world in question must (albeit in a counter-intuitive manner) 'determine' the content of the specific preconditions in some way.

Now, we can make a strategic point at this juncture, which is that the category of the synthetic a priori has never been fully accepted within the problematic of scientific modernism. Why is this? We know that *fin-de-siècle* Viennese thought, stemming from cultural decay, scientific advance and artistic audacity, gave rise to the purest renunciation of metaphysics, and to the apparently simple position that all a priori truth must be analytic. We have also seen that the subject (who observes and decides) within scientific modernity is entirely problematic. We can see that the synthetic a priori, pre-determining, as it well might, the basic schematics of the subject (who observes and decides), will be difficult to treat within any system of rational objective knowledge. It is significant that the status of ethics, as systematic inquiry into the nature of morality, has declined in significance over the last 300 years, which is precisely because the prime condition of existence of the subject within scientific modernism has been its lack of limits. It is no surprise that French poststructuralism (which seeks to bring the subject back in to some extent) has drawn extensively upon the work of Martin Heidegger, whose celebrated interpretation of Kant, *Kant and the Problem of Metaphysics*, centres on the finitude of the constituting subject. Contrast this with Strawson's *The Bounds of Sense*, in which Kant's category of the synthetic a priori, is presented as a relatively unimportant muddle.[6] The conclusion that I draw at this point is that Kant's category is of considerable interest for the postmodernity debate, and for discussions about the nature of the subject within postmodernity. The key here is that, as a category, the synthetic a priori will, when used to focus the question of postmodern subjectivity, pre-limit the subjective form. This focusing on the subject as an element of the world enables us to link the subject back into the world in a limited but real sense.

When, on this much disputed territory of the synthetic a priori, we consider the issue of Kant's thesis of the moral law, of the categorical imperative of moral behaviour, what we are doing is asking if a moral law of some kind could be conceived as a condition of existence of postmodernity. We have taken the view that postmodern subjectivity is going to be a limited and grounded form of subjectivity in opposition to the unconstrained subjectivity which is the implicit, and very powerful, model for scientific modernity. We have come to the view that there is no contradiction between postmodernity and the notion of conditions of existence because these conditions of existence are either analytic and, in the strict sense, without substance, or they are synthetic, in which case, as conditions of existence, they emerge from the existent and not the meta-existent. In other words, the synthetic a priori does not betray the axiom of anti-metanarrativity. But why should the form of the limit be a moral form? In part, that question seems just slightly the wrong one to ask. It is better formulated – in the light of our responsibility for the future – as a practical matter. Can the form of the limit be a moral form?

For Kant, the moral law was necessary if the world was to be as it was experienced in his epoch. Although ultimately derived from experience, the key thing was that the existence of morality allowed Kant (and this still applies to us as we near the end of the millennium) to make sense of this experience. It is still true today that if there were no categories of morality then the way that we experience and live in the world would be unthinkably different. Kant held that we continually make moral judgements in the world in which we live. We habitually ask of actions whether they are right or not. This is an extremely important fact. To a degree, however, this is backward-looking. Is what we want to say something like, 'As it was in Kant's day, so it is in ours'? I suggest this is not something we want to follow without some very serious re-evaluation. Do not the threats and promises of postmodernity demand that we re-think the nature of moral judgement for the next millennium? One way to proceed, and the way I will follow, will be to look at what Kant says, and to ask to what extent the twin axioms of anti-metanarrativity and limit-subjectivity are contradicted by his formulations.

Kant claimed that the moral judgements that we make are addressed neither to the action judged nor to its consequences, but to the intention behind it. Evil intentions may sometimes (ironically but nevertheless) produce 'good' consequences, while 'good' intentions may lead to disastrous consequences. Whichever way we think about these things, it is clear that *fortuna* will always play an important part in the way that things work out. Kant's response to this is a very different one from Machiavelli's. Machiavelli thought that the capriciousness of events meant that no one could afford to have both principles and ends, and that successful politicians, in pursuit of their ends had to bend with the prevailing wind. For Kant, however, we live in a world in which principles and ends are co-existing forms of social life (a Lyotardian perspective on this might say that the practical resolution of the *différend* between values and goals in some way helped to produce capitalism, and the similarity of such a view to the Weberian perspective is interesting). To attempt to deny this would be like denying the necessity of the logical law of identity. So, for Kant, the caprices of fortune mean that the target of moral judgement cannot be the outcome of events, rather it has to be the quality of the intention that lies behind the action considered. If Christianity invented conscience, as Nietzsche would later argue, Kant was the first to secularise it and make a central place for this new secular conscience in his moral philosophy.

Kant would have us believe that there are three modes of intention which may inform action. The first refers to an action done from simple inclination: I go for a walk because I feel like it. The second refers to action which is done in order to further my self-interest: I learn a foreign language so that I can increase my network of research contacts. The third mode refers to action done out of duty, this refers to that case where my intention is simply to do what is right, to do what it is my duty to do. Now, it would be too severe a demand that all of our actions should be determined by a dutiful intention. A better way of seeing the relation between the three intentional modes would be to pose the question 'does my action conflict with my duty?' Is there a test that will determine if there is a conflict between our duty and our inclination? To use Kant's metaphor, can we find some sort of moral compass? Kant is sure that we can. The test that he proposes is as follows: 'Can you also will that your maxim should become a universal law?'

For Kant, what he calls the 'supreme principle of morality' is the principle that one should 'act only on that maxim through which you can at the same time will that it should become a general law'.[7] Focusing on the third form of action, action which is formed by the good intention or the dutiful intention, we can say, following Kant, that moral action is determined by a dutiful conscience, and the test of a dutiful conscience is posed by the universalisability question: is this the way we would have everybody behave?

If that is the main question, and the answer is affirmative, then we have a formal scheme for moral certitude. It is, however, only formal at this point. It is open to a sadist or a hawkish military general to pose the universalisability test and to come up with some off-centre universal maxims, such as 'death before compromise' or 'pain restores the meaning of life'. It is for this reason that Kant offers another formulation of the categorical imperative which has more substance to it than the one we have just discussed. The simplest formulation runs as follows: 'man is not a thing – not something to be used *merely* as a means: he must always be regarded . . . as an end in himself'.[8] This second formulation of the categorical imperative is effectively derived by applying the universalisability maxim to itself. It is, as we might say today, a reflexive operation, the outcome of which is a practical rule which sets limits.

Where exactly are we? We understand emerging postmodernity to be characterised by a lack of metanarrative guidance, by the consequent proliferation of different forms of life, by an incommensurability between differently located subjects, by a prime theoretical interest in rethinking the limits of subjectivity so as to enable further movement (through reflexive understanding) into the future. Kant is being re-claimed as an enabling thinker because of his position as a philosopher of the subject, and because his critical notion of the synthetic a priori is entirely appropriate to a postmodern social economy of difference. Kant's thought on the moral law has been selected to test out this line of thought, and the question we have come to – quite precisely – is whether Kant's categorical imperative can be reformulated in such a way as to make sense for limit-subjectivity within postmodernity. The two key formulations are, 'Act only on that maxim through which you can at the same time will that it should become a general law' and 'man is not a thing – not something to be used *merely* as a means: he must always be regarded . . . as an end in himself'.

In order to pursue this, and come to some preliminary resolution, we need to consider the *différend* between postmodernity and the concepts of General law, Man and Ends. Additionally, at this point, it can be seen that a very significant theoretical territory has been encountered, and a full mapping exercise will inevitably be beyond the scope of this chapter. Nevertheless, some preliminary indications can be provided. First, with regard to the question of postmodernism and general law, it may seem clear that a general law across an enormous variety of forms of life cannot be a priori. It would have to be imposed. The imposition would risk drawing disparate forms together without preserving their differ-ences as a major priority. The rule of general law within postmodernity would have macropolitical violence and reactive terrorism as constant threats. Cross-differential policy-making should work principally to hold those threats in remission. Second, with regard to the question of postmodernism and man: we must address the anthropologism inherent in the initial formulation. If postmodernity means an epoch defined by many kinds of differences, then the very idea of universal humanity has to be placed in question. The cost of a regime of differences is the loss of the liberal agenda. 'Man' has to be replaced by forms of locally constituted subjectivity. Third, with respect to the issue of postmo-dernism and ends, ends within postmodernism would emerge from the context and reference point of the being of local others. Kant's thought tended to operate in fairly stark terms, but within an economy of difference, all must be negotiated, and no settlement will be final – even though the appearance of finality can be sustained as a mechanism for manufacturing remission.

It might appear as if the effort spent on Kant has been wasted. But, that would be too hasty a conclusion. Suppose that we reformulate the Categorical Imperative, but from within a postmodern frame. We might get two alternative formulations like the following: 'Act only on that maxim through which you can at the same time will that it should become a local law' and 'Human subjects are not things to be used without negotiation: they must always be regarded as provisional ends in themselves'. Could such formulations arise from the context for which they are meant to provide both form and content as synthetic a priori? Could such formulations be lived within different forms of life? The presumption of this essay is that the answer to both of those questions is in the affirmative.

It may be objected that if such an apparent metanarrative overview can be provided, then we are back within modernism. The proper response would be that with the notions of 'local' and 'provisional' at the heart of the alleged metanarrativity, such an accusation could not be other than a play on words.

NOTES

1   Lyotard writes, 'the avant-garde is not concerned with what happens on the "subject", but with: "Does it happen?" . . . This is the sense in which I still belongs to the aesthetics of the sublime' (1992: 103).
2   Kierkegaard (1983).
3   Butor (1970: 268).
4   Lyotard (1992: 99–100).
5   Lyotard and Thébaud (1985: 67).
6   Strawson (1966: 43).
7   Kant (1948: 84).
8   Ibid.: 91–2.

BIBLIOGRAPHY

Butor, M. (1970) *Inventory*. London: Cape.
Heidegger, M. (1990) *Kant and the Problem of Metaphysics*. Bloomington: Indiana University Press.
Kant, I. (1948) *Groundwork of the Metaphysics of Morals*. London: Hutchinson.
    Critique of Pure Reason. London: Macmillan.
Kierkegaard, S. (1983). *Fear and Trembling*. Princeton, NJ: Princeton University Press.
Lyotard, J.-F. (1974) *Economie libidinale*. Paris: Minuit.
    (1984a) *The Postmodern Condition*. Manchester: Manchester University Press.
    (1984b) *Le Différend*. Manchester: Manchester University Press.
    (1992) *The Inhuman*. Oxford: Polity Press.
Lyotard, J.-F. and J.-L. Thébaud (1985) *Just Gaming*. Manchester: Manchester University Press.
Strawson, P. F. (1966). *The Bounds of Sense*. London: Methuen.

Index

relativism, 54, 67, 77
  and feminism, 108
  see also knowledge
Renouvier, Charles, 152, 163
representation,
  artistic, 120–1
  political, 40–2
rights, 49–50, 51, 77–8
  and justice, 132
romanticism, 56
Rorty, Richard, 1, 6, 7, 31, 32, 43, 61, 63,
  64–5, 100
  Contingency, Irony and Solidarity, 86
Rose, Gillian, 10
Rosenblum, Nancy, 98, 99, 102
Rothko, Mark, 215
Rousseau, Jean-Jacques, 37, 51, 151, 161
Rowlands, Michael, 2
Ruddick, S. 140
Rushdie, Salman, 98–9
Russell, Bertrand, 32

Saint-Simon, 151, 153, 162
Sandel, Michael, 78
Scheler, Max, 167, 170, 171
Schumpeter, Joseph, 169
Schürmann, Reiner, 43
sciences, 10, 21, 56, 62–4, 212
  human, 2, 3, 4–5, 172
  natural, 8, 164–6, 169–70, 172
  social, 118
self, 38–9, 73, 135
  authentic, 20, 141–2
  isolated, 85–6, 100–1, 102, 103
  situated, 85, 88, 101–3
  see also Taylor, *Sources of the Self*
Shotter, John, 5
Simmel, Georg, 29
Simons, Jon, 8
Skinner, Quentin, 21
social psychology, 4
socialism, 5, 7, 10, 168
  ethical, 152
  market, 46
  scientific, 153
  state, 151–2, 173
  utopian, 116, 161
sociology, 2, 33–4, 172
  of postmodernity, 118
Soddy, F., 160
Soviet Union, 45
Spain, 43, 98
Spengler, 163, 166–8, 170
  The Decline of the West, 163–4
spirituality, 50, 56, 57
Spivak, Gayatri, 134

Squires, Judith, 74–5
Sri Lanka, 45, 98
Strathern, Marilyn, 8, 9, 148
Strawson, P. F., 222
Sumner, William, 4
surrogacy, 182–6, 189
  see also motherhood
Surrogacy Arrangements Act, 189
Sweden, 41, 43
Sypher, Wylie, 25

Tajfel, Henri, 4
Tawney, R. H., 79
Taylor, Charles, 1, 10, 21, 78, 88,
  141–2
  Sources of the Self, 49–58
technology, 8, 118, 147–8, 202
  bio-, 8, 173, 195–7
  Faustian theories of, 163–74
  information, 147
  Promethean theories of, 156–63
  reproductive, 9, 185–6, 187, 191–2
Thatcher, Margaret, 44
Tolstoy, Leo, 32
tribalism, 20, 31, 32–3
truth, 20, 63–9, 213

Urry, John, 2
utopias, 5–6,
  ecological, 160

values, 55–6, 137, 138
Venturi, 61
Vines, G., 200

Walzer, Michael, 78, 81, 94, 99, 100
  Interpretation and Social Criticism,
    96–7
  Spheres of Justice, 81, 87, 95–6
Warnock Report, 189
Weatherall, D., 200–1
Weber, Louis, 161–2
Weber, Max, 8, 26, 36, 50, 110, 163, 166
White, Hayden, 3
White, Lyn, 150
Williams, Bernard, 38
Williams, Raymond, 79
Wilson, Elizabeth, 133
Winch, Peter, 95
Wittgenstein, Ludwig von, 2, 22, 68, 70,
  73, 88, 94, 95, 102, 217
  The Blue Book, 83
  Philosophical Investigations, 86, 97–8
  philosophy of language, 82–4
Wittig, Monique, 134
Wolff, Robert Paul, 79,